NORTH KOREA

NORTH KOREA

The Politics of Unconventional Wisdom

Han S. Park

LYNNE
RIENNER
PUBLISHERS

BOULDER
LONDON

Published in the United States of America in 2002 by
Lynne Rienner Publishers, Inc.
1800 30th Street, Boulder, Colorado 80301
www.rienner.com

and in the United Kingdom by
Lynne Rienner Publishers, Inc.
3 Henrietta Street, Covent Garden, London WC2E 8LU

Library of Congress Cataloging-in-Publication Data
A Cataloging-in-Publication record for this book
is available from the Library of Congress.

ISBN: 978-1-58826-403-9 (paperback : alk. paper)

British Cataloguing in Publication Data
A Cataloguing in Publication record for this book
is available from the British Library.

Printed and bound in the United States of America

The paper used in this publication meets the requirements
of the American National Standard for Permanence of
Paper for Printed Library Materials Z39.48-1992.

Contents

Introduction   1

1   The Perception Approach   7

2   The Advent and Evolution of *Juche* Ideology   17

3   The Philosophical Principles of *Juche*   31

4   The Creation of a Theocracy   41

5   *Juche* Education: Agents and Methods   51

6   Conditioning the Human Mind   61

7   *Juche* as a Way of Life   75

8   *Juche* in Domestic Politics   85

9   Foreign and Unification Policy   99

10 Inter-Korean Relations: A Legitimacy War   117

11 The Unconventional Wisdom in Negotiating Behavior:
    The Weapons Controversy and Beyond   133

12 North Korea Sees Itself: Perceptions of Policy Goals,
    Strategies, and Tactics   143

13 System Stability and Vulnerability   161

14 Conclusion: The Challenges Ahead   175

Bibliography   181
Index   185
About the Book   194

Introduction

Many kinds of polities and states have experimented with many different types of governments over the course of human history. Of those that may be classified as undemocratic, some have been more authoritarian, and others have been more closed, contained, rigid, and ideological. Yet no system has crystallized all the above characteristics into its polity more completely than the Democratic People's Republic of Korea (North Korea). Since the inception of the current regime, especially after the Korean War (1950–1953), North Korea has developed a breed of socialism vastly deviant from Marxism-Leninism or, for that matter, almost any other system known in political history. Scholars and observers of North Korea have found striking similarities between today's North Korea and what was depicted in George Orwell's famous novel *1984*. Written in 1949, the novel described what human society would be like in the year 1984 and predicted rule by a tyrannical government that employed surveillance, purges, brainwashing, and personality cults in order to perpetuate control. However, a growing number of people who are knowledgeable about North Korea acknowledge that the country is not entirely misguided. North Korea and its sympathizers assert that the system is relatively devoid of the kinds of social ills typically found in developing capitalist societies; namely, income inequality, moral decay, environmental deterioration, and overreliance on external resources. Political activists and radical students in South Korea, as well as some circles of overseas Koreans, profess their belief that North Korea is largely nationalistic, welfare-oriented, and sincere about national reunification.

Leaving moral judgment aside, one is struck by the resilience of the system and the remarkable stability of state power. How many socialist

1

systems have survived the massive tide of democratization without being either derailed or significantly modified? How many political systems can survive the economic hardships that have caused mass starvation and prolonged economic stagnation, as has North Korea? North Korea is truly an anomaly.

The North Korean Anomaly

The Democratic People's Republic of Korea is an atypical system that has seldom been seen in the course of world history. The system has convincingly defied conventional wisdom and common sense with respect to its fate. The collapse of socialist systems in the late 1980s was widely believed to be a prelude to North Korea's demise. When the Berlin Wall fell, the world's watchful eye shifted its focus to the Korean peninsula, in anticipation of possible absorption of the socialist north into the capitalist south. Five years after the fall of East Germany, charismatic leader Kim Il Sung died rather abruptly, and most North Korea watchers foresaw an imminent collapse of the system. As famine and economic dislocations caused mass starvation, the vacuum created by the leader's death was expected to lead to the North Korean people forcing the Kim Jong Il leadership to an insurmountable legitimacy crisis. And finally, when Hwang Jang Yop, a Party secretary and top ideological leader, defected to the south in February 1997, many believed that this dramatic event would mark the beginning of a chain reaction of system collapse. None of the above has materialized. In this sense, North Korea is an anomaly indeed.

North Korea's uniqueness is more specifically observed in Pyongyang's policymaking behavior. At a time when all the countries in the world are eager to be part of the global economic system and develop relative competitiveness in the international market, North Korea stands alone in defiance of the law of financial dynamism in the global community. The country refused to induce reform measures to promote economic growth. Even with a large, high-quality labor pool at its disposal, North Korea chose not to utilize it for productive means but to continue politicization of the masses, keeping them away from the manufacturing sector. In the face of adverse and punitive consequences, Pyongyang has refused to compromise its rocket-missile development programs. Shortages of food and medical supplies are so acute that large numbers of people are suffering from starvation and disease, but the economy continues to orient itself toward military buildup.

Even the inter-Korean summit meeting in June 2000 was not expected to stimulate Pyongyang to initiate massive reforms and openness (this theme will be discussed later). At a time when there is every incentive to open itself and accommodate the conciliatory policies of Washington and Seoul, North Korea is resolutely determined to withstand any external pressure. Even with the realization that any military confrontation against U.S.-backed South Korea will surely bring a total destruction of the country, Pyongyang has repeatedly engaged in provocative actions against a powerful enemy. Why? Is North Korea truly abnormal beyond the comprehension of rational reasoning? Is the leadership so vicious that it cares nothing about the livelihood of its own people or so precarious and disarrayed that any kind of coordinated campaign to cope with the economic crisis is not possible? Can and will North Korea withstand the massive current of democratization throughout the formerly socialist world? These questions require an in-depth analysis into the underlying forces behind policies and policymaking and an understanding of the dynamism of the relationships among behavioral motivations, belief perceptions, political players, and the predicaments faced by the system as a whole and by the leadership itself.

In this book, I maintain that with a proper understanding of the society and people, the anomaly can be explicated. Once one is capable of *empathizing* with the North Korean mindset, no matter how unconventional it may be, the seemingly irrational behavioral pattern can be seen as being rational. The purpose of this book, then, is to shed light on the *mindset* of North Koreans that dictates the policymaking process and its output. In this process, it is imperative to examine the nature and ramifications of *Juche* ideology. This ideology is pervasive. It is more than a political system of values; it is a way of life. This book, then, is a comprehensive examination of *Juche* and its implications for policy behaviors of the political system.

Further Questions

If human history is any indication, North Korea cannot remain secluded indefinitely; the mystery surrounding this unknown system will soon unravel as the world political milieu undergoes a fundamental change and abandons the legacy of the Cold War order. Nations are moving in the direction of pragmatism and the pursuit of tangible national interests by participating in the global economic system. Because this system operates on the capitalist principle of supply and demand, many controlled systems, including the socialist ones, are reorienting themselves to facilitate their activities in the new environment. Can North Korea stay away from this trend? Can it maintain the existing system while participating in the international arena? Will North Korea follow in the footsteps of Mao's China? Now that Kim Il Sung is long gone, will the leadership of North Korea be able to maintain its hold on power? If so, for how long? Many observers still believe that the passing of Kim Il Sung will ultimately bring about the demise of the system, yet it is puzzling that there appear to be no clear symptoms of power struggle following his death. These and other questions are constantly asked, but conflicting answers are heard with equal plausibility. The present study, then, is intended to address these issues. In the next chapter, I elaborate on the thesis that a system as puzzling as North Korea can best be approached from the perspective of perceptions and motivations behind policies and politics. Accordingly, any meaningful study of North Korea should begin with an in-depth examination of the belief system that so pervasively penetrates the entire spectrum of the society and guides political behavior at all levels of the system. The specific aim of this book, therefore, is to examine the formation of the mass belief systems embedded in *Juche*. My analysis advances the premise that North Korea has developed an ideology that is comparable to a form of theology and a society that exhibits many characteristics of religious fundamentalism. I also advance the view that *Juche* is the locus of North Korean society and political culture; only with a proper understanding of the belief system embedded in the *Juche* doctrine can one explain North Korean political behavior, politics, and policy orientations. This book consists of three clusters of chapters: first, chapters in which conceptual and methodological issues designed to advance an appropriate approach are dealt with; second, chapters dealing with the nature and evolution of the ideology of *Juche* itself; and finally, chapters showing specific policy orientations and behaviors as examples.

If limitations on reliable information and references hamper scholarly inquiry, no study can be as hampered as that of North Korea. Of course, there is a large amount of material published in both South Korea and North Korea, but its reliability and objectiveness might be limited for obvious and understandable reasons. I rely heavily on firsthand information and personal observations obtained from my numerous visits to this most reclusive country. Since my first visit in 1981, I have visited North Korea more than thirty times, mostly in the 1990s. However, in many incidents, the hosting personnel desired or explicitly demanded that their anonymity be kept, and I honored their wishes and requests.

* * *

I wish to express appreciation to the Korea Asia Pacific Peace Committee, the Committee on Overseas Compatriots, and the now-defunct Academy of *Juche* Science in North Korea for their generous hospitality during my trips. I am also deeply indebted to the scholars and government officials there who provided me with a wealth of information, without which this book would not have been conceived. However, I am solely responsible for the contents and opinions expressed in this volume.

I also wish to express my heartfelt gratitude to the understanding friends and colleagues at the University of Georgia for their unreserved support when I needed to make trips even when classes were in session. They often filled in for my classes because they valued my efforts to help the cause of mutual understanding and the promotion of peace in the Korean peninsula and the Asia-Pacific region. I thank especially Thomas Lauth, head of the Department of Political Science at the University of Georgia, in this regard. I would like to acknowledge Don Rodgers for invaluable suggestions and careful reading of the manuscript. Particular appreciation is given to my wife, Wonie, and three children, Clara, Kenneth, and Sharon, for their understanding and encouragement, especially when I had to leave home for extended periods of time.

This book is dedicated to my parents, who were victims of the tragic history of a divided Korea and passed away without ever seeing again their parents and relatives who lived across the border.

1

The Perception Approach

Failure in explaining and predicting North Korean policy choices may be attributed to three sources of inadequacy: information paucity, normative biases, and inappropriate conceptual frameworks. Much has been said and written about the first two. The lack of reliable and sufficient information on North Korea cannot be understated. To label policies as unconventional or irrational can be construed as viewing the North Korean case through the prism of Western bias. However, what has not been sufficiently addressed is the fact that the study of North Korea may suffer from the usage of an incorrect conceptual framework. Most studies on North Korea have used three general approaches that have been unable to generate explanatory-predictive analyses.

The most common approach is the elite leadership approach, whereby power politics surrounding the very top leadership is given the primary emphasis. This approach is popular largely because North Korea has always been known as a centrist system where the locus of power is monolithic and centered around one person. In this case, the study of North Korea is often considered almost synonymous with the study of Kim Il Sung or Kim Jong Il. Here, personality traits of the person and his personal ties with other individuals are regarded as the key to any explanation of the system's policy behavior. The problems with this approach are numerous. First of all, securing information on North Korean leadership that is both reliable and sufficient has always been almost impossible. Second, the personality of a particular individual tends to be unpredictable and often inconsistent with actual behaviors. Third, emphasis on a leadership as the unit of analysis will be hampered by its demise or, as in the case of North Korea, the death of the leader himself. No one had predicted that the death of Kim Il Sung would come in July 1994; few predicted the leadership of Kim Jong Il to be as stable and solid as it has been in the post–Kim Il Sung period.

Another popular approach is the institutional approach, which examines the nature and structure of politically vital institutions such as the Workers' Party of Korea, the People's Army, and the government bureaucracy. One fashionable aspect of this approach is to weigh the relative power of the institutions to discern the direction of policy. Since the death of Kim Il Sung, analysts have wanted to ascertain the military's capability because they concluded that the military leadership controlled the highly controversial nuclear and missile programs. Moreover, they also concluded that successor Kim Jong Il was unable to control the armed forces and that the latter might have grudges against the leadership. The problem with this approach is the severe paucity of information on such inherently secretive institutions. In North Korea, institutional structure often does not lend itself to explanation of political dynamics because institutions tend to be ceremonial rather than substantive. Rankings of any of the institutions do not necessarily reflect the level and amount of power and influence. Thus, this approach is vastly inadequate as an explanatory tool.

Finally, there is the power politics approach, in which the international, regional, and inter-Korean political context is considered a main determinant of policy behavior. According to this approach, the forces surrounding the peninsula have decisively affected the nature and character of the system. The schism between China and the Soviet Union in the late 1960s caused North Korea to follow a path of neutrality, paving the way for the ideology of *Juche*. Major policies such as the *Chollima* campaign of the late 1950s and the Red Flag Youth campaign in the late 1960s were replications of China's Great Leap Forward and Cultural Revolution. According to this approach, the demise of the socialist systems in Europe and the massive reforms in China should have affected North Korea. This perspective, however, fails to account for the policies and political behaviors surrounding the controversial nuclear weapons and missile programs, which differ from expectations stemming from the external post–Cold War and globalization context.

To overcome some of the shortcomings of the conventional approaches, I use an alternative approach in this study, which may be called the "perception approach." It is guided by the premise that state of mind determines behavioral patterns. Therefore, it is imperative for an explanatory and predictive analysis of behavior to begin with an understanding of the belief system context in which the behavior takes place. An adequate understanding of the belief system requires the analysis of a myriad of variables concerning the nature and the process of socialization at all levels of social and cultural reality.

The perception analysis helps in understanding the attitudes of the perceiver. Too often, students of international and comparative studies have focused on institutions, power politics, and economic output as the units of analysis, as opposed to focusing on human variables such as perceptions, need satisfaction, and the process of learning and political socialization. As a result, policies and behavioral traits that are inconsistent with accepted norms in open societies and defy "rational" expectation are often characterized as being abnormal or irrational. In this way, studies on North Korea and other "rogue" systems are anchored in what might be termed as "epistemic imperialism," which insists that *they* should behave in accordance with *our* norms. In this book, I attempt to provide a different perspective, one that is derived from the "phenomenological" viewpoint in which what is perceived constitutes the reality. I contend that one should understand and react to the perceptions of reality of the North Koreans themselves. I further contend that no perception is inexplicable if one is willing and able to put oneself in the shoes of the perceiver. Only with such empathy can one begin to find rationality in seemingly irrational and random patterns of behavior.

An understanding of the cultural atmosphere of the country being examined is indispensable to the perception approach. For this reason, the cultural approach that has been developed in comparative studies of world politics must be employed. It has been used in a number of empirical inquiries since the early 1960s and is based primarily upon the work of Gabriel Almond and James Coleman (1960) and Almond and Sidney Verba (1963), although numerous definitions and applications of the concept have been developed since that time.[1] The approach arose as a response to the formal-legalistic studies of political systems dominant in comparative politics, which often were unable to provide convincing explanations for differences between developmental experiences. The cultural approach is based upon the postulate of oriented action. The assumption is that people do not react objectively to changing situations but that they react to them through what Harry Eckstein refers to as "mediating orientations," in which responses to stimuli (actions in situations) are believed to result from both the experience of objective situations and the actors' subjective processing of experience.[2]

Political culture can help to explain a particular set of beliefs or attitudes as a product of the history of a society, and it can mediate between certain socioeconomic changes and the people. Political culture can shape and be shaped by socioeconomic changes in a particular society. As Steven White states, "Its merit, discriminatingly employed, is to identify those features of political belief and behavior which are historically derivable, specific to a particular national or other sub-group, and likely to have a continuing influence upon future political evolution."[3]

Central to the conceptualization and development of political culture, then, is the notion of historical context. Political culture can be seen to develop out of and then shape the objective and subjective social, economic, and political conditions of a people. Culture and the ideologies that spring from culture do not arise in a vacuum. They are developed over long periods of history and are conditioned by the traditions, beliefs, and social practices of a people. One must be careful, though, not to become too deterministic in discussing the development of political culture. Political culture can and does change. This change can be brought about by a number of influences ranging from dramatic experiences such as war or revolution to the concerted efforts of a new regime to alter the norms, values, and behaviors of the people. Still, regardless of events, culture is slow to change. Even when dramatic socioeconomic and political changes are occurring, one should not expect a group or an individual to suddenly lose all vestiges of the past. Reactions to new objective conditions, situations, ideas, and possibilities will continue to be influenced and to some extent guided by existing subjective cultural orientations. It is in that light that we must espouse the salient culture of Korean Confucianism and the historical context in which the North Korean "perception" is formed.

The Cultural Context of Confucianism in North Korea

In an ordinary revolutionary setting in which new programs and ideologies are to replace traditional and conventional ways of life, the existence of any age-old cultural legacy is counterproductive to the revolutionary cause. In China, for instance, Confucianism was considered as an obstacle to socialist consolidation. In part this attitude prompted the Great Proletarian Cultural Revolution in the mid-1960s. But North Korea did not experience much resistance from Confucianism. On the contrary, Confucianism in North Korea helped the development of a charismatic leadership and paternalist socialism to the extent that without Confucian cultural influences inherent in the historical heritage, the system itself would not have been constructed in the way it has been. In fact, when discussing the politics, society, and culture, or more specifically the political culture, of North Korea, primary importance has to be placed on Confucianism. As Lucian Pye writes, "The evolution of Confucianism produced distinct political cultures, each with a unique approach to the concept of power."[4] Korea is commonly recognized as the most Confucian of the Confucian countries, emerging as the most thoroughly Confucianized state in Asia during the Yi (Chosun) Dynasty (1392–1910). Martina Deuchler observes perceptively that:

> Chinese neo-Confucianism, which from the late Koryo became the major intellectual force in Korea, inspired a new class of Korean scholar-officials with a particular vision of social organization and gave them the necessary guidelines to implant it in their own environment. The reorganization of Korean society thus inaugurated reached a scope and depth that were rarely attained by social action anywhere else.[5]

During the 600 years of the Yi Dynasty, there was a strong effort on the part of the elite to Confucianize the society. One distinct feature of Korean Confucianism was its emphasis on familial structure. In its teachings to children, the inward and familial relationships were emphasized far more than the outward relationships between friends and the ruler or the nation. Thus, Korean children were taught Confucian familialism almost solely, and the nationalistic or patriotic elements of Confucianism were deemphasized. The Korean texts ranked the importance of the five Confucian relationships in the following order: father-son, husband-wife, old-young, friend-friend, and ruler-subject.[6]

The behavior of the Korean people was strongly guided by this familial ethic. The centerpiece of the Korean system was the kinship system, based on patrilineal descent groups. Efforts were made to display relationships to important or influential people. Families created and printed intricate genealogies that would verify their ancestral bonds with people of significance. In order to become socially, politically, and economically prominent, one had to display properly certified lineage.

Because of the importance of the family or blood bond, children made strong efforts to bring honor to the family. Children focused on filial piety, pleasing their parents through various family-focused rituals and through the highly competitive civil service examination process. The goal of the children was to bring glory to the family through the development of a strong understanding of the Confucian texts and through the attainment of a good government position that would provide the family with wealth and power.

Great emphasis was placed on family-oriented rituals in Korea. The formality of the Yi Dynasty led to a preference for formal Confucian rituals. Ceremonies such as weddings, funerals, and other family-oriented events were quite important, but the most important of the rituals were related to ancestor worship. According to Spencer Palmer, the reluctance of Koreans to accept the finiteness and transitory nature of life led them to develop a belief that there is some sort of existence after death. This belief contributed to a complex system of ancestor worship, through which the living strive to show respect for the dead and provide for them to make the afterlife as comfortable as possible. These rituals include providing food and other necessities for the deceased and, to show devotion, observing a mourning period of three years.[7]

It is important to note that during the Japanese occupation of Korea from 1910 until 1945, Japanese influences affected the form and structure of Korean Confucianism. Although the fundamental structure of Confucianism remained the same, coercive Japanese influences did create some confusion in the Korean Confucian personality. The primary difference between Japanese Confucianism and Korean Confucianism is the rank order of importance of the five Confucian relationships. In contrast to the Korean version, the Japanese version places the greatest emphasis on the ruler-subject relationship and much less emphasis on the father-son relationship. Thus the generation born after 1919 confronted a confusing mix of Confucianism. As Hosuck Kang observes:

> Their personality orientation was both inward and familialistic (Korean), and outward and nationalistic (Japanese). Their system of relationships (role expectations) was also maintained with the ties between father and son and between ruler and subject. The value system was composed of filial piety to their parents, and loyalty to the Japanese emperor. The split personality was still in the Confucian *jen* and *i* framework.[8]

This, of course, is not to argue that Confucianism was weakened during the Japanese rule, but instead to show that perhaps the particular form of Korean Confucianism might have been predicated upon a delicate balance of the family-centered Confucian structure and the state-centered Confucian system.

The focus of Confucianism is *man* and, what is more important, human relationships. To say that the focus of Confucianism is *man,* though, is not to suggest that the individual is of great value in isolation. The goal of Confucianism is to teach individuals how they should fit into a greater social network and to ensure that they are fulfilling their role in the family and society. As Changjiang Sun states, the effort is to "integrate all people into the network of patriarchal society and make each person a node in this 'homogeneous' big network."[9] Confucian political culture, then, emphasizes above all else group loyalty, obedience, and a consensual style of rule that avoids direct confrontation. In other words, Confucianism "speaks of the desirability of negating the human error of individualism."[10] Thus, Korean Confucianism places little value on individuals acting out of self-interest separate from the collective. The individual is given worth and value only in the context of his relationship with and contribution to the family. Families are given worth and value based on their lineage or the successes of their family members. Thus, individual orientation and individual action are anathema to the development of a strong, learned, virtuous individual and to the betterment of the family and society as a whole.

Confucianism led to the development of a particular social order in Korea. In addition, it is clear that the Confucian familial and social structure contributed to the development of a distinct political culture, that is, an observable configuration of values, symbols, orientations, and behavioral patterns. Although the North Korean regime made efforts to eliminate Confucian beliefs and behavior from North Korean society and political culture, it can be argued that strong vestiges of Confucianism persist in the current North Korean political and social structure.

In short, there are a few salient and characteristic elements in Korean Confucianism that have clearly reinforced the formation and maturation of the political ideology of *Juche.* Elements such as a family-centered outlook, man (rather than matter) being the center of the universe, and the notion of life after death have all exerted profound influence in the philosophical structure of the *Juche* ideology. I will discuss this important theme further in Chapter 3.

The Historical Context

The historical context in which the ideology of *Juche* was initially conceived and transformed has undergone a series of transformations that must be identified for a plausible explanation of its belief system. The most central historical condition was the colonial experience under Japanese imperial power for thirty-six years (1910–1945). This period was preceded by centuries of Korean dynastic rule, the last of which, the Yi Dynasty, was helpless in defending national sovereignty against a militarily superior Japan. The period of Japanese rule left a profound impact on essentially every sphere of Korean life. The colonial period was one of political oppression, economic exploitation, social dislocation, demographic disintegration, and most of all, national humiliation. As will be seen, the emergence of Kim Il Sung's charismatic leadership would not have been possible without the account of his role in the nationalist struggle against Japan.

Another historical context within which the belief system of *Juche* became reinforced and further refined was the Korean War (1950–1953), in which the forces of the United States and other member states of the United Nations participated on the side of the South, resulting in massive human casualties and destruction. Following the war, South Korea has continuously been under the security protection of the United States, with some 36,000 U.S. troops being stationed in the peninsula. Because the ideology embedded in *Juche* professes nationalism, this historical condition has made it even more indigenous. Furthermore, as South Korea became a powerful economic force in Asia and the U.S.-backed military acquired sophisticated weapons, North Korea felt a great security threat from the South. It led the regime to solidify its power base and integrate the system around the official ideology. In competing with the South, North Korea needed to establish an ideology that would manifest a sharp contrast with the South Korean ideological structure.

Finally, the tension and struggle between the communist superpowers of China and the Soviet Union was yet another historical condition that affected the formation and evolution of ideology. The demise of the Soviet Union itself, followed by the breakup of Eastern European socialist systems, has also intensified the Pyongyang regime's obsession with shielding its people and society from external influences. The ideology reflected an environmental change by emphasizing the necessity of creating a new breed of socialism with Korean character. As will be elaborated on later, North Korea has been successful in making its ideology distinctly different from all other ideological expositions of socialism.

In short, *Juche* may be considered as a product of history. Had there been a different history, the nature and structure of the ideological belief system of *Juche* would have been different, if it ever came about at all.

However, historical factors may affect people's orientations and value systems, but they do not function in a vacuum. As explained in the preceding section, Korean Confucianism allied with the historical settings to produce *Juche* as the unique ideology of North Korea.

Notes

1. Gabriel Almond and James Coleman, eds., *The Politics of the Developing Areas* (Princeton, N.J.: Princeton University Press, 1960); Gabriel Almond and Sidney Verba, *The Civic Culture: Political Attitudes and Democracy in Five Nations* (Princeton, N.J.: Princeton University Press, 1963).

2. Harry Eckstein, "A Culturalist Theory of Political Change," *American Political Science Review* 82, no. 3 (1988), p. 790.

3. Steven White, *Political Culture and Soviet Politics* (New York: St. Martin's Press, 1979), pp. 15–16.

4. Lucian Pye, *Asian Power and Politics: The Cultural Dimensions of Authority* (Cambridge, Mass.: Harvard University Press, 1985), p. 254.

5. Martina Deuchler, *The Confucian Transformation of Korea: A Study of Society and Ideology* (Cambridge, Mass.: Harvard University Press, 1992), p. 6.

6. Thomas Hosuck Kang, "Changes in the North Korean Personality from Confucianist to Communist," in Jae Kyu Park and Jung Gun Kim, eds., *The Politics of North Korea* (Seoul, Korea: Institute for Far Eastern Studies, 1979), p. 73.

7. Spencer Palmer, *Confucian Rituals in Korea* (Berkeley, Calif.: Asian Humanities Press, 1984), pp. 89–90.

8. Kang, "Changes," p. 77.

9. Changjiang Sun, "Chinese Society, Chinese Confucianism, and the Modernization of China," in Silke Krieger and Rolf Trauzettel, eds., *Confucianism and the Modernization of China* (Mainz, Germany: V. Hase and Koehler Verlag, 1991), p. 392.

10. Harmon Ziegler, *Pluralism, Corporatism and Confucianism: Political Association and Conflict Regulation in the United States, Europe, and Taiwan* (Philadelphia: Temple University Press, 1988), p. 125.

2

The Advent and Evolution of *Juche* Ideology

To trace the origin of *Juche* is difficult because it depends largely on which of the various stages of the ideological evolution can be legitimately called a form of ideology as opposed to a slogan. The Korean word *Juche* is a common word that has been in use as long as the language itself. The word simply means self-reliance or self-support, which can be applied to individuals as well as groups in all situations. The term *Juche,* or *Jaju,* was commonly used during the Japanese occupation by all the nationalist leaders who lamented the incapability of the Korean people themselves to govern an independent sovereign state and attributed the colonial humiliation to this lack of self-governance. It is not surprising that Kim Il Sung allegedly used the concept as early as the 1920s because he was involved at various times in anti-Japanese campaigns.[1] However, the use of the term *Juche* does not coincide with the birth of an ideology. There were five distinct stages in the evolution of the ideology.

Before examining the five phases of the ideological evolution, it will be useful to clarify the conditions of the emergence of the ideology as spelled out by North Korean theoreticians themselves. *Juche* theoreticians in North Korea maintain that the emergence of the ideology in North Korea was not accidental; rather, the history of Korea has provided a legitimate nursing ground on which the peculiar ideas of *Juche* can be articulated. They propose two analytically distinct conditions: the objective historical condition and the subjective human condition. Only when both conditions are simultaneously present will they become sufficient.

The Necessary and Sufficient
Condition for the Birth of *Juche*

The historical environment and the world power structure surrounding the peninsula, both aspects beyond the control of the Korean people, constitute the *objective condition*. According to this perspective, the expansion of Western powers and Japan in East Asia, preceding the national partition and the ensuing development of a world power structure, caused the emergence of *Juche* on the Korean peninsula. The Opium War in China (1840–1842), the resultant humiliating subjugation of the once-proud Han Chinese to the militarily superior Western powers, and the colonization of Manchuria, Korea, and much of the Southeast Asian territories by imperial Japan (alluded to in the previous chapter), are all considered to be the direct historical forces necessitating the emergence of *Juche*.

Japanese colonial policies were designed to assimilate the Korean population, as a subservient class of citizens, into Japanese culture and society. Thus, the national independence movement was necessary to the survival of the nation itself. *Juche* theoreticians attribute the colonization of the nation to two factors: military inferiority and weak nationalism. For this reason, North Koreans have constantly been reminded that Kim Il Sung's lifelong struggle was to militarily prepare for self-defense and ideologically solidify the people through nationalism. The principle of militarism has been instrumental in the development and compilation of weapons above and beyond the country's economic means. North Korea's capability in the production of nuclear weapons and long-range missiles should be understood in the light of the country's resolute determination to strengthen military power. At the same time, Korean nationalism in the form of *Juche* has shown incremental progression from antiforeignism to an ethnocentric sense of national superiority, which guides the worldview of *Juche* itself. Therefore, it is obvious that the colonial experience under Japan was a necessary condition for the emergence of the ideology.

Furthermore, *Juche* theoreticians argue that the entire history of Korea has laid the foundation upon which the very conception of the ideology was made. The theoreticians point to the fact that the Korean history is one of exploitation by such foreign powers as the Chinese, Russians, Mongolians, Japanese, and Americans; in the process, the Korean people endured national humiliation, physical suffering, and the deprivation of human dignity, yet they maintained a strong sense of ethnic purity.[2] According to *Juche* theoreticians, the severity of these experiences incited the Korean people's aspiration for national independence and made them uniquely qualified for developing an ideology that upholds a nation's self-determination.

The national division imposed by external powers and the ensuing conflict that resulted in millions of casualties and separated families may also be seen as objective conditions. The unfortunate human trauma, in this case, is also attributed to a lack of military preparedness and the absence of national consensus on a nationalist ideology. According to *Juche*, no other people in the world has experienced the same kind and degree of human misfortune, and this painful experience has been effectively used to create this unique ideology. Another objective condition, the perpetual tension between Beijing and Moscow, especially in the late 1960s, placed North Korea in the precarious position of having to maintain equidistance from the two communist powers and forced Pyongyang to develop an ideology of neutrality by denouncing dependence on either side.

Considering the aforementioned objective conditions, North Koreans have been led to believe that such an ideology as *Juche* was naturally expected to emerge from their country. Yet, according to *Juche* theoreticians, the objective historical elements by themselves would not have been sufficient for the ideology to emerge. *Juche* theoreticians never hesitate to suggest that the presence of such a great leader as Kim Il Sung at the right historical moment provided the basis for the subjective conditions. It is hardly surprising that *Juche* is asserted to have been created by Kim Il Sung himself and refined and advanced by his son. To North Korean intellectuals, it is absurd to condone the claim that certain individuals such as Hwang Jang Yop, who defected to South Korea in 1997, had any role in its creation.[3] They believe that Kim's early activities in Manchuria for national emancipation from Japan laid the foundation of the ideology.

What makes the presence of the man Kim Il Sung such an imperative requirement for the birth of the ideology? What does this person represent in the minds of the people? Most of all, Kim represents the peasantry and working class. Mankyongdae, his birthplace in Pyongyang, is the mecca of *Juche*. At the site, household items used by his parents and grandparents are displayed to convey two themes: extreme poverty and the revolutionary consciousness of the family. From the onset, Kim Il Sung has been epitomized as a friend of the working class. His life also epitomizes nationalism; the numerous accounts of Kim's life stories and his 1992 autobiography *Segiwa doburo* (With the century) depict that his love for his country was greater than his personal ambition or his need to fulfill his family obligations. The sole purpose of his life was to ensure the collective well-being of the common people. Furthermore, Kim Il Sung is carefully portrayed as a humanist with unparalleled compassion for the needy.

In short, the presence of Kim Il Sung is the single most important subjective condition; the leader, in this case, embodies all of the qualities desirable for *Juche*, including a close affinity to the working class, revolutionary consciousness, nationalism, collectivism, and humanism. As discussed later, *Juche* itself is the crystallization of these values and principles. *Juche* theoreticians maintain that all the objective conditions would have been wasted had Kim Il Sung not been born at such a crucial time. They point to the fact that the South, in spite of all the similar objective and historical experiences, was not only unable to develop such an ideology but also moved in a direction that opposed the ideals for which *Juche* stands. In short, the fact that Kim Il Sung was born and lived at the historical juncture when the aforementioned objective conditions abounded provides the necessary and sufficient conditions for the emergence of such an ideology.

Evolution of *Juche*

Unlike a typical political ideology (such as liberal democracy or Marxist socialism) that has a discernible and constant conceptual structure, *Juche*'s conceptual or philosophical structure has shown continuous evolution. Generally, one might identify five distinct phases in its evolution. Here, one will notice the underlying rule that the ideology has had to reflect the system's aspirations or goals in the context of ever-changing international and domestic political climates. *Juche* theoreticians are never ambiguous about the fact that their ideology changes. In fact, they find a source of merit in the changing nature of the ideology. One scholar at the Academy of *Juche* Science asserted that an ideology that is alive has to change as any living being must change.[4]

Juche *as Anti-Japanism*

Kim Il Sung, as the "creator" of *Juche*, used the concept extensively from the mid-1920s to the early 1950s to express his deeply felt sentiments against Japanese colonial rule and especially against those political leaders who were incapable of preserving national independence and political sovereignty. He advocated, as did many others, that Koreans must fight to win back their nation by promoting combat capability and spiritual solidarity against the militarily stronger Japanese soldiers. In fact, the formation of Kim Il Sung's charisma began with the theme that he sacrificed his personal well-being for the noble cause of saving the country from Japanese colonialism. Even when he was a little boy at the age of twelve, he was said to be preoccupied with the aspiration for national independence. As the liberation of the country from Japanese control was the most important policy goal, the country naturally advanced the popular theme of anticolonialism. At this stage, the term *Juche* meant little more than antagonist sentiment against a specific target. In this sense, *Juche* was not established even as a rudimentary form of ideology.

Juche *as Antihegemonism*

In the decade following the Korean War, North Korea found a new enemy that helped South Korea and destroyed much of the northern half of the country with massive air strikes; the new enemy was the United States of America. In the war, the city of Pyongyang was practically leveled to the ground, leaving no physical structures untouched and millions of people killed or wounded. Ever since the war, there has been a genuine fear among North Korean residents that U.S. forces might renew hostilities. The fact that U.S. forces have been stationed continuously in the South and have performed routine military exercises jointly with South Korean armed forces has always made North Korea uneasy and apprehensive. Since the adoption of the armistice agreement in 1953, Pyongyang has persistently demanded the withdrawal of U.S. troops from the Korean peninsula. North Koreans were particularly resentful of the hegemonic expansion of U.S. military influence.

Coupled with the presence of the United States in Korea, the growing Sino-Soviet dispute in 1960, which drove the two communist giants to the brink of war, and Soviet involvement in Eastern Europe and Vietnam were instrumental in the growth of antihegemonism in the North Korean political and diplomatic orientation. Pyongyang was put in a precarious position between the two superpowers of the communist bloc; it did not wish to antagonize either of them by maintaining intimate relations with one at the expense of the other. This situation forced the Pyongyang government to declare a path of equidistance and thus self-reliance. But it was the Soviet Union that became a more convenient target of North Korean criticism because of Moscow's expansionist policy. By contrast, China provided a role model of sorts by indulging in the massive indigenization of

Marxism-Leninism during the fanatical phase of the Great Proletariat Cultural Revolution in the late 1960s. Although North Korea did not express great enthusiasm for the Cultural Revolution, it restrained itself from publicly denouncing the Chinese campaign for creating a personality cult for Mao Zedong. In fact, North Korea followed in the footsteps of Mao in instigating concerted efforts to develop an indigenous ideology and in creating a charismatic leadership for Kim Il Sung. Just as Mao criticized Moscow for its hegemonic policies, Kim expressed displeasure with the Soviet Union's interventionist policies. As pointed out in the preceding discussion, this doctrine of antihegemonism was further reinforced by Pyongyang's interest in denouncing U.S. influence in South Korea. In short, the ideological insistence of political sovereignty under *Juche* became reinforced by the political reality surrounding the peninsula.

Antihegemonism was also used by Kim Il Sung to consolidate his power and to integrate the country politically. By 1958, contenders for power challenging Kim's leadership and factions within the Workers' Party of Korea had been harshly purged under the pretension that they were leaning toward and siding with the Soviets or the Chinese.[5]

Juche *as Nationalist Ideology*

By the end of the 1960s, North Korea had become a stable regime devoid of any immediate source of opposition to Kim's authority. His leadership could not be challenged, for it was steadily gaining a charismatic quality. By this time, as pointed out above, almost all political enemies had been eliminated from leadership circles. Furthermore, the economy had fully recovered from the shambles of the Korean War. It may sound unbelievable, but until 1970, the North Korean gross national product per capita was higher than that of South Korea.

What Pyongyang needed at this historical juncture was a persuasive ideology with which to legitimize Kim's charismatic leadership and to demonstrate ideological superiority to the South. It may be generalized that once a regime is established and stability is secured, the next step taken by the regime is to expand its legitimacy through political education. During this stage of development, which may be termed political integration, the ruling elite attempts to further the basis of regime legitimacy through the introduction of an official political ideology.[6] Many newly independent countries have consistently promoted nationalism as their official ideology. North Korea was not an exception.

Nationalism began to be accentuated as the cornerstone of *Juche*. The fact that South Korea was led by Rhee Syngman, who was educated in and had been a long-term resident of the United States, indicated a strong U.S. influence on the Rhee regime and provided Kim Il Sung with the necessary ammunition to condemn the South for being shamelessly antinationalistic and pathetically subjected to foreign domination. In contrast to the South, the North was in a position to declare a policy of equidistance to its communist allies and join the nonaligned movement. Pyongyang managed to establish *Juche* institutes in nonaligned countries such as India. This political climate proved to be an ideal situation for Pyongyang to adopt ultranationalism as the foundation of *Juche* ideology.

In the mid-1960s, nationalism was still primarily antiforeignism without a coherent philosophical structure. But as the ideology was further refined in the late 1960s and much of the 1970s, goals and strategies to implement nationalism were identified. Specifically, *Juche* was defined in terms of three analytically distinct objectives: political sovereignty, economic subsistence, and military self-defense. Political sovereignty forced the regime to limit its political and diplomatic ties to those countries Pyongyang found ideologically compatible, thus limiting foreign relations to only a handful of socialist countries. It is in this period that North Korea campaigned against the South for superiority in legitimacy. Overwhelmed by nationalist sentiment, Pyongyang believed that the Seoul regime could be overthrown by its own masses on the grounds that the South lacked nationalist solidarity and thus political legitimacy. The North Korean government believed that the people in the South could be induced to participate in an antiregime mass movement only if their precarious stability was disturbed. The infiltration of the Blue House, the presidential residence in Seoul, by a North Korean commando unit in 1968 could be interpreted as the expression of Pyongyang's determination to disturb political stability in hopes of inciting mass uprisings against the Park Chung Hee regime.

The policy of economic self-reliance deterred economic growth, and North Korea fell further behind its neighboring countries through the 1970s and beyond, especially South Korea.[7] This period happened to coincide with the high-growth years for the newly industrializing countries (NICs) and the "Asian tigers," of which South Korea was one. All these countries employed the export-led strategy toward economic growth. Instead of promoting balanced growth, as was the case in North Korea, the NICs concentrated their efforts on the production of export goods that

could be competitive in the international market. But North Korea alienated itself from world economic activities in order to establish a *Juche*
economy. One should not forget that at this time there was growing support among Third World countries for the *dependencia* movement, which
proclaimed that economic and cultural independence was the only way of
avoiding certain subjugation to the industrialized countries.

What has been most economically detrimental is the principle of military self-reliance. Kim Il Sung's opinion on the importance of military
power was unambiguously demonstrated in his early years when he was
campaigning for national independence. In his Manchuria days, his group
was known for its employment of militant means for which weapons had
been secured at all costs. He criticized Kim Koo, Yo Woon Yong, and Ahn
Chang Ho, who had a broad base of support for their patriotism and
reliance on the nonmilitary/nonviolence principle. According to Kim, a
nonviolent revolution would not work in the fight against colonialism and
expansionism.[8] In fact, military self-reliance was viewed as a necessary
condition for political sovereignty. No amount of resources devoted to
building military strength was considered too large; North Korea has consistently invested an inordinate proportion of its national wealth in the
weapons industry. Kim also witnessed the dramatic event when the formidable Japanese imperial forces, which had invaded East and Southeast
Asia and Russia and eventually bombed the Hawaiian Islands, had to
unconditionally surrender to the power of U.S. atomic bombs. Thus it is
not surprising for Kim to be engulfed by his own obsessive desire for
weapons, specifically atomic bombs.

Although the military principle may have deterred economic growth
in general, North Korea's primary source of foreign currency earnings has
been the export of everything from conventional weapons to sophisticated missiles. There seems to be no shortage of demand for North Korean
weapons in the international market, especially in the Arab world. The
controversy surrounding North Korea's nuclear weapons production must
be seen in the greater context of North Korea's ideological doctrine of military self-reliance. I will deal with this issue in Chapter 11.

In short, the policies designed to adhere to the principles of political,
economic, and military self-reliance may not be designed to attain maxi-
mal material payoff. In fact, they have been largely counterproductive for
the development of industry and often detrimental to the welfare of the
society as a whole. Nevertheless, the principles were intended to promote
nationalism among the masses and to demonstrate a position of superiority for regime legitimacy over the South.

Juche *as Paternalist Socialism*

As the ideology became intimately tied to the regime as an instrument of legitimatization of power, the leadership articulated a new theoretical dimension in which the leadership itself was sanctified as the generator and embodiment of the ideology. This process not only coincided with a quantum leap in the charisma of the Great Leader but also with the regime's need for the official promotion of Kim Jong Il's leadership caliber, which began in conjunction with the Sixth Party Congress in 1980. After observing the succession process in the Soviet Union, Vietnam, and China, Kim Il Sung decided that the great flaw of socialist systems was the almost universal inability of the ruling elite to solve the succession issue. It was not accidental that North Korea selected the hereditary approach as the succession mechanism. The North Korean people had never seen a popularly elected leadership in their entire history. The dynastic systems of early modern Korea were replaced abruptly by Japanese colonial power. Kim Il Sung was quickly and naturally seen as a royal leader of sorts. Thus, deification of the leader's family was not a deviation from the age-old Oriental despotic cultural perspective. Civic education textbooks were written or rewritten with the clear ideological objective of political socialization of the masses into the belief that not only the Great Leader himself was superhuman but also his entire family line. At Mankyongdae, exhibits were designed to promote the charisma of the leader and his family. In North Korea, everyone, regardless of age, education level, geographical origin, or sex, has visited this shrine at least several times.

In Robert Tucker's theory of the process of charisma formation, a charismatic person evolves from the formative stage of "charismatic aspirant" through the progressive stage of "charismatic luminary" and eventually to the stage of "charismatic giant."[9] By the late 1980s, Kim's charisma had developed to the level of a "charismatic giant," whereby his leadership was believed to be predestined. He became a natural leader, much like the father of a family. At this point, his actual leadership defied the contractual foundation of leadership.[10] A leader who has solidified his leadership on the grounds of paternalism is not subject to impeachment of any kind because such a leadership is perceived as a matter of natural order. In the context of Confucianism, respecting the father is an obligation that constitutes the utmost virtue. This fact, regardless of the father's conduct or contribution to the family, bears profound implications. Most of all, the leadership of the "father" is not to be judged by what it does but instead by what it is. Under such a system, the basis of regime legitimacy has nothing to do with the theory of social contract, thus giving Kim Il Sung the natural right to rule.

Another significant implication of paternalism is that not only the "father" himself but the whole family is destined to rule. This idea will naturally sanctify the hereditary succession of power by the son. Thus, it was not coincidental that Kim Jong Il was officially designated as the heir apparent at the Sixth Party Congress in 1980. It is intriguing to note that the young Kim's ascension to power was initially promoted on the basis of his abilities rather than on his family ties. In fact, one scholar at the Kim Il Sung University unequivocally told me in the summer of 1981 that the legitimization of Kim Jong Il's leadership would have been easier if he had not been the son of Kim Il Sung; he explained that the son's ability and achievements tended to be discredited because of his relationship to the Great Leader. His superb qualifications, according to this scholar, stand on their own merit.[11] However, as the charismatization process advanced more quickly, the young Kim benefited from the family relationship. As his father attained charisma as the paternalistic leader, the son was naturally expected to partake of the charisma of the family. At Mankyongdae, a family museum was erected in the early 1980s in which the Kim clan is heralded as the center of the independence movement. The historical documentation ends with the young Kim having demonstrated unusual leadership quality and unparalleled patriotism.

Juche as Weltanschauung

Unlike the earlier stages of ideological evolution, *Juche* soon evolved into a legitimate Weltanschauung with a philosophical structure. The articulation of the structure of human nature and the theory of the political-social life are relatively recent developments. I do not suggest that *Juche* represents a unique and complete worldview, but it is a worldview with some coherent structure, as opposed to a mere political slogan.

The idea that man is the center of the universe is by no means a new perspective; nor is the doctrine of political sovereignty or self-determination. Furthermore, nothing is new about *Juche*'s emphasis on human consciousness as the determinant of human behavior. What is original, however, is the theory that coherently integrated yet distinctly different components of human faculty perform unique and diverse functions.

As will be discussed more fully later, human nature inherently longs to be in "the center of the universe," where man's relationship with nature and society is clearly prescribed. Nature exists solely for the sake of human beings; thus man is fully entitled to explore natural resources. Yet man also has the obligation to manage and "control" the global physical environment. According to *Juche*, science is a tool designed to utilize as well as rehabilitate nature for the advancement of human well-being for both the present and future. According to this perspective, no person should be subjected to another person's capricious control, nor should he be submitted to institutional manipulation. Institutions, as in the case of science, are designed to serve human beings rather than be served by them. Even ideologies themselves are regarded as institutional means to human well-being. Another component of human nature is faculty, which makes value judgment possible. Humans are endowed with the natural right and capability to make behavioral choices through free consciousness. Yet another component of human nature allows people to keep themselves from enslavement by material resources and social institutions.

These elements of human nature are to be cultivated and developed through socialization and political education. For this reason, ideological education becomes an integral part of human development, and such an education should be continuous throughout one's life. The practice of "education through work" in the form of a factory college should be seen in this vein. A factory college refers to the practice whereby college-level classes that would fulfill degree and certification programs in a variety of specialized fields are offered at factories. College professors from regular institutions of higher education, such as Kim Il Sung University and Kim Chaek University, are brought in as instructors. Classes routinely begin with rituals that are intended to glorify the two Kims' works and their legacy.

In 1973, North Korea introduced an eleven-year public school education in conjunction with the expansion of *Juche*, for the regime felt it necessary to provide ideological education. The eleven years of compulsory education are followed by "education through work" in all walks of life. Practically all workplaces and schools in North Korea are required to set aside at least one full day each week for study-learning (*haksop*) in which every citizen participates. A typical *haksop* day begins with the announcement of directives and instructions from the Party, followed by self-criticism by each member. In this session, workers confess wrongdoing that may have been committed during the preceding week, followed by vows to redeem themselves through deepened loyalty to the Party and the country. After this, discussion centers on *Juche*.

Juche as a Weltanschauung becomes more obvious in its exposition of the properties of the human mind. As will be elaborated in the following chapter, the human faculty is viewed as having a series of concomitant properties. They are consciousness (*Uisiksong*), creativity (*Changuisong*), and self-determination (*Jajusong*). According to this view, human dignity is attained when life is conducted in congruence with these three elements of human being. It is further claimed that *Juche* is one ideology designed to facilitate these qualities; thus, human dignity is guaranteed when life is consistent with the principles of *Juche*.

As human *Uisiksong* becomes the engineering force of human behavior, people must create specific means and programs to realize what *Uisiksong* dictates, hence, the arrival of *Changuisong*. It refers to creativity that seeks ways of implementing desirable ideas in concrete historical situations. This aspect of human nature might be perceived as a cognitive attribute. At this juncture, a rational and scientific assessment takes place in terms of the validity and effectiveness of specific approaches and concrete programs. *Jajusong*, however, prescribes the principle of self-rule at the individual, group, and national levels. This idea is extensively used in rationalizing national self-determination and self-sufficiency. According to this theory, the international division of labor is counterproductive because it perpetuates the dependence of nations with raw materials and labor upon nations with capital and technology. The ideology basically adheres to the claims of the *dependencia* school of thought, which views the world as an exploitive system as long as nations are unable to meet their basic needs and provide for military self-defense.[12] Here, *Juche* is faced with the formidable task of discrediting the achievements of the newly industrializing countries, especially South Korea, because the NICs have shown that countries participating in the international division of labor and developing export-led economies could be prosperous, thus challenging the very premises of the *dependencia* school. For this reason, North Korea was always sympathetic to the nonaligned movement and maintained close ties with the Group of 77.

However, the breakdown of socialist systems in Eastern Europe and the Soviet Union, as well as reform-oriented Chinese development, forced North Korea to dissociate itself from the nonaligned movement. The very need for dissociation from other socialist countries has been instrumental to the rapid transition of *Juche* into a unique ideological system under the banner of "socialism in our style" (*urisik sahoejuii*). This ideological position may sound similar to other forms of nationalized socialism, such as China under Deng Xiaoping and Yugoslavia under Josip Broz Tito. But what is radically unique about North Korea is that *Juche* in its advanced version is a completely different breed of ideology, as opposed to a variation of socialism.

In summary, the ideology of *Juche* that is so central to the system and helps to explain much of the political dynamics of North Korea has shown different faces over time. It has undergone a systematic evolution, eventually culminating in a form of philosophical worldview. The change, however, has not been random or unpredictable. There have always been specific reasons necessitating change. In the following chapter, I will explain further the structure and theoretical philosophical underpinning of the ideology as it is today.

Notes

1. The idea of *Juche* was clearly presented in June 1930 in President Kim's report, entitled "The Path of the Korean Revolution," at the Meeting of Leading Personnel of the Young Communist League and Anti-Imperialist Youth League. See *Kim Il Sung Encyclopedia* (New Delhi, India: Vishwanath, 1992), p. 74.

2. It is intriguing to note that Korea is ranked first in the world in ethnic homogeneity. See George Kurian, *The Book of World Rankings* (New York: Facts on File, 1979).

3. When Hwang Jang Yop, head of the Academy of *Juche* Science, defected to South Korea, Western media portrayed him as the father of *Juche* theory.

4. Li Ji Su, president of the Academy of *Juche* Science, made this remark to this author.

5. For further elaboration on this theme, refer to Suh Dae Sook, *Kim Il Sung: The North Korean Leader* (New York: Columbia University Press, 1988).

6. For a comprehensive theory of social change in which political integration is treated as one stage of political development, see Han S. Park, *Human Needs and Political Development: A Dissent to Utopian Solutions* (Cambridge, Mass.: Schenkman Press, 1984).

7. For further discussion, see Han S. Park, "*Juche* as a Foreign Policy Constraint in North Korea," *Asian Perspective* 11, no. 1 (1987).

8. Kim Il Sung's opposition to nonviolence is documented unambiguously in his autobiography, *Segiwa doburo* (With the century) (Pyongyang: Korea Labor Publishers, 1992), especially pp. 229–302. Kim criticized Ahn Chang Ho, a renowned nationalist leader, for advocating a nonviolent resistance movement.

9. Robert Tucker, *Stalin as Revolutionary: 1889–1929* (New York: W. W. Norton, 1973)

10. The social contract theory of regime legitimacy was first advanced by classical liberalists such as John Locke, who believed that the justification of power rests with the consent of the people to the terms of contract between the government and the governed.

11. Refer to Han Shik Park, "Ch'uche: North Korean Ideology," in Eugene Kim, ed., *Journey to North Korea* (Berkeley: Institute of East Asian Studies, University of California at Berkeley, 1983).

12. For a typical dependency school argument, see Andre Gunder Frank, "Capitalist Underdevelopment and Socialist Revolution," in *Latin America: Underdevelopment or Revolution?* (New York: Monthly Review Press, 1969), pp. 84–98.

3

The Philosophical Principles of *Juche*

As expected of any coherent system of ideas, *Juche* has indeed professed a Weltanschauung pertaining to guidelines for desirable (ideal) relationships in the world. Just like any other ideology, it is meant to guide behavioral orientations for the individual, patterns of institutionalization for the society, and policy directions for the government. For a mass belief system instilled by the government to be effective in guiding the course of action at various levels of the society, it must be congruent with prevailing sociocultural conditions. As discussed earlier, the sociohistorical milieu surrounding *Juche* ideology can be characterized by the historical conditions of Japanese colonialism, national independence, national division, Sino-Soviet relations, and the global politics of the Cold War era. These historical and contextual events have made a decisive impact on shaping the belief system of *Juche*, and, as a result, it has developed the ideological attributes of militant nationalism, humanism, spiritual determinism, and even a notion of eternal life.

Militant Nationalism

The most salient factor in the belief system of *Juche* has to be nationalism, as it invokes hostility against foreign hegemonic powers and promotes the sovereignty of the Korean heritage and its people. In fact, the kind of sovereignty that Pyongyang claims is more than just independence. *Juche* views Korea as a chosen land, and the people are told consistently that world civilization originated from the Korean peninsula, a theme that is portrayed emphatically in the massive thirty-three-volume history books, *Choson jonsa.*[1] When history is viewed as having been specifically designed and devoid of any accidental development, a sense of predestination sets in. Coupled with this, the notion that a people are predestined to inspire and "lead the world's oppressed peoples" makes North Korean nationalism ultra-ethnocentric.

In a Marxist socialist system, politics is supposedly guided by class consciousness, but national consciousness has guided North Korea since the introduction of the *Juche* ideology. Indeed, national consciousness supersedes all other forms of belief. Political purges and power solidification have been pursued in the name of nationalism. North Korean nationalism, however, was firmly founded on the repudiation of foreign powers, beginning with colonialist Japan and eventually moving to the "imperialist" United States. The negative foundation of nationalism carried the Kim Il Sung regime through crises and eventually to the adoption of *Juche* as the official ideology. In its present version, *Juche* is far more than a form of antiforeignism, however; it has acquired a quality of self-affirmation. The "self" in this case is the nation as an indivisible and sacred entity. The notion that individuals are not worthy of living if they are deprived of their nation has been promoted so pervasively that complete loyalty to the nation supersedes all other forms of behavioral orientation. In the initial stages of the building of nationalism, the concrete, historical reality that Japanese colonization of Korea forced the Korean people to live a subhuman life helped solidify nationalist sentiments. Furthermore, Kim Il Sung's leadership position would not have been established as solidly as it has if there were any doubt about his mythical role as a leader of the independence movement.

The nationalist sentiment is evidenced in all areas, especially in the cultural and aesthetic life. As will be discussed later in the context of *Juche* art, the quality of art is judged by its expression of and contribution to nationalism. Whatever is traditionally Korean is considered sacred and should be preserved. Traditional music, paintings, literature, sports, and just about every form of traditional cultural life are to be revered. This orientation in the cultural system has effectively barred the intrusion of foreign, especially Western, cultural influence.

Human Beings as the Locus

The phrase "man is the center of the universe" has become almost a cliché in North Korea. Originally, *Juche* was initiated to convey the doctrine that

Korea, like any other sovereign nation, should be self-sufficient. But this exclusive nationalism has proven to be counterproductive, even detrimental to economic and technological development. More recently, therefore, *Juche*'s "self-reliance" is being reinterpreted as meaning a human-centered worldview. The perception that "man is the master of nature and society and the main factor that decides everything" is the cornerstone of the *Juche* worldview.[2] *Juche* theoreticians maintain that "society consists of people, social wealth, and social relations. Here man is always the master. Both social wealth and social relations are created by man and serve him."[3] As such, man should not be subjected to enslavement of any kind, whether it is due to economic poverty, political subjugation, or military domination by fellow human beings.

North Korea's emphasis on technological development as part of the heralded "Three Revolutions Campaign" is intended to convey the theme that technology should contribute to the emancipation of man from the constraints of nature and society.[4] *Juche* theoreticians consider the technical revolution to be "an important political task to help relieve the working people of exploitation and oppression and to cast off the fetters of nature . . . as a part and parcel of the cause of human emancipation."[5] Kim Il Sung himself maintained that "the technical revolution is a momentous revolutionary task which will relieve our people, free them of exploitation from hard work, enable them to produce more material wealth while working easily, and ensure them a richer and more cultural life."[6] Furthermore, human beings should never be manipulated by institutions, material conditions, or mythical beliefs such as religious dogmas, according to *Jajusong*. The doctrine that man is the master of the universe suggests that society, along with its many institutions, is created by man and should serve the well-being of its members. This, however, is not to suggest that North Korea does not promote collectivist views in the relationship between society and individual members. What it suggests is that the nature of a society should be determined by the ideals and "consciousness" of the people, although isolated individuals detached from the society are given no raison d'être (this theme will be elaborated upon later).

Spiritual Determinism

Though it may sound ironic, *Juche,* as an ideology of socialist and self-proclaimed Marxism, defies the material determinism of history. The Marxist premise of economic or material structure as the "substructure" upon which all "superstructures" will be founded is unequivocally denounced. Instead, spiritual consciousness determines the course of history, and it alone underlies all other structures. In fact, *Juche*'s fundamental deviation from Marxism begins at this point. According to this doctrine, human behavior is guided not by the conditions of mode and relations of production but by the direct guidance of the "brain" (*noesu*). The concept of brain here requires clarification. According to *Juche* theory, the brain of a sociopolitical organism performs a function for the country that is equivalent to what the central nervous system of a human body does for a human being. The term *brain* is used in this book with this particular connotation.[7] It should be understood in the context of the term *political-social body*. Likewise, social change occurs in accordance with the command of the society's *noesu*, as opposed to being dictated by the forces and relations of production. In this way, a direct analogy is made between the human body and the social organism. This analogy enables the theory of the political-social body, in which a triangular relationship is advanced among the people, the Party, and the Great Leader.[8] The leader in this case performs the function of the brain, which makes decisions and commands actions for the various parts of the body; the Party acts as the nerve system that mediates and maintains equilibrium between the brain and the body; the people themselves implement decisions of the brain and channel feedback to the leader.

The central concept in this context is *Uisiksong,* a quality of man that makes human beings unique and distinguishable from all other living species. *Juche* theoreticians perceive consciousness "in relation to man's independent and creative abilities to reshape and change the world"; they define consciousness as "a mental activity, a special function of the brain that directs man's independent and creative activities in a unified way."[9]

Man is meant to be conscious of his place in the universe as dictated by the aforementioned *Jajusong,* which guides all forms of relationships in the living world and helps discern problem areas when the world is not guided by this concept. In fact, this theory of human quality is based on *Juche*'s interpretation of human nature. According to this doctrine, man consists of the body and the spirit. The spirit enables man to cultivate and develop consciousness, and the spirit ultimately commands the body, not the converse. Consciousness, however, will not develop without concerted efforts by the individual to educate himself and to continuously internalize the collective will of the society as represented by the guidance of the leader and the Party. In this way, *Jajusong* facilitates dialectical synthesis between *Uisiksong* and *Changuisong* in order to create the political-social body of the living world.

Although the aforementioned *Uisiksong* refers to metaphysical or spiritual preparedness to further the development of human nature, *Changuisong* is an active, mobile, and engineering force of human action. If *Uisiksong* is static and philosophical, *Changuisong* may be understood as dynamic and functional. This quality of man enables him to apply abstract principles to concrete reality by creatively adapting the principles to the specific conditions of the society. Kim Il Sung defines creativity as "a quality of man who transforms the world in keeping with his independent aspirations and requirements."[10] Accordingly, *Juche* maintains that it is this quality of man that has developed Marxism-Leninism to work in the peculiar, indigenous situation of Korea, thus advancing the ideological system to a greater perfection. Conversely, if political ideologies and institutional arrangements are copied from foreign experiences without adjusting them creatively to the concrete, indigenous conditions of each society, they will exhibit irregularities and symptoms of maladjustment. Therefore, a society of creative people must not blindly adopt foreign values or institutions. In order to be creative in this regard, one must first scientifically study one's own society and fully understand the historical and cultural traditions. Doing so further encourages the nationalistic perspective in educational programs and cultural activities.

Collectivism

The seemingly perennial dispute on the relationship between the whole and its parts has been resolved in North Korea. It is the whole that makes its parts meaningful and empowers the constituent parts. This holistic perspective is central to the theory of *Juche*. In the early phases of the ideological evolution, the relationship was regarded as dialectical, or "one for all and all for one." But since 1986, when the doctrine of the political-social body was introduced, it has always been the whole that makes the parts not only meaningful but possible. According to this doctrine, isolated individuals without a collective group are analogous to fish detached from the fishbowl. The fishbowl is the nation, and the fish are individuals. It is the nation that gives life to its citizens. It has every right to demand absolute loyalty from the individuals whose ultimate worth lies in the ability to submit themselves to the state. It is a form of totalitarianism, with not just pragmatic justification but philosophical sanctification. As alluded to above, a person has two lives, a biological life and a political-social life. Everyone will have a full biological life, but they will have to work at earning the political-social life. The latter is attained when they identify their lives in the context of the collective entity. If they sacrifice their biological lives for the collective body, they will attain the life of the political-social body that will live as long as the nation exists. In this way, the people's sacrifices to the nation are given almost a theological meaning and are made to seem in the ultimate interest of the people. Nowhere in the history of political theory has this level of rationalization for collectivism been articulated.

Transcendentalism

With the advent of the concept of the political-social body in 1986 and the ensuing establishment of the Academy of *Juche* Science, the ideology of *Juche* has been rapidly transformed into a religious doctrine and theology. Obvious questions in this context are whether and how the political-social body will be maintained in the post–Kim Il Sung era and even in the post–Kim Jong Il era. Although it is obvious that Kim Jong Il has securely succeeded King Il Sung as the brain in the body, the questions remain unanswered because, no matter who the occupier might be, the lifespan of the brain will coincide with the physical existence of the leader. A senior scholar who is widely regarded as the architect of the ideology and its most profound theoretician commented to me that "*Juche* will not be perfected as a philosophical system without being 'religionized,'" a point that has never been made until recently. Indeed, unless it acquires a religious character of sorts, the theory of the political-social body will self-destruct when the brain disappears from the scene.

It is in this context that the Pyongyang leadership has allowed Christian churches, and many *Juche* theoreticians have been deeply involved in studying the possible linkage between *Juche* and Christian theology.[11] One should not be surprised by the fact that *Juche* theoreticians have even advanced a "theology" of an eternal life as well as the concept of a supernatural being or God of sorts. The eternal life proclaimed here is attained when a biological (isolated) individual acquires a political-social life by overcoming innate human desires and an egoistic lifestyle and integrating himself thoroughly into the life system of the national community, thus becoming part of the immortal political-social body. An example of this process is found in people who have sacrificed their lives for national and social causes and are remembered in the conscience of the people throughout history. In this way, martyrdom is sanctified as a path toward eternal life.

As to the nature of the supernatural entity, *Juche* theoreticians envision that such a being is embodied in a symbolic construct that can be inferred from a perfected existence that cannot be realized but only imagined. Professor Li Chi Su, a leading *Juche* theoretician, conceptualized that the spiritual and moral qualities of man have made steady improvement over the course of history, as evidenced by the fact that the killing of another human being in a fight is no longer institutionalized, as was the case with the medieval jousts. If, as expected, human moral quality develops continuously despite inevitable fluctuations in the short run, we can envision the perfection of human nature in the remote but imaginable future. This imagined state of a perfected mankind helps portray the characteristics of God. According to Li, man should strive to expedite the process in which human nature is perfected. It is *Uisiksong* that allows man to extend his imagination beyond existential constraints, thus enabling man to envision God. In this sense, one might infer that human development or the quality of man in this ideological system is assessed in terms of its proximity to that perfected state of human nature.

The difference between a political doctrine and a theology is that the latter addresses the question of solving the human predicament of mortality. A doctrine that has an organized theory concerning the afterlife distinguishes itself as a religious doctrine rather than a political ideology. In this sense, North Korea's *Juche* has indeed acquired a theological quality.

The term *eternal truth* has long been used to refer to the ideology, but the notion of an *eternal life* is relatively new and has become the cornerstone of the theological aspect of the belief system. According to *Juche* theoreticians, a biologically mortal human being will acquire an immortal life when his or her existence is integrated into the society itself. The society, unlike the individual, does not perish but endures and outlives individual members of the society. Thus, individual achievement, whether intellectual, material, or political, will "evaporate just like the morning fog" with little meaning and value, unless the achievement is integrated into the life of the society itself.[12] Immortal life is gained when one's individual life has an affect on society and history. In other words, when a person makes a lasting contribution to society, his presence will not disappear merely because his biological existence ends. National heroes, martyrs, artists, intellectuals, workers, and even peasants who have made tangible and enduring contributions to the social life itself can attain eternal life. In this perception of immortality, there are several important questions: Are there varying degrees of eternal life, depending on the magnitude and significance of the contribution? If one's contribution is not recognized by other members of the society at the present time but rather in the future, will such a contribution acquire immortality at the time of rediscovery or at the time of the work itself? What if a potential contribution is never recognized because of an accidental disappearance of the pertinent record or the insensitivity or ignorance of people? These questions have never been addressed.

Nevertheless, the notion of eternal life is very concrete and apparently realistic to the mass public in society. North Koreans are told that the state of human nature is ever imperfect and that one can improve the quality of human nature by cultivating an attribute for which the image of God calls. Their God is inseparable from human beings. In fact, God is the extension of man, in that a perfected man is the realistic perception of the ultimate embodiment of the transcendental being. According to *Juche,* God is caring, compassionate, and above all loving rather than commanding or controlling; nor does he have a grand blueprint for a predestined human history.

North Koreans believe that human beings have made steady improvement over the long course of history in terms of compassion and love being perceived as admirable qualities. In early and medieval times, the physical, coercive capability was the sole determinant of leadership, but as history progressed, humans found virtue in living together through love and compassion. What ties society together is no longer sheer power but rather persuasion and values such as liberty and equality. The scientific mind of mankind has made even more dramatic progress toward perfection. Here, the perfection may never be attained but is always pursued and approximated; the imagined, perfected state, however, represents the quality of God, expressing that he grows within and by mankind itself.

When I attempted to convey to a leading *Juche* theoretician that the Christian God supersedes human achievement in society, he responded by asking me how one can maintain an unwavering faith in such a God when he is so vague and cannot be explained scientifically. The North Korean God is experiential because he is inferred from the existential nature of human beings. Their God is also practical and functional because he causes people to improve the quality of life. To the extent that an individual becomes perfected as he attains the political-social life by becoming an integral part of the community, human development is a process of acquiring eternal life.

The death of Kim Il Sung and his lingering impact on every facet of social and political life of the North Korean system must be seen in this context. When he died in 1994 as a result of a heart attack, the abrupt death shocked the entire land for many days. All the billboards and slogans wishing him "a long life and good health" were quickly replaced by words conveying that "the Great Leader lives *forever* with the people." Since then, we have seen what is called in North Korea "government by legacy" (*yuhoon jongchi*), whereby policy directives and instructions by the Great Leader become policies themselves. For example, every working desk in government offices and public places is furnished with a daily calendar, in which policy directives fill every page. These policies are revisited and often implemented in all workplaces as directed by the government.

Viewed in the above context, it is not so accidental that North Korea's official calendar regards the beginning of history as coincident with the birth year of Kim Il Sung. As he was born in 1912, the year 2000 is referred to as *Juche 89*. Because the Gregorian calendar began with the year of Christ's birth, North Koreans consider that using it is thoughtless and inconsistent with the doctrine of *Juche*. For official communications abroad, the *Juche* year is used with the Western calendar year in parentheses.

There may be numerous logical inconsistencies and philosophical inadequacies, but the issue is not the "objective" persuasiveness of this "theology"; the central issue here is whether the masses in North Korea believe in the doctrine. If so, who are the true believers, and how many could there be? Considering the rigorous requirement of ideological preparedness for members of the Workers' Party of Korea, it might be reasonable to conclude that most of the party members are true believers, which accounts for 15 percent of the population. Additionally, the young people who have gone through a complete process of ideological education, including membership in the Socialist Youth League (*Sarochong*), could well be true believers. Even a conservative estimate suggests that 20–30 percent of the 22 million North Korean people might have developed an unwavering faith in this aspect of *Juche*. They are the fanatical supporters of the Kim leadership as well as the hereditary succession of power. When we consider the reality of religious fundamentalism in Western society and the proliferation of sectarian religious groups throughout the world, including the United States and Japan, it is not too difficult to imagine the "success" of a quasi-religious development in this carefully managed system.

In short, *Juche* is more than a simple slogan. It may have begun as such, but in the course of evolution, a system of beliefs and values has evolved into a grand ideological structure. To characterize the ideology as a convenient device with which to justify Kim's power and leadership is an incomplete understanding. *Juche*'s evolution into the present form has been a long and pervasive process. There was a time when the ideology was merely a political slogan, but to understand it only in that restricted vein is far too inadequate to account for the recent reality of North Korean politics and policies. This being the case, one must understand the nature of this aspect of the belief system in order to comprehend North Korean behavioral traits and policy orientations.

Notes

1. *Choson jonsa*. Written by the Research Institute of Social Sciences, 33 vols. (Pyongyang: Encyclopedia Publishers, 1979–1982).
2. Kim Il Sung, *Works*, English ed., vol. 27 (Pyongyang: Foreign Language Publishing House), p. 491.
3. Kim Il Sung, *Encyclopedia* (New Delhi, India: Vishwanath, 1992), p. 85.
4. The Three Revolutions Campaign includes science, technology, and culture. This campaign is believed to have been advanced by Kim Jong Il.
5. Kim Il Sung, *Encyclopedia*, p. 262.
6. Kim Il Sung, *Works*, English ed., vol. 15, pp. 178–179.
7. An elaborate discussion of the concept of brain can be found in Kim Il Sung, *Encyclopedia*, p. 109.
8. "Great Leader" here refers to both Kim Il Sung and Kim Jong Il.
9. Kim Il Sung, *Encyclopedia*, p. 79.
10. Kim Il Sung, *Answers to Questions Raised by Foreign Journalists*, English ed., vol. 3 (Pyongyang: Foreign Language Publishing House), p. 285.
11. There are two Presbyterian churches and one Catholic church in Pyongyang that hold weekly services regularly. The largest, the *Bongsu* Church, draws approximately 150 members each Sunday.
12. This expression is commonly used in the Korean language. The same expression is widely used by *Juche* scholars.

4

The Creation of a Theocracy

In the previous chapter, I established that the North Korean ideology of *Juche* is not an ordinary political ideology; it is indeed a complex system of values that are intriguingly utilized for the purpose of political mobilization and regime legitimacy. One might ask how stable and salient this system of values is to the mass public of North Korea. Are they "true believers"? Can their beliefs be readily dismantled when they are confronted with information and facts that might be vastly inconsistent with their own perspectives? These questions cannot be definitively answered without a careful assessment of the process in which such beliefs are formed. In fact, one might say that the level of their saliency will be determined by the extent to which their values have penetrated into the belief structure of the people. If a belief is salient, new information to which the believer is exposed is likely to be filtered and "interpreted" so that the belief may be reinforced without causing psychological dissonance. However, if the belief is not as salient, any new information that might challenge the validity of the belief could cause psychological discomfort and attitudinal cross-pressure to the extent that the old belief may be reevaluated or even discarded. Therefore, it is essential to examine the level and nature of the saliency of belief before predicting the course of the future development of a system such as North Korea's. In this chapter, I advance the view that the North Korean belief system of *Juche* and the way that people are inculcated into that system is similar to what might be observed in a religious community.

The literature on "brainwashing" shows that a process of intense socialization or indoctrination requires a set of requisite conditions that are common to a variety of cases and are mutually reinforcing for the common goal of changing human dispositions and the character of a community. They include, among other things, the presence of a cult personality, the pervasive appeal of a doctrine or scripture that prescribes moral and ethical standards in human conduct, and a notion of a higher order of universe accompanied by a faith in eternal life. Furthermore, the requisite forces for an effective brainwashing include a sense of threat from the massive force of the "evil" world to the extent that a siege mentality becomes a normal phenomenon.[1] It does not take too much imagination to see that North Korea is a country that has all the requisite conditions on a scale that has never before been witnessed in human history. For the sake of analytical rigor, I categorize those requisite conditions into contextual or environmental conditions and human and experiential conditions. I concisely examine each of these requisite conditions as they have been observed in the North Korean experience.

The Contextual Conditions

The contextual conditions include factors such as historical experience and geopolitical characteristics that are present at the time of the formation of a religious community. Literature on religion, especially the sectarian variety, identifies several basic and common requisite conditions, including hardships in life situations, identity crisis, and fear of external hostility.

Difficult Times

People are made vulnerable to religious persuasion when they suffer from economic and political hardships. Most charismatic political figures have emerged as a result of difficulties associated with the colonial experience, during which indigenous people were politically tormented and exploited by colonial authorities. In fact, such difficulties are conducive to any form of religious development because religion provides a sublime sphere where political manipulation and intervention can be blocked out.

Korea has had such a historical experience. As discussed earlier, Japanese colonial policy was intensively disruptive of indigenous life for Koreans for nearly forty years. With the intention of annexing the peninsula as a source of rice and other agricultural products, Japan attempted to uproot the cultural heritage of the Korean people. The Japanese did so by forcing all Koreans to discard their national identity by adopting Japanese names. It also officially banned the use of the Korean language and rewrote textbooks to teach that Korea was a part of Japan. In that process, Korean economic sources were depleted, valuable historical treasures were shipped to Japan, and manpower was mobilized at exploitative rates, not to mention the trauma of the "comfort women."[2] Many Koreans had to abandon their homes and were taken to Japan for resettlement. These people and their descendants comprise the bulk of the Korean minority ethnic group in Japan today. It is noteworthy that Kim Il Sung, with the persistent banner of nationalism, appealed to these people in Japan for their loyalty and support, which he was able to muster throughout his political tenure.

The economic and political difficulties experienced by the Korean people during the Japanese colonial period helped the North Korean government to solidify its legitimacy on the grounds that it had established a republic that claimed to be "a paradise on Earth." However unrealistic and deceptive this claim may sound to outside people, the North Koreans strongly believed in and advocated it, at least until the death of Kim Il Sung in 1994, because their only comparative reference was the colonial situation. Throughout the 1970s and early 1980s, North Korea promoted the Paradise on Earth slogan. The basis of rationalization of this slogan was unambiguous and simple, as typified by the following remarks commonly made by common people: "Throughout the nation's history, our ancestors thought a paradise to be a society where people enjoy three things: being able to eat white rice, live under a clay-roof, and educate children. These three 'privileges' were the life-long aspirations for our ancestors. Now we have achieved all three under the wise leadership of the Great Leader."[3] Since famine and food shortages became pervasive problems in the second half of the 1990s, North Korea has not mentioned that "paradise" claim.

Identity Crisis

Studies of religious movements, especially cults, identify what they call "spiritual isolation" as a condition conducive to inculcation.[4] Generally, as a person finds himself in a state of identity crisis, he will be most vulnerable to religious indoctrination and often searches for the opportunity to restore identity by joining a religious community.

One has to remember that Korea was not a sovereign state for several decades. During this period, the Koreans had nothing with which to identify themselves. Even the independence that came about as a result of Japan's defeat in World War II did not provide the people with a sense of national identity because the United States and the Soviet Union divided the peninsula for the purpose of accepting Japanese surrender and providing an environment in which the Korean people could establish an independent government. But such a government never materialized as Cold War politics imposed its own world order on the Korean peninsula. The two halves of Korea became subjugated to the major powers of the United States and the Soviet Union. South Korean governments have maintained their close ties with the United States to the point of developing dependency in all areas of political and economic life, whereas the Pyongyang regime has experienced difficulties in relationships with the communist world powers. These difficulties originated from the tension between the Soviet Union and China. North Korea was initially aided politically and economically by Moscow, during the years when Kim Il Sung had to solidify his power base. However, Kim's strong personal ties with the Chinese leadership and Mao's involvement in the Korean War paved the way to an increased role for China in North Korea. Pyongyang's dilemma soon became evident as the two communist superpowers developed territorial disputes; Mao was not inclined to accept the position of a junior to the Soviet Union, especially in the post-Stalin era. Through the late 1960s and 1970s, the relationship between the communist powers progressively deteriorated to a point at which North Korea could not side with one without antagonizing the other. As discussed earlier, Pyongyang's decision to proclaim a position of equidistance in dealing with Beijing and Moscow was an inevitable consequence of Sino-Soviet tension.

Coupled with this international political climate was Pyongyang's need to wage a "legitimacy war" with Seoul. Whatever South Korea stood for was denounced and demonized. Pyongyang did not hesitate to upbraid the Seoul regime for its dependence on "imperialist" powers. Kim Il Sung was able to appeal to the people by instilling in them the belief that his leadership was founded on nationalism and self-reliance. This strategy worked in part because of South Korea's vulnerability to foreign influence. In short, an isolated position in the international environment and the competition with the South gave North Korea an identity crisis.

Physical Isolation and a Hostile Environment

At the individual level, physical isolation is often seen as a condition for effective religious indoctrination. At the community level, perceived or actual hostility from external sources not only encourages collective cohe-siveness but also ultimately promotes a siege mentality.[5]

The fact that the North Korean people have been isolated from the outside world needs no elaborate documentation. Physically, North Korea has been secluded not only from the Western world but also from its socialist allies. Until the late 1970s, Pyongyang maintained diplomatic relations with only a handful of hardcore communist systems, such as the Soviet Union, China, Cuba, Albania, and North Vietnam, and the volume of interaction was negligible. Since the demise of the socialist systems in Eastern Europe and the Soviet Union, along with reforms in China in the late 1980s, North Korea has even further alienated itself from the rest of the world. The fact that there are only two weekly commercial flights each way between Beijing and Pyongyang demonstrates the extent to which North Korean citizens are out of contact with foreigners. There is no such thing as tourism, except for extremely limited groups or "delegations" invited by the government agencies for specifically stated purposes. North Korea's isolation is not limited to physical seclusion. In fact, there is lit-erally no channel, other than what is provided by the government, through which citizens can receive information about the world or even about their own society.

The isolation observed in North Korea is of a peculiar kind in that it is reinforced and accompanied by the fear of threats from hostile enemies. The people are constantly reminded of the threat posed by U.S. support of South Korea. The realization that South Korea is economically and tech-nologically far more advanced than the North, coupled with the fact that the population in the South is twice as large, makes the Pyongyang lead-ership nervous. The actual or imaginary presence of external hostility helps a regime in consolidating its power and securing support from the people. This phenomenon has never been more convincingly demonstrat-ed anywhere in the world than in North Korea.

In order to perpetuate the leadership, especially in the post–Kim Il Sung era, the government will be hard-pressed to keep the people from external contacts that might cause "cross-pressures" to an insurmountable degree. Cross-pressure occurs when a person is subjected to new infor-mation that is contrary to old knowledge, thus creating cognitive disso-nance. It may lead to an instinctive effort either to reinforce the previous belief and knowledge or to alter the cognitive system.[6] The direction in which the North Koreans' belief system will move in response to infor-mation from the South and capitalist societies will be determined by the degree of the previous belief's saliency, a point I discuss later in this book.

The Human Conditions

In addition to contextual and environmental conditions, there must be more specific requirements for a religious movement. These include the presence of a leader equipped with a charismatic personality, a "holy" scripture, a sense of mission, and faith in salvation or eternal life.

The Charismatic Personality

A visitor to Pyongyang during the first week of November 1994, some 100 days after Kim Il Sung's death, remarked that "it is hard to believe that Kim Il Sung is dead in North Korea." There are still signs of his presence in every facet of individual and collective life in North Korea. As alluded to earlier, all the slogans that used to express the people's desire to see Kim's "long life" have been replaced by another proclaiming that "the Great Leader *lives* with us *forever!*" Television programs are full of his public appearances and instructions that are revered to the point that they are sacred. Policies are derived from his "living will," which is shown in numerous speeches and writings that are being revisited with heightened vigor.

Is Kim Il Sung dead? Obviously, he is physically dead, but *Juche* has long promoted the notion of political-social life that does not end when the physical body dies. It is this political-social life of Kim that is supposed to remain alive in the minds of the people. Whether Kim Il Sung is comparable to a truly religious figure such as Jesus Christ defies common wisdom, but the fact that Kim has acquired a status of immortality in the belief system of *Juche* is undeniable. For the last ten years or so, Kim Il Sung has been depicted as having achieved everything a man can achieve without being God himself.

The Holy Scripture

Every religion is furnished with a holy scripture to which the believers render absolute authority and consider as the ultimate source of guidance for their behavior. Does North Korea have such an undisputed body of "teachings"? To this date, no such "Bible" in a one-volume book form has been written. However, there is a body of written "works" that carries tremendous weight in people's daily lives and provides concrete guidelines for policymaking. The term *works* here refers undoubtedly to those endorsed by the Great Leader himself. Given the longevity of his life and leadership, Kim's teachings over the years involved virtually every conceivable sphere of life in North Korea. They are everywhere and omnipresent. As observed earlier, since his death, his "teachings" are given the new term *yuhoon* (The will of the deceased). In fact, the policy of the Workers' Party of Korea is to elevate the teachings of the late Great Leader to the level of *yuhoon,* at which point they become sacred.

The Sacred Mission

Yet another theological dimension of *Juche* involves the notion that this doctrine can save humanity from certain extinction following a calamity. This aspect of the belief system shares the views of many sectarian or fundamentalist religious doctrines. As the only genuine socialist system left, according to *Juche* theoreticians, North Korea has a historical mission to save humanity from capitalist materialism, consumerism, decadent culture, and moral decay. North Koreans are told that they have a sacred mission that must be fulfilled, or human history will end. The world will be hostile toward them out of fear of being overwhelmed by the virtuous ideology of *Juche.*

Members of a fundamentalist religious community tend to see the world in the dichotomous terms of "good versus evil" and believe that good is outnumbered and overpowered by evil.[7] The massiveness of the evil force is such that the world will "drift" away, leaving no alternative to the certain collapse of the human species itself. Believers in such a religious creed tend to contend that only they have the ability to save humanity by fighting off the evil force. This mission is sacred and cannot be compromised. This belief has been further emphasized since the epidemic collapse of socialist systems in Eastern Europe and the Soviet Union. When asked, children in North Korean public schools almost habitually define the purpose of their study as carrying out the sacred mission of saving humanity from the evil forces of imperialism. Moreover, this belief is reinforced by the notion that they are a chosen people.

The Eternal Life as the Ultimate Reward

No religious belief is complete without a common belief, by all members of the community, in salvation or an everlasting life. Such a life is to be earned through hard work and devotion to certain causes and by enduring difficulties in earthly life. This notion of salvation contrasts with the Christian notion that an eternal life is "given" by the grace of God (although not all denominations subscribe to this idea). The *Juche* theology prescribes concrete guidelines for social and organizational behavior as well as attitudes and norms necessary for ultimate emancipation. These guidelines are always consistent with the principles of collectivism, self-determination, and spiritual determinism. Any conduct that may be construed as being selfish is condemned. Any form of behavior that is devoid of self-control and submissive to external influence is denounced, and any action guided by material consumerism is harshly punished. These principles make it possible for North Koreans to withstand economic difficulty, diplomatic isolation, and ideological containment.

As one attains the quality of a political-social life and becomes fully integrated into the society and completely altruistic, then one's life will not end with the passing of one's body. This elevated quality of living is congruent with the aforementioned guiding principles of behavior. Although certain behavioral qualities are conducive to eternal life, others are considered "sinful." Generally, attitudes and behaviors in the interest of the entire society and nation as opposed to self-interest are considered virtuous and consistent with expectations for eternal life. The extent to which a person attains such salvation is reflected in the enrichment of his political-social body.

As discussed earlier, Kim Il Sung, along with many other historical heroes and heroines, is widely regarded as having attained such an eternal life. According to this doctrine, the eternal life lives in the remembrance of the people; nevertheless, it is not limited to the fact that people remember and pay tribute. As one *Juche* theologian expressed, "The Great Leader lives on regardless of what might happen to the people's recognition, because it is an objective and factual truth."

God: A Supernatural Being

As expected in any religion, North Korea's religious life must include at its center a notion of supernatural power. In the North Korean belief system, there exists a God of sorts, the image of a perfected human being. The nature of this perfect being can only be inferred from observations of virtuous people, for such a being cannot be expected to have lived in reality. Nonetheless, this superbeing is inferred from experience as opposed to embodying a quality that is superimposed from abstract and metaphysical constructs. In this way, *Juche* still remains an atheistic worldview. This one area has not been developed with any degree of conceptual clarity or theoretical consensus. With this somewhat ambiguous conception of a super-

natural being, however, North Koreans are socialized to idolize this perfected being and are encouraged to emulate it. Now that Kim Il Sung is
gone, the imaginary being is concretely described as having been epitomized by the Great Leader himself. As this perfected being is only imaginary and does not function as the creator or omnipotent and omniscient
being, *Juche* is devoid of the concept of God comparable to that of
Christianity; but it contains a sense of God in that there is a conceived being
who is so perfect and truthful that it cannot be historically realized. Whether
this notion of a supernatural being is sufficient for a religious community to
function as such in a longer historical context is yet to be seen.

Thus far, we have established the fact that North Korea may have
formed a community that resembles a religious society. A central question,
then, is to what extent do the people in the various walks of life come to
believe in the doctrine? How does such a belief affect the people's attitudes and behaviors? These questions require a more rigorous examination of the process of education and political socialization, a topic
addressed in the following chapter.

Notes

1. On conditions for the emergence of a sectarian religious group, a number of
references are available including: Robert Jay Lifton, *Thought Reform and the
Psychology of Totalism: A Study of "Brainwashing" in China* (New York: W. W.
Norton, 1961); Theodore L. Dorpat, *Gaslighting, the Double Whammy,
Interrogation, and Other Methods of Covert Control in Psychotherapy and Psycho-
analysis* (Northvale, N.J.: J. Aronson, 1996); Thomas W. Keiser and Jacqueline L.
Keiser, *The Anatomy of Illusion: Religious Cults and Destructive Persuasion*
(Springfield, Ill.: Thomas, 1987); William W. Sargant, *Brainwashing* (Garden City,
N.Y.: Doubleday, 1957); Denise Winn, *The Manipulated Mind: Brainwashing,
Conditioning, and Indoctrination* (London: Octagon Press, 1983).

2. A dramatic account of the atrocities committed by Japanese soldiers
toward Korean young women was provided by Therese Park in her novel, *A Gift
of the Emperor* (Duluth, Minn.: Spinster's Ink, 1977).

3. One professor at Kim Il Sung University offered this observation to me in
1981 when I visited that university.

4. Edward M. Levine, "Deprogramming Without Tears," *Sociology*
(March–April 1980), pp. 34–38. For an analysis of North Korea from this per-
spective, see Helen-Louise Hunter, *Kim Il Sung's North Korea* (Westport, Conn.:
Praeger, 1999).

5. Donald J. Ottenberg, "Therapeutic Community and the Danger of the Cult
Phenomenon," *Marriage and Family Review* (Fall–Winter 1981), pp. 151–173;

Robert W. Balch, "Looking Behind the Scenes in a Religious Cult: Implications for the Study of Conversion," *Sociological Analysis* 41, no. 2 (Summer 1980), pp. 137–143.

6. On the theory of cognitive dissonance, see Leon Festinger, *A Theory of Cognitive Dissonance* (Evanston, Ill.: Row, Peterson, 1957).

7. Francesca Alexander and Michele Rollins, "Alcoholics Anonymous: The Unseen Cult," *California Sociologist* (Winter 1984), pp. 33–48; Balch, "Looking Behind the Scenes in a Religious Cult," pp. 137–143.

5

Juche Education: Agents and Methods

A political ideology is meaningful only to the extent that it provides for the legitimization of a political system and its leadership. Whether the ideology is philosophically or scholarly convincing is not of vital significance. Thus an ideology should be examined in terms of the degree to which it is adhered to by the people. Doing so requires an analysis of the process and outcome of political socialization.

Political education and socialization in North Korea begin at the earliest possible stage of human development, certainly at infancy, if not before birth. All the songs and instrumental music aired through loudspeakers at every conceivable public place are orchestrated to convey the personality cult of the Kim family and to promote *Juche* doctrine. The process continues through eleven years of formal education, workplaces, community groups, party organizations, mass media, and ceremonial mass events. I briefly examine these socialization "agents."

Schools

Preschool Education

Workplaces are equipped with nursery facilities and day care centers. Additionally, there are many "week care centers," where parents leave children for several days when their work requires them to be away from home for a prolonged period of time. Activities and programs at these centers are designed for the effective political socialization of children. A typical center shows oversized portraits of Kim Il Sung and Kim Jong Il in every room and incorporates into the curriculum stories depicting heroism displayed by the leaders when they themselves were children. They teach songs and involve the children in plays intended to inculcate them with patriotism and devotion to the party and leadership. As the children are fed, they will be told that they are fortunate to be given food when children in South Korea and all over the world are starving; for this they are thankful to the Great Leader and the Dear Leader as well as the Party.[1] The food they eat, the clothes they wear, the toys they play with, and all the supplies they use are attributed to the leader's benevolence and personal caring. By the time these children are old enough to enter public school, they will have acquired almost unconditional loyalty to the leader and the Party.

Primary Schools

Since the mid-1960s, North Korea has mandated public education for eleven years, which is longer than school terms in most countries in the Third World. Even in South Korea, compulsory public education is limited to six years.[2] On the first day of school, all children participate in an opening ceremony during which uniforms that are the same throughout the country and school supplies are "handed down" by the leadership that "passionately loves and cares for each child." All schools use common textbooks that are filled with pictures, anecdotes, stories, and musical compositions about the Great Leader, the Dear Leader, the Party, and the nation. At the same time, the educational materials are loaded with contents condemning imperialists and puppet regimes, especially the United States and South Korea. Even mathematics books use illustrations and calculation problems that are designed for political socialization.

The regular curriculum for public schools ends in the early afternoon and is followed by extracurricular activities. These activities, lasting at least three hours, are programmed to provide special training in athletics, arts, and scientific fields. Each child is required to "master three skills" in these areas. The exemplary model is demonstrated at the Children's Palace in Pyongyang. Selected children from various schools in the area come to this massive marble building, which is equipped with modern facilities. The swimming pool has an elevator for divers and can accommodate 300 children at the same time. There are also drawing rooms for both Oriental and Western paintings, sewing rooms, music rooms for a variety of instruments, computer rooms, science rooms for chemistry and physics, table tennis rooms, and a gymnasium for various sports and other events. In addition, there is a huge concert hall where selected children's groups perform regularly. The theater, which has 1,500 seats, is filled with students for a variety of performances. The front row seats are reserved for dignitaries and foreign visitors. As dignitaries and foreign guests enter the hall, the students extend welcoming gestures by applauding, often giving standing ovations. The content of all the performances is unambiguously aimed at promoting loyalty to the Great Leader and the Dear Leader, as well as to the Party and the nation. When the flowers signifying either Kim Il Sung or Kim Jong Il or a picture of the sun is beamed on the screen behind the live performance, the entire audience applauds instinctively and simultaneously.

Training and performing are routine practices on campuses throughout North Korea. The children have no leisure time; they are fully and exhaustively engulfed by these extracurricular activities. Competition, which is always organized by collective units such as schools, is fierce. The symbolic payoffs for winning in the competitions are great: the winning schools are recognized with special awards that are given out in elaborate ceremonies by the top leadership. Visitors hear from the host that there is no juvenile delinquency in the country because all children are fully committed to educational programs.

As in the case of the preschools, school uniforms and supplies are periodically provided by the state. At ceremonies for the "handing down" of these "gifts" by the leadership, pupils are led to pay tribute to and show appreciation for the benevolent caring for each person by the state. Students are often so moved that they weep or jump up and down. Usually these ceremonies are extremely emotional, memorable occasions for the children.

Colleges and Universities

Three types of higher education have developed in North Korea: comprehensive universities; technical and vocational institutions; and "factory colleges." Government authorities maintain that every college-age person is "enrolled" in an educational institution of one form or another.

Only one institution falls into the first category of a comprehensive university, and that is Kim Il Sung University, which was founded in 1946. Most political leaders have attended this university. Currently, there are approximately 12,000 students, including 5,000 female students, who are recruited through rigorous entrance examinations. Of the fifteen disciplines, the Department of the Works of Kim Il Sung is the most competi-

tive and draws students of the highest quality and soundest ideological orientation. In assessing applicants' qualifications, the political character of
the family is most important, especially in that coveted department.[3]
Contrary to the common belief that most of the students are from the
Pyongyang area, where residents are rigorously screened, 70 percent of
the students at this elite university come from provincial areas.

Technical and vocational institutions are of various sizes, ranging
from the Kim Chaek Technological University to various vocational
schools. Regardless of the field, all students are subjected to a political
curriculum for ideological education. One of the weekly working days is
set aside for political discussion, self-criticism, and the study of *Juche*. In
addition to these institutions, there is the "factory college." Every factory
has living quarters with apartments, and workers are generally required to
live there. At the workplace, college-level programs are incorporated into
the work schedule, and teachers regularly visit from other institutions,
including colleges and universities. At the "factory college," workers pursue degrees of higher education. In the curricula at these unconventional
"colleges," ideological education designed to inculcate *Juche* ideas is central. The educational forum is also used as a "self-criticism" session, in
which the health of the political and ideological orientation of workers is
assessed. Books and references used for education include collections of
speeches and writings by Kim Il Sung and Kim Jong Il, as well as video
materials about the leaders and other patriotic figures. World news is carefully filtered for the singular purpose of condemning the imperialist systems and the "revisionist" socialists of the former Soviet Union and
Eastern European countries. The students often participate in simulation
games and produce theatrical performances with strong political themes.

Mass Media

The Korean Central News Agency monopolizes all media. Basically, there
are two forms of mass media, the *Rodong Sinmun*, the one and only daily
newspaper for the general public, and the television. All citizens are routinely and extensively exposed to them.

The Rodong Sinmun

As the official publication of the Party, this daily paper is the primary
source of both domestic and international news. It is six pages long, except

for special issues. The first two pages consist mostly of reprints of congratulatory messages for the leadership. The typical heading for virtually every column used to read "The Great Leader Kim Il Sung Receives Delegation from China," with a photograph. Since the passing of the Great Leader, the centerfold photograph of the leadership has not appeared with any degree of regularity. Instead, Kim Jong Il is heralded. On these initial pages, editorials are occasionally written that are almost always political, either condemning South Korea and the United States or heralding North Korea's achievements. The third page reports economic news, typically praising agricultural production and industrial construction. Model workers and work units are often recognized with esoteric stories about their hard work and patriotic attitudes. The fourth page typically reports on political heroism on the part of the Party and its leadership; often, the praises are made by foreign observers. The last two pages are mostly devoted to attacking U.S. imperialism and the "puppet" regime of the South. The newspaper is solely an instrument of political socialization for the masses; it does not appear that the Pyongyang authorities intend to influence the opinions of foreigners or even their southern compatriots. The primary target audience appears to be the working class of North Korea itself.

Although it is hard to estimate the circulation, it is fair to suggest that practically all citizens have easy access to the paper. The reality is that the citizens read the "news," for it is usually the only available source of written information about their "world."

Television

All citizens in North Korea have access to televisions in homes, town halls, or workplaces. At department stores, various television makers and brands are displayed for sale, and many people purchase them. The price of a television set ranges from several hundred to several thousand wons, depending on the brand and maker. Considering that the exchange rate to the U.S. dollar is approximately 2 to 1, and in view of the fact that an average monthly salary for clerical and professional occupations is 70–150 wons, the price for a television set is extremely high. Contrary to the expectation that anti-Japan sentiments might bar commodity items imported from Japan, there are several models with Japanese labels such as Toshiba, National, and Panasonic that are widely available in department stores.

There are no more than three TV channels, and only two seem to offer programs on a regular basis. There are no programs during the daytime;

they begin in the evening. A typical program is made in reverence of the Great Leader and the Dear Leader, the Workers' Party of Korea, and the patriotic working class. Often included are musical programs introducing new songs and performances, feature films and documentaries, and interviews with Korean War veterans and heroes and heroines of anticolonial campaigns. For example, in the spring of 1993, one year before the death of Kim Il Sung, a new song designed to glorify Kim Jong Il was introduced with the title, "Please Receive Our Salutes"; scores of musical and performance celebrities appeared on television to provide an analysis of the song as fitting the character of the benevolent Dear Leader. In fact, these programs have a common theme in that they all pay tremendous tribute to the selfless leadership of the Party, the Great Leader, and his son.

Watching television is an integral part of life for average citizens. After a day's work, it is the most common way to spend the evening. In fact, practically everyone seems to be watching the same programs, and conversations that take place in the family often center around them. In this way, political socialization and ideological education take place in living rooms, workplaces, and public places such as gymnasiums, barbershops, and restaurants. Interestingly enough, radio sets are not sold anywhere in North Korea. One reason for the conspicuous absence of radios is that South Korean broadcasts designed to denounce the system of North Korea can reach the populations through short and midrange sound waves, and controlling the airwaves is practically impossible. In contrast, television broadcast programs from the South can be easily blocked or scrambled.

Entertainment and Performing Arts

North Korea does not seem to be wasting any of its resources from the point of political education and ideological consolidation. Indeed, public entertainment and performing arts such as music, movies, and theatrical plays that are intended to provide the public with some leisure and enjoyment are heavily orchestrated for ideological and political socialization. There are ample opportunities for the public to spend "leisure" time for entertainment. In Pyongyang city alone, there are at least a dozen theaters and performing halls that are large enough to house more than 1,000 people at a time. The Dear Leader is also credited for numerous major compositions for songs and opera music. The famous opera *Sea of Blood*, for instance, is alleged to represent a synthesis of all forms of musical expositions and the crystallization of *Juche* music. Through the music, the audience appreciates the ingenuity of the leader and his unwavering love for the people. The public facilities for entertainment arts are heavily used by people of all walks of life. Weekly and monthly tickets are distributed free of charge to factory workers, teachers, soldiers, bureaucrats, farmers, and students. They are often required to attend these entertainment events, for public discussions about them are likely to ensue at their workplaces. In fact, most people look forward to and are anxious to view coming events.

Indeed, for *Juche* education, these performing facilities are essential, as places to introduce indigenous art to the people in the most concrete forms. Under the slogan of *Jucheization,* every single performance or program is interpreted as being a manifestation of the ideology. It is in these public places that the people will be observing and learning the nature of *Jucheization* in a variety of forms, a topic that will be explicated in the following chapter.

The Workers' Party of Korea

The proportion of Party members in North Korea is estimated to be 15 percent of the total population, by far the highest percentage among all the communist systems that have ever existed. The ideological training within the Party is most rigorous and intensive. Meetings are regularly and frequently called for at various levels of the structure. At the very basic level, Party cells, self-criticism meetings are held on a daily basis. The Party organization and membership penetrate deeply and extensively into the population; at every workplace, there is a Party cell with its secretary. In fact, the Party secretary within each workplace is very powerful and mediates between the Party center and the grassroots level. He or she is also expected to be accountable to the Party and the government. Regardless of the secretary's occupation, he or she makes decisions affecting the lives of all members. Promotion or demotion, even severe punishment, may be based on recommendations of the Party secretary. At frequently held meetings, government directives and materials for political education are transmitted to the rank and file through the Party organs.

One intriguing fact is that the secretary or leader of a workplace is not necessarily more educated or more established socially than other members of the Party. As was the case in China during the early phase of Maoist revolution, the underprivileged and traditionally deprived people have been aggressively mobilized by the Workers' Party in North Korea.

Sons and daughters who lost their parents to the Japanese in their struggle for national independence and to the Korean War have been actively recruited and promoted to elite ranks in the Party. One of the deputy ambassadors from North Korea to the United Nations in the 1990s declared that his loyalty to the Party was unconditional; he was willing to do anything it needed him to do because he "would have been nothing had the Party not picked him up and raised him in the benevolent hands of the Party when he was an abandoned orphan." He reminded me that a large proportion of those who are committed to the Party are of humble family origins and feel eternally indebted to it.

Most Party members go through a similar regularized course, beginning with membership training in the Socialist Youth League (*Sarochong*), which consists of secondary school children ranging from twelve to eighteen years of age. In order to be inducted into this prestigious youth organization, one must pass rigorous examinations, including those on political consciousness and especially the ideas embedded in *Juche*. Being selected in this initial process is regarded as a high honor because it ensures that one will move up the ladder of success. Two or three years of ideological and physical training will prepare the future leaders for productive Party membership. The training typically involves group activities, camping, and political education through participation in manual labor. It is commonplace throughout North Korea to see groups of *Sarochong* members engaged in public rallies, sport events, and a variety of public services such as sweeping streets.

Mass Rallies

Mass rallies are held throughout the country on several major occasions, including the birthdays of Kim Il Sung and Kim Jong Il; the occasions commemorating the inauguration of the state, the establishment of the Party, and that of the People's Army; and Labor Day. These rallies are always accompanied by "mass games" demonstrating the people's love and devotion to the leadership and the country. Visitors are often impressed by the "mass games," which have the reputation of being the most spectacular extravaganza that any society in the world has ever exhibited. The people spend weeks and months preparing for the occasions.[4] In these rallies, the people are "conditioned" to reaffirm their devotion to the leadership in a truly emotional display of loyalty. Many foreigners, including dignitaries and especially Koreans living abroad, are invited to participate in these events. The visitors come to Pyongyang to pay "tribute" and respect to the Great Leader, the Dear Leader, and the fatherland. Mass rallies are not limited to certain memorable days of the year; they are also part of sports events. There are several major sport arenas in Pyongyang alone, including May Day Coliseum, which has a 150,000 seating capacity, and North Koreans are known for their devotion to competitive sports. No event will take place without elaborate symbolic programs designed to show their solidarity in support of the leadership and the Party. In summary, political beliefs are formed and reinforced throughout one's life in the controlled context of various life environments. Because of the stability and longevity of the leadership, this process has been remarkably consistent since the very inception of the regime itself.

Notes

1. Kim Jong Il has been referred to as the Dear Leader consistently since the Sixth Party Congress in 1980.

2. The Kim Dae-jung government announced only in 2001 that the length of public schooling will be expanded to nine years, which will be implemented in phases over a three-year period.

3. This information was obtained during interviews of faculty members at the university.

4. Perhaps the most spectacular event was the one staged at the May Day Coliseum in October 2000 on the occasion of the fifty-fifth anniversary of the establishment of the Workers' Party of Korea. U.S. secretary of state Madeleine Albright witnessed the event and called it spectacular.

6

Conditioning the Human Mind

North Korea as Human Nursery: A Controlled Life World

Citizens of North Korea have been effectively shielded from the uncontrolled environment of the external world. They are not only physically confined but also mentally isolated within their own surroundings. Their environment is created and maintained by the government, and their minds are nourished with "food" provided by the leadership. In this way, their minds are induced to be exactly the way the leadership designs them to be. The masses are exposed selectively to the external environment. They are led to perceive selectively and induced to retain information selectively. The selection is guided by the ideology and made by the leadership.

The extent to which North Korean citizens are physically limited to their own immediate life environment is hard to document with any degree of scientific accuracy. However, even cursory observation suggests that North Korea is incredibly closed to and isolated from other societies. Foreign travel for ordinary citizens is practically nonexistent. Graphic evidence of this is that there are only two commercial flights coming out of Pyongyang to Beijing in a week, and each plane is small, with a capacity of not many more than 100 passengers. This has been the case since this author's first visit in 1981. Most of the passengers are either diplomats or foreign visitors with some official functions in Pyongyang. A similar situation is observed in the flights to other destinations such as Moscow, with even less frequency and volume of passengers.

61

Perhaps the greatest number of travelers abroad occurs at the border with China, where some commercial activities happen, but this route is also limited and irregular. When China explored relations with South Korea in the early 1990s, border traveling was almost completely shut down. Relatively frequent and steady visitations are also made by Koreans in Japan, such as members of the Federation of Koreans, who have established long-standing, sympathetic relations with Pyongyang. Students of Choson University in Tokyo, which was established and is operated by North Korea sympathizers, make routine trips to North Korea as a part of their normal curriculum. These students are given special treatment during their visits. They are always welcomed by dignitaries and entertained by performing groups; they also visit scenic places and participate in sports events and educational sessions in which the main theme is always *Juche* ideology.

As far as ordinary North Korean citizens are concerned, they are simply not exposed to the outside world. What they learn about the world comes only through the aforementioned television programs and news reports by the government-operated Korean Central News Agency. In this way, the public is extremely susceptible to manipulation of opinions and beliefs by the Party and leadership, who have complete control of information. The people are provided with information sanctioned by the leadership. For most people, it is not likely that they even imagine the possibility of alternative patterns of life that might be superior to theirs, nor are they disposed to create an alternative life on their own initiative. This phenomenon is analogous to children within a family who are totally dependent upon and protected by the family institution and their parents.

Just as a parent is not to be chosen, the leader is not to be selected by the "free" will of the people. The leader becomes one by virtue of what he *is* rather than what he *does*. In this context, the Great Leader or Dear Leader is not selected from among contenders by "rational" calculation; rather, he becomes a leader just because he *is* different. One must not forget that the public has never been exposed to a republican system, whereby leadership recruitment is competitive and regime legitimacy is based on the principle of social contract. To illustrate this point, I remind the reader of a refreshing experience: when I had the opportunity to state that President Kim Il Sung might have contributed greatly to the country but he, too, has made many mistakes, one professor at Kim Il Sung University proclaimed that "even if a father makes terrible mistakes, he still is the father!"

Longevity and Consistency

The "human nursery" phenomenon becomes stable and effective when the life environment is not challenged by alien input over a sustained period of time. One must remember that Kim Il Sung and his son Kim Jong Il have been the only heads of state since North Korea gained independence in 1945 and technically since the inception of the regime in 1948. Most citizens who are active in the workforce have been educated within the same political and ideological environment.

The North Korean people's belief systems have grown along with the evolution and development of the *Juche* doctrine itself. This fact makes the process of indoctrination even more effective and lively. When a new component of *Juche* is created, as happened with the introduction of the theory of the political-social life in 1986, political education gains new vitality. Following the introduction, all the organs of political education were activated for prompt and intensive education of the masses. The same can be said with respect to the notion of an eternal life that was developed in conjunction with the political-social life theory. In this way, everyone moves at the same time on the same "boat" toward the progressively greater intensification of their belief systems.

In such a situation, there is only reinforcement, never cognitive dissonance that might lead to attitudinal or cognitive cross-pressure.[1] Once a belief system is formed and never challenged but rather consistently reinforced, it becomes a rigid dogma. Furthermore, when the dogma transcends the restrictions of time and space, it becomes a matter of religious faith. As discussed earlier, *Juche* has indeed become a religious doctrine. This development would not have been conceivable without the longevity of the regime and its leadership.

Without interruption in the progression of socialization for several decades, *Juche* has been able to deeply penetrate and assimilate itself into the mass belief systems. The degree of rigidity and saliency of beliefs may have reached a point at which external disturbances may not easily cause psychological dissonance. Instead, alien ideas and discomforting information can be easily and effectively eliminated before they disturb the equilibrium of belief systems. No one knows for sure whether the period of time has indeed been long enough and whether the saliency of beliefs has attained the kind of stability that can endure the test of time. But all indications show that the North Korean belief system is perhaps more coherent than any other politically engineered belief system that has ever been witnessed in history, including German Nazism, Japanese ultranationalism before World War II, and Maoism during the Cultural Revolution in China.

Positive Reinforcement: The Confucian Appeal

As I alluded to in the opening chapter, the nursing ground for *Juche* has been the cultural legacy of Confucianism. Although it is an overstatement to say that *Juche* is only a contemporary manifestation of Confucianism, to reject the notion that the salient cultural base of Confucian heritage did influence the process of political socialization in North Korea is equally erroneous. It is undeniable, as in the case of the Chinese communist revolution, that the new revolutionary regime in North Korea considered the traditional cultural legacy to be counterproductive to achieving its political goals. Yet, ironically, like Mao's China, Kim's North Korea aspired to establish a new system that was based on the strength and uniqueness of the indigenous society, without reverting to the original traditional ideals and norms. If China emphasized rejecting the Confucian value system as epitomized by the Cultural Revolution, North Korea has skillfully utilized the Confucian value system and cultural legacy selectively to reinforce the new cultural system of *Juche*. As discussed earlier, there are a few central areas of continuity between the Korean brand of Confucianism and the values and norms advocated by *Juche*.

The first area of continuity between the two value systems is the theme that man is the master of the universe and should be able to transform society, nature, and people. The human-centered worldview and the idea of the independent social being (*Jajusong*) should not, however, be interpreted as an individualistic conceptualization of political and social life in the Western liberal tradition. *Juche* and *Jajusong* are presented as a form of self-affirmation, but in this case the "self" being referred to is the nation. The belief is that the nature of the society should be determined by the ideals and the consciousness of the people. It is in this light that the aforementioned political-social body theory of *Juche* was developed. It is clear, then, that *Juche*, like Confucianism, rejects the material determinism of Marxism-Leninism. The political-social body theory argues that the course of human relations and history are determined by direct thought and consciousness. Thus, individual thought is important to the development of society, yet only in the context of its relationship to the whole of society. The society is perceived as a single body with the people, the Party, and the leader acting as parts of the whole.

The second area of continuity is found in the concept of leadership (ruler). In the context of political-social life, the leader is the brain and the Party is the nerve center. Thus, the people must respect and obey the leader and the Party. In return, the leader and the Party are obligated to listen to the will of the people and provide for their well-being. It is here that we see a direct link between Confucianism and *Juche*. In the Confucian system, the leader, or king, is given authority through the mandate of heaven. The leader, then, has the obligation to be a good and virtuous leader and to provide for the well-being of the people. The Confucian idea that a leader is not subject to choice by the people and rules by mandate of heaven is clearly consistent with the sanctification of the leader in *Juche* beliefs.

Another constant theme running through the *Juche* ideology is the notion of collectivism, and a parallel is found here as well. As in traditional Confucian thought, the individual is given value only in the context of the collective whole or through the contribution that the individual can make to the benefit of the society. Confucianism is based on the belief that to maintain social order, people must play their assigned roles in a fixed structure of authority. It is clear that the same concept applies in the political-social body theory. The creative and independent social being must act in the context of the greater society. When the leader or the party makes a decision, it is the duty of the individual to obey that decision. The individual can only be granted value and even eternal life as a component of the collective body. If one acts according to the directives of the leader and the party, one strengthens the entire body and brings honor to oneself.

In this context in the North Korean political system, the Party, or the whole of the political-social body, has replaced the traditional family as the beneficiary of virtuous or honorable behavior. Hence, as in traditional Confucian society, individuals do not act out of pure self-interest but rather out of concern for how their actions will affect the greater whole. More directly, in the past, young people would bring honor to themselves and their families by practicing filial piety and learning the Confucian texts. In modern North Korea, young people bring honor to themselves as a greater part of the whole by practicing filial piety toward the leader and by memorizing the writings of Kim Il Sung and Kim Jong Il.

As an extension of collectivism, another striking similarity between modern governments in Confucian nations is the existence of and commitment to a single, strong party. North Korea is certainly no exception to this. The Confucian political culture stresses consensus and harmony more than a particular form of government. The dominance of a single party has been the norm not only in the communist nations of Asia; even in countries like Japan, Taiwan, and South Korea, which have developed stronger forms of pluralism, there exists the dominance of a single political party. As Harmon Ziegler argues, these parties tend to be recognized as the "vessel of the accumulated wisdom of the country," and the "keeper of the faith."[2]

That is certainly the position of the Workers' Party of Korea. The Party is perceived to be the only entity that has the ability to act as the nerve center of the political-social body. Although the individualism and creativity of the people is essential, the full potential of the people will never be realized without the strong guidance and leadership of an enlightened Party. Throughout his discussion of the Party, Kim Jong Il constantly refers to the ideal that the Party must be unified and monolithic and that there should never be any opposition to Party actions once policy decisions are made. The relationship between the Party, the leader, and the people is represented with the people as members of the collective and the leader as the representative of the collective.[3] Thus, the Party is seen as the center of accumulated knowledge and power in the North Korean system, demanding, and for the most part receiving, the unconditional loyalty and obedience of the people.

The current structure of North Korean ideology, with the state as an extension of the family and the head of state as the "father" of the nation, is closely linked to the strong patriarchal nature of Korean Confucianism. For example, one need only look at the people's relationship to Kim Il Sung to see how he adopted the role of the father. An Indian author, T. B. Mukherjee, gives us a clear picture of this belief when he describes how he met Kim Il Sung. He states that Kim is loved and respected by the people for his reciprocal love for them. People consider him as their father.[4] In describing his meeting with Kim, he writes, "the meeting was surcharged with love and affection as if it were a meeting of a father with a long lost son," and "I looked upon him as a dear father and requested him to bless me in the Indian way by putting his hand on my head."[5] These types of descriptions of the Great Leader are a constant theme in North Korean political culture.

Other symbols of the fatherly relationship of Kim Il Sung or Kim Jong Il to the people are the titles given to them. Kim Il Sung had both official and unofficial titles. The official titles included *tongji* (comrade), *wonsu* (marshal), *changgun* (general), *susang* (premier), and *suryong* (leader). These, of course, refer to his various official positions and titles in North Korean government and society. In addition, Kim has two unofficial titles: *oboi* (parents) and *aboji* (father). These titles indicate blood ties to the Great Leader and suggest that the leader is an extension of the family and therefore is to be paid the same respect and filial piety that a Confucian child would pay to his or her true father. Thus, although the official North Korean position promotes the elimination of traditional familial ties, at the same time these types of ties are advocated for the people's relationship with Kim Il Sung and Kim Jong Il. It is unlikely that such a relational structure could have developed in North Korea in the absence of the strong patriarchal Korean Confucian tradition. Other relationships in North Korean society have taken similar forms. For example, soldiers in the military are instructed to look at the military as a family. Leaders are to act as parents, comrades are instructed to act as brothers, and the Party is to be looked upon as the people's mother.

Even some of the traditional Korean Confucian rituals have been carried into the North Korean political system. Although traditional rituals such as ancestor worship (*manismus*) have been discouraged by the North Korean leadership, in an effort to build up the leadership of Kim Il Sung, the worship of the Great Leader and his family was allowed. There are monuments in North Korea celebrating the accomplishments not only of Kim himself but of his family. It is an accepted practice to bow to the graves of Kim's family and to worship his ancestors.

The concept that the state is an extension of family is most blatantly demonstrated by the hereditary succession of power and the delay in Kim Jong Il's taking official control of the country after the death of his father. The hereditary succession is consistent with the age-old dynastic practice in the Confucian tradition. Concerning the delay in formally assuming power, the North Koreans initially stated that Kim Jong Il would wait until the appropriate three-year mourning period had passed. Kim Il Sung has been referred to as the father of the Korean people, as the savior of all oppressed people, as the greatest philosopher of all time, and as a messiah. It is clear from this and other examples that Kim Il Sung created a cult of worship similar to the Confucian cult of worship. Again, it is highly unlikely that such a deeply rooted cult of personality and such a rigorous political and social ideology and structure could have emerged and taken such firm hold without the presence of the strong tradition of Korean Confucianism. In short, although North Korea never openly celebrated the Confucian legacy as being desirable for the realization of revolution, it has effectively used Confucian values and practices for establishing the unique kind of political system that it has.

Politics of Fear

Another strategy for effective political socialization is provoking a sense of fear in the masses. The nation is surrounded by hostile and militarily superior powers. The stigma of being labeled a rogue nation by the United Sates and much of the Western world has helped the regime in Pyongyang solidify its power base and consolidate public opinion to create an absolutely monolithic system. The thesis that the presence of actual or imagined external foes is conducive to internal unity has become an axiomatic truth in any political system. In fact, nations such as Iraq, Libya, and Cuba have charismatic leaders and stable systems because of, not despite, the fact that they have been ridiculed and alienated by Western countries. North Korea's fear stems from the presence of U.S.-backed South Korea, which houses U.S. ground troops and has a security arrangement with the United States. Further, the United States, Japan, and South Korea have consistently maintained a stable security alliance system, with North Korea as its primary source of threat. Coupled with these threats is the loss on the part of the Pyongyang government of the communist bloc as a support system. Isolated from, alienated from, and demonized by the rest of the world, North Korea has sought and found a powerful incentive to guard itself from collapse.

The fear on the part of the North Korean people is not just conceptual and theoretical. They feel the fear in the most concrete terms. They are consistently reminded that South Korea is preparing for a surprise attack with sophisticated weapons, including nuclear bombs, supplied by the Americans. Their fear is consistently substantiated as a real possibility on the occasion of the Team Spirit or other military exercises that have been conducted routinely by the South Korean and U.S. armed forces. Even though the exercises have been suspended at times when inter-Korean relations have shown either improvement or a brighter prospect, North Korea has never assumed their permanent cessation. In these exercises, the most sophisticated weapons are demonstrated in a simulated warfare, and some new weapons are tested. Every spring, around the time of the Team Spirit exercises, North Korea mobilizes emergency measures under the assumption that the target of the exercises could instantly become North Korea itself. The emergency measures include alerting the entire military, with standby orders to react to any provocation by the South, and evacuation practices for the entire population, especially in Pyongyang. These emergency measures always disturb normalcy in all sectors of the economy, polity, and society. Furthermore, the presence of some 36,000

U.S. ground troops backed by naval fleets with air strike capabilities is a tangible source of fear and uneasiness on the part of the entire North Korean population.

To defend itself from certain hostility, the Pyongyang regime has made concerted efforts to prepare for the worst scenario. One might note in this context that the underground subway system in Pyongyang is between 70 and 100 meters deep. The extraordinary depth, which must have incurred enormous construction costs, must have been intended to provide bomb shelters. Additionally, roads in Pyongyang, including Tongil and Kwangbok Streets, are at least 100 meters wide and straight, without medians, suggesting that they were built as aircraft runways. It is believed that every village throughout the country is furnished with bomb shelters sufficiently deep and large enough to accommodate all villagers. Additionally, schools and public buildings are also similarly prepared. These are physical demonstrations of the psychological uneasiness and fear of possible attack.

The fear has more recently been provoked by rhetoric in the United States surrounding the construction of the national missile defense (NMD) system. In an attempt to rationalize the enormous costs for building the NMD system, both the Clinton and Bush administrations and the advocates for the system used the threat from North Korean missiles as the primary justification. Once again, despite all the seemingly conciliatory gestures from Seoul and Washington following the historic inter-Korean summit meeting in June 2000, the stark reality for North Korea is the fact that the world is hostile and its survival is precarious. It may sound ironic, but the display of military muscle by the United States and security preparedness on the part of South Korea have helped North Korea in strengthening its political and ideological stability.

New Identity, Pride, and Self-Esteem

As discussed earlier, the initial impetus for *Juche* was the empirical reality that North Korea needed to maintain a posture of neutrality at a time when China and the former Soviet Union were vying for supremacy and Pyongyang was unable to favor one over the other. Thus, from the beginning, the ideology gave North Korea an identity. As socialist systems around the world were experiencing difficulty maintaining their existence, North Korea needed to take off the straitjacket of the internationally recognized form of communism and to avoid the tide of endemic collapse of socialist systems. In other words, North Korea needed to distance itself from other socialist systems and their ideologies. Here *Juche* became rejuvenated as an ideology unique to North Korea.

In the minds of its believers, *Juche* is not only an ideology that is a useful tool for the elite to govern the people, but more significantly, it is a worldview shared by the entire population. As discussed earlier, the reason that *Juche,* which is commonly referred to as "the eternal truth," emerged in North Korea is that the land is different from any other country—it is "blessed" with both objective and subjective conditions. In this sense, North Korea is perceived by many to be a special place and its people a "chosen people."

There are two large museums in Pyongyang, the National Museum of History and the Museum of Revolutionary Struggle. The former, a massive marble structure in the center of the city, houses archival documents that are designed to portray the notion that human civilization originated from Korea and that Korean ancestors enjoyed a position of physical and cultural superiority. In the museum, for example, stone-age tools are displayed with the inscription that they were excavated in northeastern China, which was formerly inhabited by ancestors of present-day Koreans, and the tools predate any archaeological finds known to mankind. Regardless of the issue of authenticity, this physical "evidence" is effectively used to bolster the people's sense of pride and ethnic superiority.

The self-centered people defy any comparison. In fact, when they evaluate their present situation in terms of economic and political life, they compare only with the past, as opposed to comparing themselves with other peoples or other nations. The popular slogan "We Are Never Envious of Anything in the World" is meant to indicate that their present condition reflects a marked improvement from the darker days under Japanese colonialism or the imperial establishment of the Yi Dynasty. North Korea refuses to subject itself to a quantitative comparison with any other system, especially South Korea. It views its system as being qualitatively not only unique but superior to all other ideological systems.

To the North Koreans who have gone through the normal course of socialization, the nation is worth protecting at all cost and their cause is worth dying for. The ideology of *Juche* provides the people with a deep sense of pride and esteem. One might think it absurd to imagine any sense of pride when large numbers of people are struggling to survive starvation. But economic condition has little bearing on legitimizing the regime (this theme is discussed further in Chapter 10).

When an ideology provides the people with a sense of mission, the inculcation process is more effective when it gives them a sense of pride and self-esteem. In fact, if the values and beliefs taught in the indoctrination process are mere prescriptions of behavior and desirable patterns of interactions in the society, as the case might be in Confucian teachings, the learning process will be void of emotional enthusiasm. However, if the ideology prescribes a sense of mission for the society and history, the believers can be more emotionally involved and socialization can attain greater effectiveness.

The mission in which North Koreans believe is no less than saving humanity from imperialist and inhumane exploitation by capitalist materialism. *Juche* theoreticians maintain that capitalist development has systematically converted man from the status of master of the universe to that of slave and that no existing ideology can reverse the course of social development from the process of degeneration. A new ideology has to emerge if humanity is to be saved and sustained, and the new ideology is *Juche*. With this sense of mission, North Korea has organized numerous research institutes throughout the world, especially in many nonaligned countries of the Third World. Since the establishment of the International Institute of *Juche* Ideas in Tokyo in 1978, a great number of institutions have been formed in locations virtually all over the world.

Conditioned Reflex

Earlier in this book, I observed that the process of charismatic formation for Kim Il Sung may have transformed him into what Robert Tucker terms a "charismatic giant." There is no question that the level of personal and family charisma has reached a point at which the Great Leader has attained the status of a religious leader. As discussed earlier, unlike charismatic political leaders such as Fidel Castro, Mohandas Gandhi, and even Mao Zedong, Kim Il Sung has acquired a quality of immortality because *Juche* is believed to be a theology with a notion of eternal life. He is the closest manifestation of God himself. Kim is more like the founder of a "religious" persuasion with a 23-million-person membership than a mere political leader. For example, a high-ranking diplomat reflexively professed: "American missionary workers are persistently trying to come in and propagate their God but they should realize that we already have our God in the Great Leader."[6] Kim Il Sung's personal credentials are such that only a supernatural being can possibly exceed them. With such a leader, obedience is not coerced; it is perceived by many to be for the people's own good, and their submission to his authority is voluntary.

One intriguing method for inducing a collective and emotionally charged mindset is the use of musical orchestration. It is comparable to the use of hymn songs in Christian churches, melodic recitation of religious scriptures in Buddhism and Hinduism, and vocal affirmation of one's faith using music in a variety of religious rituals. Psychologically speaking, a state of hypnosis is achieved through this mechanism. In North Korea, songs are sung in all walks of life throughout the country. Most of the popular songs express reverence for the leadership, specifically either Kim Jong Il or Kim Il Sung. Occasionally, the Workers' Party of Korea is praised, along with the military. As will be discussed in the following chapter, North Korean music has attained a self-proclaimed reputation as "*Juche* music." Just as music is a reflexive, as opposed to contemplated, response to certain stimuli, many forms of official resolves and declarations are memorized and cited over and over again in such a way that many symbolic expressions appear spontaneous and reflexive.

In summary, the factors identified in this chapter can be effectively used to control the mind. This phenomenon is hardly unique to North Korea. Intense indoctrination of schoolchildren and mass politicization have been evident in a wide range of societies. China under Mao Zedong, especially during the Cultural Revolution, and Cuba under Fidel Castro are good examples. Even in the United States, public school children were induced to read certain kinds of books that prescribed faith in their own government and nation.[7] Considering these practices in relatively open societies, it is not difficult to understand the religious aspect of North Korean mass beliefs and its behavioral manifestations. Where the people are shielded from the outside world, information is strictly filtered and controlled, a sense of threat from alien and evil forces is pervasive, the people are inculcated with a sense of mission, and a strong cultic leadership is established, a religious community is bound to prosper. This is exactly what has happened in North Korea during the last half century.

Notes

1. The analytical concept of cognitive dissonance introduced by Leon Festinger is applicable here. See Festinger, *A Theory of Cognitive Dissonance* (Evanston, Ill.: Row, Peterson, 1957).

2. Harmon Ziegler, *Pluralism, Corporatism and Confucianism: Political Association and Conflict Regulation in the United States, Europe, and Taiwan* (Philadelphia: Temple University Press, 1988), p. 132.

3. T. B. Mukherjee, *The Social, Economic, and Political Ideas of the Great President Kim Il Sung* (Pyongyang: Foreign Language Publishing House, 1983), p. 107.

4. Ibid., p. 284.

5. Ibid., pp. 286–287.

6. This remark was made by an official from North Korea's mission to the United Nations at an informal dinner in New York in March 2000.

7. This practice is portrayed in John H. Westerhoff, *McGuffey and His Readers* (Nashville, Tenn.: Parthenon Press, 1978).

7

Juche as a Way of Life

Juche is not just a political ideology designed to rationalize political orientations or a philosophical belief system officially promoted by the ruling elite. It is a way of life in North Korea, a vocabulary that is inseparable from North Korean life. In virtually every sphere of life, one finds the
presence of *Juche*. As a result, the process of political socialization whereby *Juche* is instilled in people's belief system is greatly reinforced by the
fact that the idea is not just perceived and thought about, but more important it is *lived* in an array of tangible life situations.

Juche Music

The most significant aspect of aesthetic life in North Korea is music.
Every possible sound wave carries musical melodies. All performing
facilities are fully in use to induce "thematic entertainment" (entertainment with purpose) through music and other forms of entertainment.
Music is an important vehicle for political and ideological integration. In
fact, so-called *Juche* music graphically demonstrates what the ideology is
all about. Theoreticians in North Korea insist that *Juche* is not a form of
antagonism; it is rather a synthesis that transcends the limitations and
shortcomings of the self as well as those of others. This claim is substantiated by the fact that orchestral music in North Korea incorporates both
Western instruments and generic Korean musical instruments to "create"
music that overcomes limitations in the artistic expression of either musical world. Furthermore, *Juche* music advances the concepts of *bang-*

75

chang and *jolgawha* as the creative refinements of the Korean heritage and culture.

Bangchang integrates vocal music with instrumental compositions, similar to what Ludwig van Beethoven did in *Symphony No. 9*. In the instrumentalists' chamber hidden behind (or below) the stage of an opera, singers are commonly seated along with the instrumentalists. The notion here is that neither the human voice nor musical instruments can be complete unless they are in harmony with each other, which is claimed to approximate the grand unity of the universe. In some cases, the entire audience participates in the singing to dramatize the effect of unity.

Jolgawha refers to the rhythms of phrasings. In the traditional Korean system of poems, called *shijo,* such rhythms as 3-4-4-4, 3-4-3-4, and 3-3-4 are believed to parallel the human body's rhythm of breathing. These patterns were commonly used in traditional *shijo* and folksongs; the famous folksong *Arirang* is a typical example of such a phonetically structured expression. The widely acclaimed opera *Pibada* (Sea of blood) is filled with the same rhythms and *bangchang*. The same principle is adopted in compositions of contemporary music, including operas and numerous other musical outlets such as songs written in reverence of Kim Il Sung, Kim Jong Il, children, mothers, soldiers, and the Party.

Yet another example of *Juche* music seeks an integrated harmony of sound and visual arts. Invariably, performers on the stage are attracted to the scenes of Kim Il Sung flowers and the sun itself, which signifies the Great Leader. Sets change constantly to coincide with the theme of the performance. At times, a poem will appear on the screen line by line as the performers sing along. The notion here is a great unity and harmony of sights and sounds, which *Juche* theoreticians consider to be a more integrated and thus more perfected form of art.

The extent to which schoolchildren from nursery to secondary school are involved in music may be unprecedented anywhere in the world. Every child participates in musical programs, either as a singer or an instrumentalist. In fact, at schools and extracurricular educational venues, every child is required to choose and study a musical instrument. Almost every day, students remain at school after classes to practice and rehearse performances. Each school will prepare a team of performing artists to represent the school at regional and national competitions. The schools that win these competitions will have the honor of performing at the Children's Palace in Pyongyang annually or quarterly. At selected performances, important government officials and even the Great Leader or Dear Leader are present. As observed previously, the typical repertoire for any musical event includes songs about the Great Leader and Dear Leader as well as the Party and the People's Army. New songs are introduced on a continuing basis. In fact, most young people in North Korea are capable of singing a great number of songs that are politically and ideologically engineered, but their repertoire is extremely limited in other areas, even in traditional folk music. They simply have not been exposed to any range of songs. All television programs, radio broadcasts, and live performances are almost exclusively guided by ideological imperatives as called for by *Juche*.

Juche Architecture

The epitome of *Juche* architecture is the People's Hall of Great Learning (Inmin Dae Haksopdang), located in the center of the capital city. According to North Korean theoreticians, this building's external appearance exhibits traditional Korean architectural forms, while at the same time, contemporary simplicity and functional efficiency are contained within the structure. In fact, inside the building, halls and rooms have extremely high ceilings and are covered with marble stones throughout. Theoreticians explain that the "creative mixture" of the traditional aesthetic beauty and modern convenience is the mark of *Juche* architecture. Most public buildings incorporate the same principle. Even in the countryside, many private homes show what they claim to be a unique style of roofs and eaves. The style is different from either the Chinese or Japanese traditional styles. To the foreign eye, the difference might seem negligible, but it becomes more evident once explained. In this way, North Koreans are incessantly reminded that Koreans are unique and that they have maintained a rich heritage that is distinctive and distinguished.

Juche Literature

According to Kim Il Sung, "literature as *Juche*-oriented humanics is the philosophy of life; it gives answers to human questions by artistically describing the lives of people."[1] Since literature is humanics, it must describe man and human problems, and it must provide solutions to these problems. In this sense, literature as well as art must bear epistemological and educational functions that are expected to "bring home to the people the meaning of life and to contribute to the formation of their world outlook."[2] Accordingly, literature must contain political and ideological meanings that are instructive of sound "moral" judgment; when literature lacks such meaning and purpose, it tends to appeal only to sentimentalism and will inevitably become decadent, paralyzing the spiritual health of the society. In novels, short stories, and even poems published in North Korea, it is the norm that heroes and heroines are depicted for their display of patriotism. Literary achievement is judged by its success in promoting ideological goals dictated by *Juche*, as opposed to any other artistic criterion. A cursory survey of *Chosonmunhak* (Korean literature), a monthly magazine, will find that most of the short stories, life histories, poems, and even comics are filled with ideological and political messages. Selected storybooks are often required to be read and then discussed in the weekly "study day" sessions at workplaces. On this day, virtually all workers and other citizens are required to participate in preprogrammed discussion sessions conducted at administrative units at the grassroots level.

Another significant example of *Juche* literature is the series *Minjok kwa Unmyong* (Nation and destiny). In it, dozens of individuals in the course of North Korean history who have displayed patriotism of unusual quality are heralded as national heroic figures. They include individuals in various occupations and life environments, ranging from artists to prisoners of war. Entries in this series are growing. Once a novel is written on a chosen person, the work will simultaneously be made into a film for national distribution to theaters and on video. Among recent subjects are Yun Isang and Ri In Mo.

Yun, who passed away in 1995 in Germany, was a world-renowned composer who used Berlin as his base. Born a South Korean, Yun achieved his acclaimed position as a composer through his activities abroad. He was abducted by the military government of South Korea from Berlin and imprisoned in Seoul in 1966–1967 on charges of treason. He was released only after an international uproar that included a petition bearing the signatures of dignitaries such as former German chancellor Willy Brandt, Nobel Peace Prize laureate Andrey Sakharov, and scores of European composers and performing artists. He was praised by Kim Il Sung himself as "a nationalist artist" and heralded as "a pride of the nation." A music hall was constructed bearing his name, and a residential mansion was also built in Pyongyang for him and his family. A resident orchestra, named Yun Isang Symphonic Orchestra, was established. All these arrangements persist even after the death of both Kim and Yun. There still are some 400 musicians working at the Yun Isang Institute.

Yun's life is glorified because of his nationalism and his fight against the South Korean military dictatorship. Yun has never confessed himself as a socialist or communist but always insisted on his nationalist perspective.

Ri In Mo is yet another person featured in the series. Ri is a former North Korean soldier who was captured during the Korean War. He spent over forty years in a South Korean prison. His refusal to denounce the North forced him to remain in prison for such a long period of time. When Kim Young Sam was inaugurated in 1992 as president of South Korea, his minister of unification, Han Wan Sang, persuaded the president to make a conciliatory gesture to the North by returning Ri In Mo, who was struggling with his advanced age and poor health. The moment Ri returned to his home in the North, he instantly became a national hero because he had never compromised his loyalty to the North and had refused to give in to the torturous dictatorship for such a long time. The story became an instant best-seller that reached every family throughout the country. Ri has been given special care by the government, including being sent at a huge cost to the United States to receive medical treatment in 1997.[3] This man, like Yun, never insisted on his socialist or communist orientation. He was seen as an example of unwavering loyalty to the "right" cause. The right cause in this case as well is nationalism and heroic resistance to the "wrong" system of South Korea.

In addition to this series, which portrays more recent exemplary individuals, there are a host of novels, movie scripts, and short stories designed to reinterpret historical figures, such as the renowned anti-Japan independent fighter, Ahn Joong Keun, who assassinated the Japanese governor of the Korean colony, Hirohito. In the newly interpreted story, before his death Ahn laments the absence of a great leader in Korea who will emancipate the oppressed Korean people from Japan and makes a prophetic remark that such a leader will come to rescue the country. Undoubtedly, the great leader on the horizon is Kim Il Sung. A similar account is seen in the story of Kim Koo, a well-respected, popular national figure following the surrender of Japan in 1945. He is depicted here as a public figure who shows a great deal of admiration for Kim Il Sung and the desirability of socialist nationalism.

Since the passing of the Great Leader in 1994, the most popular literature is the series *Segiwa doburo* (With the century), the autobiography of Kim Il Sung. Kim started writing this series in 1992 on the occasion of his eightieth birthday. By that time, the daily business of running the government had been transferred to his son Kim Jong Il, allowing Kim Il Sung to enjoy well-deserved leisure time to write about his own life and thoughts. Six volumes in the series were published in 1994. Since Kim's death of an unexpected heart attack that year, additional volumes have been published, and the series now comprises eight volumes in all. The autobiography is extensively incorporated into the life of the public. The work is presented on television every night in a variety of forms, including a lady in a traditional Korean costume reading the series. Students and workers are regularly engaged in collective deliberations and scholarly analyses of the literary values of the work.

Juche Sports

In all sports, what is referred to as the "*Juche* method" is applied. It ensures that any kind of sports training includes mental and ideological preparedness as a key component. Physical fitness and athletic skill will not be sufficient. One must first have a complete understanding and knowledge of the sport in which one is preparing for competition and find a reason to be proud of engaging oneself in a particular sport. In other words, one must train oneself for the clear purpose of bringing glory to the nation and the leader. When sixteen-year-old Kye Sun Hui won the gold medal in judo at the 1996 summer Olympic Games in Atlanta, she told reporters that the key to her success was her determination to win for the glory of her fatherland and the Dear Leader and to show the world that North Korea was a force to cope with in any field.

Tae kwon do is promoted as the sport that best exemplifies *Juche*. It is documented as originating in Korea, and its spiritual component is consistent with the philosophical outlook in traditional Korea. Thus, the sport has been promoted as the national sport. At every level of educational institution and in every workplace, rigorous training, competitions, and exhibitions are commonplace. Also, tae kwon do is an integral part of military training, and all military personnel are required to reach a certain level of mastery in this sport. In addition, *Juche* is heavily emphasized as the backbone of tae kwon do tactics and movements. According to *Juche* theory, tae kwon do is designed to destroy a physically superior and imposing enemy—the hegemonic powers of the world. For those who have mastered this art, there will be no enemy too strong to destroy. Furthermore, believers in this martial art advance the view that the unifying force of the sport can facilitate national unification across the border and throughout compatriot communities around the world. As a symbolic example, Choe Hong Hee, a martial arts guru and long-time resident of

Canada, has been received by North Korea with utmost respect and popularity. He has provided instruction in Pyongyang for many years and has gained a large number of disciples.

In addition to tae kwon do, boxing, judo, shooting, and table tennis are important on the sports scene in North Korea. According to *Juche* thinkers, these sports share a common attribute in that they all require the training of the mind as well as of the body. Only when the mind and body achieve harmony can one begin to understand the secret of the sport. In fact, North Koreans steadily improve at those sports to reinforce their beliefs in this regard. One might notice here that this notion of harmony between the body and the mind is consistent with the Confucian outlook. The Confucian teaching that "when the spirit overwhelms oneself, there is nothing that cannot be achieved" resonates throughout sport arenas in North Korea.

Juche Medicine

Every hospital in North Korea is equipped with both Eastern and Western medical facilities. The educational curriculum for medical science includes both, but the two are integrated rather than dealt with separately. The "synthesis" of these two medical science ingredients is referred to as *Juche* medicine. According to advocates of this practice, it is largely responsible for maintaining a high life expectancy, comparable to those of Western industrial countries and South Korea, in a country that is economically far off from the ranks of the developed world. This innovative approach, according to one well-known cancer patient, has helped him cure the disease. Kim Hyong U, a former North Korean ambassador to the United Nations, left his post in 1997 after being diagnosed as having an advanced case of lung cancer at a hospital in New York. He left with the understanding that his cancer was inoperable and that he was returning home for a final rest. The medical team in New York predicted that he would live six months. But he returned after two and a half years as the head of a delegation to a symposium on U.S.–North Korean relations, held at the University of Georgia in November 1999. He gave a press conference at the UN Plaza Hotel on December 2, where he declared:

> There is not a single cancer cell in my body. I am no longer a cancer patient. When I left this city some two and a half years ago, no one thought my return to be even a remote possibility. But I am here thanks

to my fatherland's superior medical science and the benevolent country and Dear Leader Kim Jong Il who personally looked after me. It is all because of *Juche* medicine. From now on, the medical field the world over that is watching me at this time will pay attention to the advanced medical science and health care in my country. I assure you that I am not a ghost who came back to life from my grave.[4]

Whether the claim made by the ambassador has any scientific credibility is not the issue here. The important fact is that North Koreans seem to believe in the merit of this kind of medicine.

Other Expressions of *Juche* Life

The realization of *Juche* in concrete life situations can be seen in a number of areas in addition to the ones discussed above, such as dance, agricultural methods, costumes, and even hairstyles. For instance, there is such a thing as *Juche* dance. It is characterized by body movements that are limited to the upper body, especially the arms, hands, and shoulders. One theoretician who specializes in dance suggests that this form of dancing clearly contrasts with Western dance, which relies primarily on the movement of the lower body; it is also distinctly different from African dance, which employs the movement of the entire body. Traditional or *Juche* dance is widely taught at schools. All schoolchildren are expected to have training in this area before leaving school. Another activity used to express the notion of *Juche* is acrobatics. In fact, North Korean acrobatics is widely recognized for its level of difficulty, but the insertion of ideas into acrobatic performances that are allegedly generated from *Juche* is not as widely understood. Many forms of choreography are claimed to have combined sports and arts that in turn are explained by *Juche* principles.

In any performing art, including acrobatics, the stage is extensively used to show visual symbols and scenes of *Juche* ideas. North Koreans claim that their stage decoration is truly indigenous and superior to that of other countries. Using smoke and other substances as well as revolving objects, they create dynamic scenes on the stage. All these deviations from the conventional are seen as the expressions of *Juche*.

North Koreans have developed a sense of the proper way to maintain their physical appearance, monitoring their dresses, hats, shoes, and even hairstyles. Diverse expressions are not allowed, for conformity to the norm is imperative for the citizens to avoid comparisons and possible competition. Schools of all levels require students to wear uniforms, which often include hats. Uniforms are provided free of charge twice each year. Normally, children tend to outgrow their uniforms before the time for another distribution. There are specific codes for hairstyles for schoolchildren, sometimes varying slightly depending on the age and grade. Even adults tend to wear certain kinds of acceptable hairstyles. Women's hairstyles, for example, are limited to a few variations. At a salon, one will find pictures of a few recommended hairstyles posted on the wall and will simply indicate one's preference. In fact, these accepted styles are called *Juche* styles. The North Koreans attach to these styles not only aesthetic but ideological values. Once an ideological value is attached, any deviation is difficult, for it may be interpreted as construing a disobedient attitude toward the state.

As alluded to earlier, perhaps the most drastic and tangible aspect of *Juche* is the introduction of a new calendar. According to this calendar, time began with the birth of Kim Il Sung. The year he was born, 1912, is *Juche* year 1. Thus, the year 2000 would be *Juche* 89. The *Juche* calendar is used in every home and office and even in the New Year's greeting card. It was instituted in observance of the death of the Great Leader, who is credited with creating *Juche* philosophy. On a daily calendar, the teachings of both Kim Il Sung and Kim Jong Il are printed on each page, which also reiterates their guidance given on that particular day in earlier years. Needless to say, this practice is analogous to using the birth year of Jesus Christ as the initial year of the Western calendar.

Another example of the application of *Juche* to daily life can be observed in the agricultural sector. The phrase "*Juche* farming method" is used extensively. This method refers to the government practice of distributing baby plants rather than seeds to individual collective farms. According to government officials, this method guarantees that germination of seeds will be maintained at the highest level and that productivity will be maximized. Included in this method is the concept of utilizing every bit of the arable land in the country. In fact, visitors to North Korea are amazed at how farmers create plots on steep hillsides and at high elevations. The campaign of converting every inch of the land into farmland helped increase productivity until the late 1980s. Since then, hillside and mountaintop plots began to lose topsoil, and the frequent flooding that devastated food production throughout the 1990s can be attributed at least in part to this practice.

In short, North Koreans live in an environment that is colored all around with *Juche*. What they hear, say, feel, and see is heavily tinted by

Juche ideas. In order to imagine this process of cultural saturation, one must see such a life environment in the context of a complete closure from the external world.

Notes

1. Kim Il Sung, *The Mission of Contemporary Literature,* English ed. (Pyongyang: Foreign Language Publishing House, 1986), p. 2.

2. Kim Il Sung, *Encyclopedia* (New Delhi: Vishwanath, 1992), p. 304.

3. Ri In Mo, *My Life and Faith: Memoirs* (Pyongyang: Foreign Language Publishing House, 1997).

4. Kim died in February 2000, some three months after this interview.

8

Juche in Domestic Politics

In the previous chapters, I examined the nature of the mass belief system, the extent of its penetration into the lives of the people, and the methods used to achieve that penetration. In the following chapters I show its ramifications for and impact on domestic, foreign, and inter-Korean policies and politics. On the domestic scene, the structure and nature of leadership, political succession, legitimacy, and power politics in the bureaucracy, the Party, and the military have all been most profoundly affected by the doctrine of *Juche*.

Leadership and Legitimacy

As I have shown in this book, the formation of a charismatic leadership in North Korea has been systematic and progressive. The principle of *Juche* has made the leadership an integral part of the body politic. The justification for power is based on the benevolence of the leadership rather than on republicanism, and its performance is evaluated through public opinion. Political leaders are chosen not for their abilities to carry out proposed policies but for their ideological stance and adherence to paternalist authority. Kim Il Sung, and now Kim Jong Il, are the fathers of their country, and the people are the children. These leaders take care of their "children" just as a benevolent father would.

When Kim Il Sung died suddenly of heart failure in July 1994, the entire nation was completely overwhelmed by unending waves of grief. Schoolchildren, college students, teachers, workers, housewives, and even soldiers could not suppress their sorrow, which was witnessed by the out-side world on CNN's live broadcasts. Many viewers, including some South Koreans, voiced their cynicism about the uncommon display of emotion over the death of a political leader by suggesting that the grievers were mobilized by the Party to show their loyalty. Many more believed that the "mourning" would be temporary and that things would get ugly as the inevitable power struggle surfaced. However, the grief was genuine. Every citizen showed his or her emotion at the death of the leader, much the same way as children would express their sorrow at the sudden loss of their father. The mourning period lasted longer than the traditional three years, includ-ing the year he died. In fact, official mourning took four years. People could not overcome the loss of the only leader they had been accustomed to. Upon his death, the office in which Kim performed his official duties was con-verted to a gravesite, where his body was laid in a glass coffin. Within a few months, an impressive building along with a long enclosed corridor was built as an annex. Streams of mourners constantly poured in from all cor-ners of the country. Most of them, even military officers, could not hide their grief. The people refused to accept the reality that Kim Il Sung was no longer with them. The charisma surrounding him became so absolute that he could not be wrong and whatever he did attained automatic legitimacy. He became the only source of righteousness and legitimacy.

In a way, no one, not even Kim Jong Il, could find legitimacy in isola-tion from Kim Il Sung. One has to assume that the leadership made con-certed efforts to create a charismatic leader in Kim Jong Il, but his father's legacy was too overwhelming to be replaced even by his own son. In the end, the country chose to integrate the two leaders as though they were one. In the mid-1980s, when Kim Jong Il was being groomed as the coming leader, the official scenario was that the young Kim was so independently qualified to lead the people that he should not be regarded as benefiting from his father's position. As I recall from a personal interview of a scholar of *Juche* philosophy, the official position with regard to the power succession was that Kim Jong Il's leadership capability should be viewed independent-ly from his father's.[1] But in the post–Kim Il Sung era, Kim Jong Il is viewed by the people as the embodiment of Kim Il Sung, as expressed in the doc-trine that *one is the essence of the other*. Today, it is safe to say that Kim Jong Il's leadership is inseparably entrenched in the legacy of Kim Il Sung. The paternal bond between the two is finally advocated unambiguously. It is sim-ply that a father and his children are inseparable, and their relationship can-not be destroyed because of hard feelings and misconduct on either part. To this extent, the legitimacy of the government is not subject to evaluation.

In general, a political system's stability depends on its legitimacy. However, there is no consensus among scholars on the question of what makes a regime legitimate. A multitude of factors may affect the political legitimacy of any leadership, among which ideology and performance are crucial. To establish an ideally and normally stable leadership, both ideological appeal and tangible material achievement are essential. In reality, however, different systems have chosen one of the two bases of regime legitimacy as being more salient.[2]

In the case of North Korea, political legitimacy is derived from ideology. Practical achievement in terms of economic performance has little bearing on the question of whether the government is entitled to rule. This "despotic" notion of regime legitimacy might help one to understand the unconventional phenomenon that severe economic hardship, including food shortages, has not caused any appreciable degree of popular unrest or a legitimacy crisis.

Government by Legacy *(Yuhoon jong chi)*

A peculiar thing happened after the death of Kim Il Sung. North Korea became perhaps the first country in world history where the deceased still rules. Almost all policies in almost all areas in the country have been generated from Kim Il Sung's "guidance" and directives. Since the longevity of his leadership spanned nearly half a century, he was able to touch on practically all conceivable areas and situations.

On collective farms, farmers are equipped with guidance books covering every phase of growing all farm produce, such as rice, potatoes, wheat, corn, and vegetables. The same is the case with the livestock industry. Kim Il Sung was supposed to be an expert on agriculture because he was the son of a farmer and engaged in farming throughout his life. The day before he passed away in 1994, he gave instructions to officials of collective farms. His directives are absolute and are always obeyed. For instance, following his guidance, farmers throughout the country are raising white goats. Visitors will notice white goats meandering around everywhere in the country, even in the suburbs of major cities. Saltwater fish farming is a popular line of work that also was promoted by the leader. The industrial factory is another site where the teachings of the Great Leader are vividly displayed, recited, studied, and adhered to. Some factory sites are singled out as model factories because of the simple fact that the Great Leader visited and provided "on the spot" guidance. Places

where he visited are "enshrined" with appropriately inscribed signs showing the date he made the visit. These model sites are used as training sites
for farm or factory officials and planners.

Another example of Kim Il Sung's legacy is the new constitution,
promulgated on September 5, 1998, and referred to as the Kim Il Sung
Constitution. Among its new features, two are worth mentioning. First, it
is the first constitution with a preamble. The preamble praises the late
Great Leader as an immortal figure. Second, the constitution abolishes the
position of the presidency (*jusok*). The peculiar reasoning behind abolish-
ing this position is that "the Presidency is eternally reserved for the Great
Leader Kim Il Sung." Since the position is permanently occupied by the
"deceased" who "lives with the people forever," no one else can possibly
occupy that position. The wording of the constitution leads one to suggest
that the presidency has not been abolished; instead there is a permanent
president of sorts. The North Korean leadership and many common people share this interpretation.

Yuhoon (legacy) policies are never criticized because they "cannot be
wrong" and because any criticism undermines Kim's authority and wisdom. This kind of policy rigidity may prove to be counterproductive, but
it also contributes to political stability and system maintenance.

"All for One and One for All"

I explained earlier that *Juche*'s theory of the political-social body is an
aspect of political culture that provides a theoretical foundation upon
which absolute collectivism is rationalized. Individuals are worthless
unless they are integrated into the body of the community. Since the political-social body is considered to be the natural order, its constituent parts
maintain a state of equilibrium by performing different functions that are
commanded and coordinated by the "brain." Thus, the brain and other
organs are to be integrated as mutually indispensable parts. Their relationship is not contractual but natural. It is in this context that we must
understand the leadership of Kim Il Sung and his successors as the brain.
In this same vein, the Party is seen as the mediator between the mass public and the leader. The Party is the functional arm of the leader for conveying his will to the mass public. At the same time, the Party is designed
to aggregate and represent the will of the people to the leadership. Thus,
as discussed earlier, the authority structure of North Korea is perceived as
a natural organismic structure, as opposed to a product of a contractual
arrangement between the ruler and the ruled.

Although in theory society exists for its citizens, it is the individuals that are always subjected to the leader's benevolence. The individuals have a solemn obligation to reciprocate the leader's benevolence with unconditional love and loyalty. The leader, however, cannot be a capricious dictator for the obvious reason that the brain cannot function in defiance of the body's feedback. The hereditary succession of power was not seen as unusual in North Korea; the people accepted the commonsensical idea that the brain had regenerated itself and that only one who had lived in the family of the Great Leader and maintained close functional interaction with him could attain the qualities necessary to function as the brain of the sociopolitical organism. No other person could be more naturally qualified than his own son.

In addition, the idea of hereditary power succession is hardly deviant from the traditional practice in Korea, where such a succession is viewed as natural. One must realize that North Korea has never experienced any other kind of leadership succession because the present leadership was the first one following the Japanese colonial period, which was preceded by the age-old dynastic regimes. In a sense, the political-social body doctrine has provided a theoretical justification for the traditional practice of hereditary power succession to which Koreans are accustomed.

Furthermore, collectivism in North Korea should not be viewed as an entirely deviant and accidental ideological configuration. Citizens gain a sense of identity only by participating in a political-social life, which undercuts the rewards of acting with hedonistic individual selfishness. Ethnic homogeneity in North Korean society provides the people with a natural source from which to establish their identity as a group. In this sense, North Korean collectivism is more than a cognitive belief system or a metaphysical artifact. It coincides with their existential quality itself.

The much-publicized notion of "all for one and one for all" should be seen in the context of the political-social body doctrine, as opposed to understanding it as a government's ploy to induce absolute loyalty of the people to the state. The doctrine is naturally integrated with an almost pure nationalism rooted in the remarkably homogeneous ethnic population.

The Party and the Bureaucracy

The bureaucracy in North Korea is no more than a functioning arm of the Party without any political power generated from within. Symbolic ranks and official positions in the bureaucracy seldom bring with them any amount of political power or authority in the hierarchy. The Party is the sole repository of power and authority. In every administrative unit, there is a Party representative who is responsible for mediating between the Party center and bureaucrats. He or she transmits policy directives from the Party, evaluates job performances of bureaucrats, and reports to the Party. In fact, this practice is not limited to the government bureaucracy; it is pervasive throughout all work units in every sector of the society. The Party representative, referred to as the secretary, is in charge of the political education of the members of his or her unit. He or she is an ideologue ("red") who is thoroughly educated in the official ideas of *Juche*. In fact, the separation of "reds" from "experts" is a vital practice without which political stability would be endangered. The mechanism of "reds over experts" was practiced in China, especially during the Cultural Revolution, but the Chinese version was merely a political device intended to solidify the government's power base and maintain political integration; in no way was the Chinese practice given ideological or theoretical justification. But in North Korea, the role of the Party is given a unique legitimacy as the mediator between the brain and other functioning organs. Since the structural hierarchy in the bureaucracy itself does not coincide with the real power hierarchy, the bureaucrats are more or less equal to one another, each reporting directly to the Party representative. Thus, positions within the organization are not meant to generate an orderly relationship to maintain institutional stability. Rather, organizational positions are defined mainly in terms of their functional obligations. The conventional form of bureaucracy inhibits the effectiveness of a centralist authority through its excessive compartmentalization and by allowing functional expertise to acquire authority. Superiors in the North Korean bureaucratic setting are not given power in certain important personnel matters such as recruitment, dismissal, and promotion. In this way, the leadership attempts to promote what is known as the "antibureaucracy campaign."

Policy Goals and Priorities

Policy goals and priorities are determined by the principles of *Juche*. The ideology has always been consistent in promoting three related areas of self-reliance: (1) military self-defense; (2) economic self-sufficiency; and (3) political self-determination. These three are mutually reinforcing and inseparable. Without a military self-defense capability, a nation cannot be sustained. In this case, neither political self-rule nor economic self-reliance is attainable. Without both military capability and political self-rule, economic self-sufficiency is impossible, given the exploitive nature of the global economic system. Without economic self-sufficiency, people's lives are dependent on external resources and political self-rule becomes impossible. In pursuing policies relevant to these areas, North Korea has shown a series of peculiar policy tendencies. One outstanding example is that the chairmanship of the military committee of the government has become the most important position in the country, whereas the position of president has been abolished under the current constitution.

Military Self-Defense

The impetus for North Korean nationhood was generated from anti-Japanese colonial politics. In his autobiography, Kim Il Sung lamented the lack of military strength during the Yi Dynasty that invited Japanese invasion, and throughout his struggle for independence, he always resorted to guerrilla warfare against the militarily superior Japanese police. Furthermore, the Japanese surrender itself was attributed to the superior military power of the Allied forces, as demonstrated by the use of nuclear bombs. Since the country was given independence as a result of the Japanese defeat, Kim Il Sung held the unwavering belief that national emancipation would be precarious if the country were incapable of defending itself from external aggression. As a result, North Korea has consistently maintained an exorbitant amount of military expenditure. The recent controversy over North Korea's suspected capability to produce nuclear weapons cannot be fully comprehended without considering the doctrine of military self-defense as a matter of national survival. If North Korea had not developed the nuclear weapons production program, the government would have been illegitimate in view of the *Juche* ideology. National defense, according to *Juche,* is not subject to compromise; it cannot be negotiated away for economic gains or political acceptance in the international community. Such an uncompromising posture was clearly demonstrated in the bilateral talks with the United States in 1993 on issues pertaining to Pyongyang's refusal to allow the International Atomic Energy Agency's special inspection of nuclear facilities in Yongbyon (see Chapter 11).

In order to realize the doctrine of military self-defense, North Korea has had to tolerate an enormous degree of sacrifice and discomfort in matters of economic life and diplomatic relations. The emphasis on the military industry favored only the heavy industrial sector at the expense of the production of consumer goods and the service sector. North Korea's pri-

mary foreign currency earnings come from arms sales. It is a widely recognized fact that Pyongyang has been producing conventional weapons,
including rather sophisticated missiles that a number of countries, such as
Iran, Iraq, Libya, Syria, and Pakistan, have imported regularly and in large
quantities to use in recent wars. As a country without a broad industrial
base, North Korea has fostered military preparedness, mainly because of
the uncompromising doctrine of self-defense called for by the *Juche* ideology. An added value is the economic payoff from the export of weapons.

Military self-defense also requires mental and spiritual preparedness.
Here, ideological education becomes an integral part of military training,
which involves *Juche* education as much as combat training. Soldiers are
told and many believe that the greatest honor is for a soldier to sacrifice
his or her life for the nation. As discussed earlier, the nation is what makes
the political-social body for an individual possible, and dying for the
nation will elevate the individual to eternal life with the nation. North
Korean soldiers in general seem to have been indoctrinated with this belief
system. In numerous encounters with frontline soldiers in the late 1990s,
I was struck by the level of determination and ideological preparedness on
the part of both officers and enlisted men. They uniformly expressed the
resolve and, more important, the desire to die in action to attain an eternal
life and to be with the Great Leader Kim Il Sung.

To the North Koreans, there is no permanent ally or permanent enemy,
but there will always be imperialist powers prepared to conquer smaller
countries that are not capable of self-defense. South Korea is depicted as
such a country unable to protect itself from foreign domination.

Economic Self-Sufficiency

According to *Juche,* basic needs for physical survival must be produced
within the country if its people's lives are to be independent of foreign
domination. For the promotion of economic self-sufficiency, the doctrine
advocates two policy objectives: balanced growth and distributive justice.[3]

Besides the heavy industrial sector that has gained prominence
because of the imperative of self-reliance, agriculture occupies a most
prominent position in the North Korean economy. The shortage of arable
land has always been a North Korean dilemma. Most farmland on the
Korean peninsula is in the southern region, and the North is left with mostly mountainous areas and is also climatically unsuitable for the production
of the main staple, rice. To remedy these natural limitations, North
Koreans have developed what is referred to as the *Juche* agricultural

method. It is designed to maximize productivity by having the government distribute rice plants and the farmers grow them. Each collective farm is allocated a certain number of plants, and the average productivity for each plant becomes a comparative yardstick with which to assess each collective farm's output. Since North Korea is an intriguingly competitive society, although the competition is never on the individual level, collective farms always compete for greater production. Superior performances are recognized by rewards and mass publicity, and inferior outputs are criticized in public. Rewards take a variety of forms, including material prizes such as television sets, refrigerators, and even money. But more likely, prizes are medals and commendation certificates from the Party or even from the Great Leader himself. Additionally, small tracts of land around residences are allotted for private use, but they are seldom used for private purposes; their harvest is often added to the collective output.

Three specific efforts to promote production merit a mention. First, irrigation systems, especially dams, have been extensively constructed, including the most heralded one at the West Sea, called Suhae kap mun. Second, the effort to expand arable land by filling in the shallow sea basin along the west coast has brought tangible results. Third, mountainous areas have been converted into arable land by clearing out forests. Although the third effort soon backfired because the loss of trees and natural vegetation resulted in erosion and frequent flooding, North Korea has generally been able to maintain food self-sufficiency, although it had to struggle throughout the 1990s with extensive famine and poor harvests.

In addition to farming, raising livestock has been emphasized, especially poultry, pigs, and lately goats. Some hog farms are equipped with modern facilities. High-yielding breeds have been introduced from abroad. At the time of the inter-Korean summit meeting in June 2000, the North Koreans took a South Korean delegation to a model hog farm to show off their advanced livestock industry. Upon returning from the meeting, the South Koreans told reporters that they were impressed with what they saw. Moreover, farm households commonly raise chickens and pigs in their backyards and on public land.

Light industry is regarded as the producer of goods that may not be as essential as farm products or as important as heavy industrial products. Thus, this sector has been accorded the least significance. The quality and quantity of commodity goods are extremely low, but this situation is by design. Because the *Juche* ideology considers luxury to be harmful to human development, the economy is never encouraged to produce commodity goods of great appeal to the consumer. A leading *Juche* theoretician reflected on this issue by articulating the view that excessive wealth is just as dangerous as excessive poverty. He further observed that poverty may ruin the human body, but excessive wealth ruins the human soul.[4]

When the economy is devoid of market competition, at least in the domestic arena, the light industry sector is not expected to develop. At the same time, in order to discourage waste, prices are set extremely high for commodities consumed beyond the amount of government distribution. In fact, commodities sold in department stores are not basic necessities but luxury items, and their prices are excessively high for casual purchases. For instance, the price for a black-and-white television set is approximately double the average worker's monthly salary.

As discussed earlier, heavy industry, especially as it involves weapons production, is given the highest emphasis in the North Korean economy. Despite the relatively backward technology and poor industrial base of the country, this sector has been promoted to ensure military self-reliance. Electrical power generators, tanks, artillery, and short- and medium-range missiles, among other heavy industrial products, are manufactured not only for domestic consumption but also for export. Despite the international efforts to discourage North Korea from developing and manufacturing weapons of certain types, this trend is expected to continue as long as *Juche* remains the guiding principle.

Another component of economic self-sufficiency is found in the policy of distributive justice. Distribution is done in accordance with people's needs and the principle of equality. In determining the amount of food to be rationed, not only the number of family members but also their ages and occupations are considered to achieve a need-based distribution. *Juche* theoreticians maintain that never before has any country implemented the Marxist ideal mode of distribution as closely as has North Korea. Furthermore, North Korea might indeed be the most equal society in the world in terms of income distribution. For most workers, regardless of occupation and educational background, the beginning salary is uniformly determined by the state; presently the initial salary is about 120 won per month, which is equivalent to approximately U.S.$60. Within a work unit, salary discrepancy is minimal; the highest salary seldom reaches twice as much as the lowest pay. At universities and colleges, beginning instructors are paid more than half the amount paid to deans and endowed professors. At leading hospitals, top administrators and senior physicians are rarely paid more than twice the salary for beginning doctors. The same situation is observed in factories and farming organizations.

There is widespread speculation among casual observers of North Korea that this country, like the former socialist systems in Eastern Europe, has a severely skewed class structure in which Party officials and government bureaucrats enjoy special benefits and a luxurious lifestyle. But this speculation is misleading and unfounded. Most high-ranking government and Party officials live in high-rise apartments in Pyongyang, where ordinary office workers, teachers, and even factory workers reside as well. In fact, each apartment floor consists of multiple units with residents from all walks of life. These residents form and belong to the voluntary administrative entity called *ban* that is obligated to convene weekly meetings. The *ban* elects its head (*banjang*). He or she is likely to be a person with the most spare time, not the most powerful official in the government. Members of a *ban* are so familiar with each other that they are unable to maintain any secrecy about personal wealth and lifestyle. Any perception of obvious inequality may cost the "privileged" their credibility and reputation and even their positions. Furthermore, wealth in the form of capital does not mean much in North Korean economic life. Because the society is tightly shielded from the outside world, North Korean money does not accord any purchasing power abroad and little enough within the country itself. In fact, accumulated wealth can often be a liability. This policy of equal distribution is designed to guarantee the satisfaction of basic needs for all citizens, a necessary requirement of economic self-sufficiency. When the economic base is weak, any appreciable degree of inequality may produce larger numbers of people who are deprived of basic needs. Thus, Pyongyang finds it imperative to maintain a distributive structure based on need and equality.

Furthermore, the ideology defies the export-led economy that has become an effective prescription of developing economies such as South Korea. An export-led economy typically develops some leading sectors in industry to give them a comparative advantage in competitive world markets. In order to enhance the quality of products and financial viability, the economy tends to be integrated into the international financial and technological system and is thus inevitably dependent on external forces. This situation would directly undermine the doctrine of economic independence called for by the *Juche* ideology. But it is precisely because of the adherence to this doctrine that the North Korean economy has suffered, at a time when neighboring capitalist economies achieved unprecedented growth, realizing what is commonly referred to as the "miracle of the Asian tigers." The North Korean doctrine has been costly indeed.

The ensuing economic isolation, coupled with Western economies' alienation of North Korea from technological cooperation and assistance, has virtually strangled the country's economy. The effect of this economic isolation has been felt even more keenly as the socialist bloc countries have either abandoned or drastically reformed their economic systems following the collapse of the Soviet Union. Economic aid and development assistance from China and the Soviet Union stopped almost overnight. The massive food shipments from northeastern China, which continued for many years, were phased out by the late 1980s. Since then, China has demanded cash for food, which North Korea has been unable to pay, thus aggravating further the chronic shortage of food throughout the 1990s. Food is not the only item that is in short supply. In fact, all consumer goods are in severely short supply throughout the country. There is virtually nothing one can see in daily life that is imported from other countries, except for automobiles and certain appliances. But imported appliances are relabeled with Korean generic labels, such as *Moranbong* and *Jindalle*, to convince the public that the economy is self-reliant and self-sufficient. Nevertheless, this kind of deception is the exception. Stores, even department stores in Pyongyang, have little merchandise, and commercial activities are very slow and stagnant. Furthermore, power shortages are evident: public buildings, including even elementary schools, are not heated in the winter months. Even lighting is in severely short supply, as evidenced by dark streets, buildings, and homes throughout the year.

In the final analysis, the price for a self-reliant economy significantly contributed to economic stagnation and hardship, including mass starvation. Is the doctrine worth that price? Even the most faithful *Juche* advocate must be raising this question. Could the summit meeting of June 2000 and the ensuing developments be seen as a genuine effort on the part of North Korea to get out of economic isolation? This question will be answered in Chapter 10.

Political Self-Determination

In order to comprehend North Korea's desire for political independence and self-determination, one has to understand the intensity and pervasiveness of the Japanese colonial manipulation of the Korean people as well as the way in which the North Korean people are led to perceive it. This desire is seen in all forms of *Juche* arts and literature. The autobiography series written by Kim Il Sung, *Segiwa doburo* (With the century), which is revered and extensively read in all circles, advances the theme that if a nation loses political sovereignty, the people become enslaved and their existence becomes worthless. Political self-reliance is not subject to compromise, although economic interdependence and military alliances may be accepted to the extent that political sovereignty does not suffer. This flexibility is an intriguing aspect of "neo-*Juche*" in the post–Cold War era. Allowing a controlled degree of economic and political interaction with foreign countries and South Korea was seriously advocated by Hwang Jang Yop, who defected to South Korea in 1997 after a long tenure as one of the foremost intellectuals and *Juche* theoreticians.[5]

The energy devoted to instilling the doctrine of self-determination into the people is enormous indeed. As discussed in the previous chapter, schools at all levels, from day care centers to universities, maintain political curricula intended to inculcate students with the political consciousness of self-determination. Every form of art provides a heavy dose of nationalism and political sovereignty. A typical example is found in the much celebrated opera *Pibada* (Sea of blood), which is designed to portray one theme and one theme only: a lack of military strength and national solidarity forced the Korean people to be helplessly subjected to humiliation and death by the Japanese. In the play, the Korean people painfully realize that unless they help themselves, no country will come to rescue them at the risk of its own national interest, as is demonstrated by the opportunistic position taken by the United States.[6]

Another powerful display of nationalism can be seen in the video and movie series *Minjok kwa Unmyong* (Nation and destiny). In this ongoing series, a number of public figures are heralded as national heroes and heroines because of their struggle for national sovereignty. In the previous chapter, I discussed the story of Ri In Mo, a prisoner of war during the Korean conflict who was sent back to North Korea after having been detained in the South as an "unconverted prisoner" for nearly half a century. A recounting of his saga will illustrate the importance of self-determination to the Korean people. Ri, who was old and in failing health, was sent back to his family in North Korea. As soon as he crossed the border and landed in the North, he was given a hero's welcome. There was massive national festivity and public parades glorifying Ri's uncompromising nationalism and iron-willed loyalty to the cause of North Korea. He was given the highest medal of honor for military service and awarded the title of "Hero" personally by Kim Il Sung himself. Ri's story is read, heard, and discussed throughout the country by people from all walks of life, often in the context of the weekly study group. Ri's and other stories in the series have been distributed on video and studied in every conceivable context of political education.

One theme that is pervasive throughout the series is that the North is ideologically, morally, and socially superior to the South. Indeed, socialization of the masses in North Korea is such that they regard South Korea as a pitiful colonial territory of the United States. According to them, South Korea is pathetically dependent on the United States in all spheres of life, including defense, economy, culture, and politics. The North Korean people are told and led to believe that it is their mission and destiny to liberate their southern compatriots from the imperialist yoke. According to the North, once a nation develops a dependence on external influences, the nation and its people will become progressively incapable of self-determination, and South Korea is pronounced to be such a system.

In short, the *Juche* principle of political self-determination has created a belief system that advocates liberating the southern half of the fatherland from imperialist forces. This belief underpins Pyongyang's unification and foreign policy.

Notes

1. Professor Min Byang Ju of Kim Il Sung University observed in 1981: "Had Kim Jong Il not been a son of Kim Il Sung, his own leadership attributes would have been demonstrated more clearly."

2. Refer to Han S. Park and Kyung Ae Park, "The Bases of Legitimacy in North and South Korea," *Korea Observer* 11, no. 2 (1987), pp. 33–44.

3. For a comprehensive discussion on the theory of *Juche* economy, see Han Chang Mo, *Jarip kyungje riron* (Theory of economic self-reliance) (Pyongyang: Publishers of Social Science, 1984).

4. This remark was made to me by Professor S. J. Koh of the Academy of *Juche* Science in November 1993.

5. Hwang Jang Yop, who invited me to the Academy of *Juche* Science on several occasions in the early 1990s, conveyed the new aspect of the ideology as he rationalized the dynamic change of *Juche* to keep pace with the changing international environment produced by the end of the Cold War and the domestic economic difficulties.

6. According to the official North Korean view, the United States could have effectively stopped Japanese maneuvers to annex Korea but chose not to intervene because of its own national interest.

9

Foreign and
Unification Policy

It is intriguing that North Korea's foreign and unification policies have closely corresponded to the evolution of the *Juche* ideology itself, further evidence that Pyongyang's policies have always been guided by the ideology. Because of regime stability and the continuity of the *Juche* idea itself, Pyongyang's foreign and unification policies have been relatively stable and continuous. Furthermore, its policies have been predictable.

The grand policy principle has consistently been self-reliance as it applies to all domains of foreign policy. In the economic arena, avoidance of dependence on other nations has guided Pyongyang's policy strategies; in the political arena, North Korea has always had a fraternal relationship with the nonaligned bloc; in the cultural domain, the North Korean leadership has made concerted efforts to avoid Western influence. This policy posture has been dramatically demonstrated by Pyongyang's negotiating behavior with the United States, Japan, and other Western countries. Nowhere has North Korea's insistence on self-reliance been seen more clearly than in the controversy over nuclear weapons and long-range missile programs for much of the 1990s.[1]

With regard to unification policy, the goal of self-determination has underscored all policy strategies and tactics. The elimination of foreign influence, beginning with the withdrawal of U.S. troops from South Korea, has been regarded as the prerequisite for national unification. The ultimate state of a unified Korea is envisioned to be similar to North Korea as far as the self-reliance posture is concerned.

Policies Toward the Major Powers

It is undeniable that Kim Il Sung's leadership was orchestrated and made possible by the Soviets' desire to exert influence on Korea. It is also true that Chinese involvement in the Korean War rescued the North Korean communist regime from certain defeat. During the Cold War era, the superpowers of the communist bloc rendered generous assistance to North Korea. Militarily, both Moscow and Beijing signed mutual defense treaties providing sophisticated weapons and technical cooperation, even to the point at which Pyongyang's suspected capability to produce nuclear weapons would not have been conceivable without their cooperation. Economically, it is no secret that North Korea has benefited from grants and a variety of economic and technical assistance from its communist allies.[2] However, what is less known to the outside world is the fact that the Pyongyang leadership has guarded against developing structural dependence upon the economies of China or the Soviet Union. For instance, neither country has become a major market for North Korean products; by the same token, North Korea has seldom been a market for foreign commodities. In fact, it has consistently condemned the politics of "dependency" allegedly practiced by multinational corporations of industrial countries against many Third World countries. Here, Pyongyang's orientation toward the major economic powers has essentially been one of dissociation and avoidance. With the exception of selected key strategic areas, such as the weapons program and heavy industrial equipment, North Korea's economy has been isolated from international economic dynamics, even within the communist bloc itself. Its meager trade activity with the communist countries is a direct result of this self-containment policy, which was maintained through the early 1970s, when Pyongyang's diplomatic and economic relations were limited to a handful of communist systems.

China

China has always been a most significant country for North Korea for a number of important reasons. First and foremost, geographical proximity allowed the formation of an ethnic Korean community in northeastern China. The Korean community began forming in the northeastern region of China even before the Japanese occupation. Economic difficulties emerged on the peninsula, where arable land was limited to the western coastal area in Cholla Province. At times, entire village populations migrated to the plains of Jilin, Liaoning, and Hailongjiang Provinces in

China. By the end of World War II, the number of Koreans living in China numbered nearly 2 million, which would have been approximately 8 percent of the total population of Korea. These immigrants introduced rice farming to the region, which became the region's major crop. The aforementioned three provinces have since become known as more affluent areas in China, but the economic situation for Korean residents during the early phase of their migration was deplorable. Most of them became farm laborers and house servants. In order to survive, most of the Korean farming families leased land for cultivation, and the rent was paid with portions of the harvest. It was commonplace that the rent was as high as 75 percent of the crop, leaving little for the farmers to live on.

The Koreans soon were attracted to the ideals of socialism and eventually the Maoist movements. In fact, early socialist campaigns by the Chinese communists were enthusiastically embraced and participated in by the Koreans, who were among the most oppressed of the citizenry, along with the "untouchable" social groups of local soldiers, salt producers, butchers, hooligans, and entertainers.[3] Some historians suggest that the communist revolution in China would not have been successful without its early success in the northeastern region and that the region's revolutionary campaign would have been futile without the active participation by the Korean residents.[4] Thus the revolution was indebted to the Korean community, and in the early years after the revolution, the Chinese communist government did not forget that debt. In 1952, the area in which the Korean community lived was designated an autonomous region, and that status has carried over to the present.

The second reason for a close connection between China and North Korea is the fact that the Chinese reciprocated Korean support by sending massive numbers of soldiers to help—indeed, rescue—North Korea from certain defeat during the Korean War. In that war, Mao Zedong lost his own son, which was truly remarkable evidence of the level of commitment and friendship. And North Koreans have not forgotten that. Third, the shipment of grain from northeastern China as needed in agriculturally poor North Korea has made China the guarantor of the livelihood of the people. Contrary to official claims by the authorities, food shortages were always a reality, even before the natural adversities struck the land in the mid-1990s. China, however, has had a surplus of food and has been able to store grains, indicating that supplying food to North Korea hardly causes an unbearable burden on the country's food sustainability. Discouraged by the lukewarm support from the international community for alleviating the food crisis, the leadership in Pyongyang has come to value China as a source of food even more in recent years. On the occasion of the fiftieth anniversary of the 1949 Revolution in China, Pyongyang sent Kim Yong Nam, speaker of the Supreme People's Assembly and also the de jure head of state (in accordance with the Constitution of 1998). China regarded his visit as an official state visit and treated it with the appropriate protocol. Beijing soon reciprocated by sending the Chinese foreign minister to Pyongyang. Furthermore, the much-publicized "secret visit" by Kim Jong Il himself to Beijing and selected industrial sites in China in spring 2000, followed by Kim's visit to a Shanghai industrial complex in 2001, laid a solid foundation for rapprochement between the two socialist governments, whose relations had been strained since the normalization of Seoul-Beijing relations in 1992.

The United States

The United States is viewed by North Korea as an imperialist power but one too important to ignore. In fact, Pyongyang views its relationship with Washington as being paradoxical, in that it wishes to keep away from the United States for the fear of disruptive influence, and at the same time it wishes to improve relations that may help alleviate economic and diplomatic difficulties. This paradox has been a root cause of Pyongyang's seemingly inconsistent and unpredictable policy behavior. It is clear that as long as the United States maintains its ground troops across the border and retains a security alliance with South Korea, Pyongyang's denunciation of Washington will not cease. Because the stationing of foreign troops and security dependence on external forces contradict the very principle of *Juche,* denouncing such practices is imperative for North Korea. It is imperative because it is a matter of system legitimacy. One has to realize that no price is too high for the ruling elite if regime legitimacy is at stake.

The aforementioned paradoxical dual interests have guided Pyongyang's policy toward Washington, forcing Pyongyang to display a range of divergent policy behaviors, at times conciliatory and at other times hostile. Generally, the rule is that when the leadership in Pyongyang perceives an incoming overture from the United States to have been intended to undermine its legitimacy or threaten regime stability, it will refuse to be involved in any kind of interaction. The much-criticized "diplomacy of brinkmanship" should be understood not as a preferred policy option but as a consequence of the regime's dual interests.

North Korea considers the United States to have leverage and influence, not only over a host of developing and developed countries but also on global financial organizations such as the International Monetary Fund and the Asia Development Bank. Without U.S. cooperation, Pyongyang feels that no financial institution will provide development loans, and without such loans, the pace of North Korean development will be hindered. Although making loans and being indebted to international funds may not be consistent with the *Juche* idea of self-reliance, Pyongyang has always complained about U.S.-led international financial organizations "strangling its throat" and suffocating the economy. Faced with economic difficulty at home and the reality that no economy can prosper without participating in the global market system, Pyongyang has advanced a policy of rapprochement toward the United States as a top priority of its foreign policy. The announcement by U.S. president Bill Clinton of the lifting of economic sanctions against North Korea on September 17, 1999, was received by Pyongyang with enthusiasm and a sense of diplomatic victory. As the North Korean economy is more likely to be integrated into the global market in the coming years, it will be interesting to see how Pyongyang deals with the discrepancy between economic interdependence and the doctrine of self-reliance.

Numerous issues need to be addressed before a full-fledged diplomatic tie can be established. Among them are the issues of U.S. troops in South Korea, the suspected nuclear weapons and long-range missile program in North Korea, and the atrocities allegedly committed by U.S. soldiers during the Korean War. Each of these issues has great ramifications, and they are expected to cause some stumbling blocks in forging a normal relationship.

The U.S. military has continuously been present in South Korea since the division of the country in 1945. During the occupation period (1945–1948), U.S. troops were stationed there along with Soviet troops to play the caretaker role during the transition from Japanese surrender to the establishment of a new Korean government. Instead of one Korean government, the division of the country led to the formation of two governments, one in the North under the tutelage of Moscow and the other in the South under the supervision of Washington. Before the withdrawal of all U.S. troops from the southern half of the peninsula could occur, the Korean War ensued, inviting massive involvement of U.S. ground troops, which have been maintained ever since at the level of at least 36,000 ground forces. Although the primary rationale for the stationing of troops in Korea was and still is to deter North Korean aggression, the presence of U.S. armed forces in the peninsula has taken on additional functions. One of them is the symbolic display of U.S. influence and power throughout the world. As the only remaining superpower, the United States wants to flex its muscles, even though there is no apparent threat to the security of the country. Such a presence may foster regional and local stability where anti-U.S. sentiment is still marginal and superficial, as is the case in South Korea. Another function is the protection of U.S. economic activities abroad. U.S. investors naturally feel more secure and comfortable when U.S. interests in the region are backed by the presence of armed forces. U.S. firms have extensive economic interests in South Korea and throughout the region, making political stability and military security in the region essential for a continued U.S. business presence. Related to the economic incentive for deploying U.S. troops is the marketing of weapons and exportable dual-use technology to the region. While maintaining the security alliance, the United States has upgraded and expanded weapons purchased by South Korea.[5] The Seoul government has even taken up part of the expense for maintaining U.S. troops there.

Pyongyang views Washington, not Seoul, as its counterpart in negotiating the stalemate on the peninsula. On the armistice agreement, the United States, China, and North Korea are the signatories. South Korea was never represented at the talks leading to the truce agreement, and Pyongyang insists that Seoul is not a legitimate party with which to negotiate. Furthermore, North Korea feels that South Korea is not in a position even today to negotiate with the North on issues pertaining to peace and security on the peninsula because it does not command its own military forces. Legally, U.S. armed forces, on behalf of the United Nations, have held commanding authority over the Korean military. Pyongyang's persistence in holding bilateral meetings with the United States in matters regarding security arrangements on the peninsula was recognized in late 1999, when the United States agreed to stage bilateral negotiations with Pyongyang to discuss the missiles issue.

Furthermore, Pyongyang agreed in 1994 to terms proposed by a consortium of countries, including the United States, Japan, European countries, and South Korea, which included the construction of two light water nuclear power plants in exchange for North Korea's relinquishing the graphite-powered nuclear plants that had been under construction at Yongbyon. The multibillion-dollar project was to be contributed to by the consortium nations, called the Korean Peninsula Energy Development Organization (KEDO). This plan includes the shipment of crude oil by the United States until one of the two plants is constructed. Although more than 70 percent of the needed resources for the construction were to be provided by South Korea, Pyongyang successfully blocked Seoul's efforts to lead the consortium. It had to be the United States that assumed the leadership position, and companies operated by the South Korean government were regarded by Pyongyang merely as subcontractors. In fact, the KEDO plan, formed in 1994 as a result of the Geneva Agreement, was scheduled to be completed by 2003, but the construction has been interrupted by numerous incidents. To name a few, Pyongyang's infiltration of submarines into the southern sea border, Washington's inability to keep up with the schedule for supplying crude oil in the amount of 50,000 tons annually, and North Korea's manufacturing and testing of long-range missiles. In spite of these interruptions, the KEDO project is still alive, and the construction is under way.

North Korea's desire to improve relations with the United States and the significance of Washington's success in curtailing Pyongyang's production and dissemination of weapons of mass destruction (WMD) are such that the bilateral relationship is bound to move forward. Furthermore, Kim Dae-jung's government in South Korea made a substantial contribution to creating a political climate that would make the United States comfortable in dealing with North Korea bilaterally without directly involving the South. The Clinton administration advanced a policy of "engagement" rather than deterrence or alienation with regard to the reclusive regime in North Korea in this context. This policy orientation seems to have become the guiding principle for the Bush administration as well.[6]

The engagement policy of the United States is consistent with the South Korean "sunshine policy" toward North Korea. The former is intended to induce the reclusive system to engage with the international community in various areas so that the system might be exposed to life environments that are different from its own. In so doing, it is hoped that the system will become more open to the outside world. It is further hoped that engagement might encourage the system to initiate economic and political reforms to adapt itself to the norms and practices of the international community. Thus, tension reduction in the peninsula may be promoted. South Korea's sunshine policy is also intended to ease tension by providing humanitarian assistance and promoting economic and cultural interaction with the North, a rather drastic deviation from the conventional policy of alienation and isolation.

Yet the Pyongyang government views these policies from Washington and Seoul as threatening. According to its view, both engagement and sunshine policies are designed to force the Pyongyang government to give up the present system and accommodate reforms and restructuring in line with capitalist civil society. By attributing the collapse of the Soviet Union and Eastern European socialist allies and the extensive reform measures in China to the capitalist West's influence, Pyongyang has closely guarded itself from falling into the same "trap." Its policy response to the post–Cold War political environment has been geared toward protecting the system from following in the same footsteps as its Cold War allies. It has even intensified ideological education programs to fend against "spiritual pollution" that might result from the influence of the capitalist West as well as South Korea. Market economy consumerism is criticized for its "decadent" effect on the human spirit.

Since the fall of Second World communist systems in the late 1980s and early 1990s, North Korea has found itself isolated and lonely. It has felt a greater need for ideological education and political control and guidance of people's thoughts and behaviors. This domestic political imperative forced the system to develop a dualism of sorts. On the one hand, the leadership has intensified reclusive politics at home, and on the other hand, it has searched for cooperative interaction with Washington in order to alleviate its stagnant economy. This dualistic approach gives the appearance that the system is divided between hard-liners and soft-liners. The military establishment adheres to the hard line, whereas professional diplomats and government bureaucrats tend to pursue pragmatic policies. This tendency should not be seen as the breakdown of authority structure or as a power conflict within the leadership. It should rather be viewed as a strategic approach to cope with the challenges of the time.

In 1999, the Clinton administration appointed William Perry, former secretary of defense, as special emissary to Pyongyang and charged him with working out a comprehensive proposal designed to implement the engagement policy. Following a series of negotiations and consultations with South Korea, Japan, and China, as well as various circles in Washington, Perry produced a report referred to as the Perry Report. This report advised Washington to ease trade sanctions and work toward full normalization of diplomatic relations, in exchange for Pyongyang's giving up all the programs relating to the production and dissemination of weapons of mass destruction and missiles. There was widespread support for the report among all parties concerned, except in North Korea itself. The agenda imbedded in the report was not acceptable to Pyongyang's belief that a nation's capability for self-defense is not subject to compromise. Yet the lifting of economic sanctions and eventual normalization of relations with the United States are too valuable to be dismissed on the part of poverty-stricken North Korea. Thus, Pyongyang's response has been consistently ambivalent. Pyongyang continues to participate in several negotiations, such as the Four-Party Talks and the missile talks in Berlin and, most significant, had agreed to conduct high-level bilateral talks with the United States in Washington and elsewhere throughout the year 2000. These talks, which were convened on several occasions, can be seen as a potential breakthrough. They were preceded by North Korea's declaration that "there is neither an eternal foe nor an eternal ally." In total, these developments mark quite a step toward rationalizing a policy of rapprochement toward the United States.[7]

Despite the positive developments outlined above, there has been a new focus by Pyongyang on atrocities committed by U.S. soldiers, who massacred a large number of civilians during the Korean War. According to the documentation at the Shinchon Museum, U.S. soldiers under the command of General Harrison D. Madden killed civilians by the thousands in the town of Shinchon and nearby villages. In a nearby village, there were a couple of gas chambers where children and their mothers were allegedly separated from each other and burned to death, which echoes the most horrible scenarios of the Nazi Holocaust. The museum and these sites are presented to the public as a vivid reminder of the crimes committed by Americans, and more important, they are shown to enlighten the people about the tragic consequence of being a militarily weak country that is unable to destroy foreign aggressors. However, the alleged atrocities have been used for domestic consumption rather than to propagandize against the United States. This cautious approach may have been due to either the need to improve relations with Washington or, as some suggest, the doubtful authenticity of the allegations.

Japan

Relations with Japan represents yet another peculiar situation for North Korea. Along with anti-U.S. sentiment, anti-Japanese sentiment is deeply entrenched in the mass belief systems of the citizens. Ever since the regime was established in 1948, North Korea has generated the driving force for political integration and consolidation of Kim Il Sung's leadership from anti-Japanese sentiment. As discussed earlier in the context of the evolution of *Juche,* Kim's leadership was established from the very beginning on the grounds that he was a nationalist hero who single-handedly liberated the nation from the yoke of Japanese colonial rule. Throughout the formation and every subsequent phase of the establishment of the republic, anti-Japanese sentiment has been used to overcome adversity and hardships. Textbooks for every level of school and popular literary sources are full of stories about Kim's struggle and colonial oppression. Japan has indeed been demonized in the belief systems of North Koreans for decades. Unlike in South Korea, all known nationalist activists and their descendants are recognized and given preferential treatment in such areas as housing assignments, educational subsidies, rationing of consumer goods, and occupational considerations. In documenting these cases of nationalist resistance, hostile feelings toward the Japanese aggression are consistently reinforced. Before it tries to mitigate these hostile sentiments against the former colonial power, Pyongyang insists that Japan must at the minimum satisfy a set of conditions that cannot be compromised. One is a formal apology from the Japanese government, which cannot be superficial or in abstract terms. It must be specific and directed toward all Korean people. Second, those who suffered specific wrongs at the hands of the oppressive imperial forces must be duly compensated, including those women who were forced to serve the military as "comfort women." Third, Japan must pay reparations to North Korea, the amount of which is yet to be determined upon careful and thorough investigation but is estimated to be in the range of U.S.$30–50 billion. Japan is not likely to comply with these demands for a number of reasons, including its domestic political climate, especially in the wake of resurging nationalism with the election of Koizumi Jun'ichiro as the prime minister in 2001, an important topic that is beyond the scope of this book.

A major sticking point is the long-range intercontinental ballistic missile incident in August 1998, in which a North Korean three-stage booster rocket (Taepodong) was launched over Japan. The Japanese were furious about the event, and Japanese public opinion showed a significant change toward favoring rearmament because of fears that North Korea could launch an effective attack.[8] North Koreans, however, declared that the rocket was not a missile designed for military use but carried a satellite with the name Kwangmyong Ho, which was launched successfully into orbit. Pyongyang even "revealed" the exact course that it traveled, which did not breach Japanese airspace.[9] Whether it was a missile or a satellite is not an important issue, however. The hard fact is that North Korea demonstrated the ability to launch multistage booster rockets. This technological ability enhanced Pyongyang's bargaining power, which was exactly what North Korea intended to achieve. Furthermore, the rocket technology made potential buyers of missiles more interested in North Korea.

In short, Pyongyang's relationship with Japan is uniquely clouded by the history of colonialism that has decisively affected the formation of political culture in North Korea. Therefore, normalization of the diplomatic relationship with Japan is expected to be a slow and difficult process. Much depends on Japan's ability and willingness to accommodate the aforementioned North Korean demands.

The Nonaligned Bloc

As the ideology of *Juche* was becoming a more legitimate self-reliance doctrine, Pyongyang expanded its diplomatic relations and functional interaction with nonaligned Third World countries outside the socialist bloc. In 1968, Kim Il Sung made a memorable speech entitled "The Great Anti-Imperialist Revolutionary Cause of the Asian, African, and Latin American Peoples Is Invincible." In this speech, he maintained that "the non-aligned movement is a powerful anti-imperialist revolutionary force reflecting the main trend of the era."[10] In fact, North Korea made consistent efforts to "export" the ideology of *Juche* to these developing countries by helping them set up institutes of *Juche*. Their leaders are invited to attend the *Juche* symposium held annually in Pyongyang; at the symposium, Kim Il Sung is praised as the creator of the ideology that speaks for all the world's oppressed peoples against imperialist powers. This event serves as the catalyst for regime legitimacy, especially in comparison with the Seoul regime. It is important to understand that there are sympathizers with the principle of *Juche* and that the Pyongyang leadership does not find it so difficult to get international support from the nonaligned bloc.

As a result, Kim Il Sung, the creator of *Juche,* is promoted as a world leader of the nonaligned movement. His massive two-volume *Encyclopedia* was published in 1992, not in North Korea but in India, not in the Korean language but in English, and not solely containing contributions by North Korean scholars but also involving scholars from such countries as France, Britain, Denmark, India, and Peru. This publication was intended to convey the message that Kim Il Sung's leadership is indeed recognized beyond the territorial limits of North Korea. The book itself is nothing more than a comprehensive account of *Juche* ideas. There are numerous other publications on *Juche* in different languages, many published in foreign countries. What is important is the fact that the North Korean people seem to believe quite firmly that their Great Leader is highly respected throughout the world. They are also led to believe that foreign leaders come to Pyongyang to pay tribute to him; at the International Exhibition Hall located at Mt. Myohyang, a variety of gifts from foreign dignitaries are displayed, with the inscription that the visitors brought them to pay tribute to the Great Leader. North Korean citizens, especially students, regularly visit the exhibition hall as part of their "on-site training"; they are constantly reminded of Kim's status, which gives them a great sense of pride and the impetus to elevate their respect for the leader.

Another reminder of the greatness of *Juche* as a global ideology is seen in the *Juche* Tower in Pyongyang. The tower was deliberately built higher than the Washington Monument in the United States, and most of the countries in the world have contributed to the construction with funds and materials. All the contributors' names are inscribed on the side of the tower facing the street, which gives citizens the distinct impression that the tower was a product of reverence and admiration for the Great Leader and the "immortal" idea of *Juche* by all the people, not only of the non-aligned countries, but of the whole world.

Overseas Koreans

North and South Korea are unique in that the number of their expatriates is large and their contribution to the homeland is significant. There are some 670,000 Korean residents in Japan; some 2 million Koreans in China who are Chinese citizens; another 2 million living in North America, mostly in the United States, of whom 250,000 are U.S. citizens; and 500,000 living in Europe, South America, and other parts of the world. Altogether, nearly 6 million Koreans live abroad, or about 8 percent of the entire population of North and South Korea. The overseas Koreans can be divided into two distinct groups, those in Japan and China and those in North America and everywhere else. The former populations resulted from mass immigrations before the end of World War II, mostly during the Japanese colonial period. The latter emigrated to North America and other open societies only from South Korea after the division of the country, mostly after the Korean War.

Those living in China and Japan have always been significant to North Korea. During the Korean War, Koreans living in northeastern China volunteered in large numbers to participate in the "Liberation War" to free their South Korean compatriots from U.S. imperial occupation.[11] The Koreans mobilized in the war were believed to have constituted a majority of the Chinese army that came to assist North Korea. As discussed earlier, for this reason, the Korean community in northeastern China has been treated well by the Chinese government and has even been granted the status of an autonomous region. All those who desired Chinese citizenship received it, and most of the Koreans chose to become Chinese citizens. Their relationship with North Korea has been largely consistent with China's political situation and Beijing's relations with Pyongyang. Since South Korea normalized diplomatic relations with China in 1992, North Korea has suffered from the increasingly pro–South Korean sentiment among the Koreans in northeastern China, who actively sought opportunities to prosper economically. The presence of the South Korean labor market was so attractive to them that many of them chose to find jobs in South Korea, where they worked as manual laborers at places where South Koreans were disinterested in working, places that earned the stigma of "3Ds" (dangerous, dirty, and demeaning). Many of them were able to make quick money in South Korea and open shops at home upon their return. However, South Korean economic and social practices and the presence of new entrepreneurs who were politically corrupt and morally degenerate negatively influenced the once innocent Korean community in northeastern China. As a result, many in China have become critical of South Korea's indiscriminate economic and social intrusion. Many of them, especially intellectuals, became more sympathetic to North Korea for no other reason than the absence of decadent culture there. North Korea has been watching the changing dynamics in the Korean community in China with keen interest.

Koreans in Japan are different from their counterparts in China. Although they too immigrated during the Japanese occupation, they often were forcefully taken to Japan by the occupying colonial government for labor and other purposes. They were not treated well, nor were they even considered for Japanese citizenship. They were marginalized in every domain and had to suffer from the derogatory label *Chosenjin* (Koreans). Two things happened to them. First, Kim Il Sung felt special concern for the Koreans in Japan because he regarded them as victims of Japanese oppression. He provided considerable resources to them for the establishment of educational institutions patterned after North Korean schools, using its textbooks and bringing children to North Korea for educational tours and nationalist education. He even established Choson University in Tokyo. The word *Choson* (*Chosen* in Japanese) was the name of the country but was never used by South Korea; thus, the university was identified with socialist North Korea. Kim Il Sung's benevolent policies made the Korean residents in Japan overwhelmingly sympathetic to North Korea, and thus they were disliked by the South Korean regime for decades.

Second, the Koreans in Japan began to accumulate huge amounts of cash. They provided almost all the slot machines at casinos and central cities. They also ran restaurants throughout Japanese metropolitan areas. They carried the stigma of indecency by filling occupations and running businesses that were traditionally unattractive to the Japanese and often considered demeaning. The result is that there are a large number of Koreans who are culturally and socially marginalized in Japan yet have great material assets. They are favorably disposed toward Pyongyang, and some are extremely loyal to the North Korean leadership. When they visit Pyongyang, they are given the red carpet treatment. They are often housed at luxurious villas and are recognized by the government for their patriotic activities. The leadership of the Korean community in Japan has always been invited to important national events. In return, they do not hesitate to give their hard-earned fortunes to their beloved fatherland. It is estimated that some U.S.$250 million annually has been poured into North Korea from this source. In order to coordinate relations with Koreans in Japan and Koreans overseas in general, Pyongyang instituted the Committee on Overseas Compatriots, which has considerable leverage in government decisionmaking pertaining to policies toward Japan.

The Korean ethnic communities in North America and other parts of the world, which are primarily of South Korean origin, are mostly disorganized and scattered about their host countries. They came out of South Korea to explore better living conditions and prosper economically, as opposed to being interested in political agendas of their home governments. Therefore, it is practically impossible for North Korea to win their support. Nevertheless, Pyongyang has not been negligent in trying to orchestrate organized support from Koreans in North America. It feels that Koreans abroad are assets of the nation and that they could be effectively mobilized for its political and diplomatic causes.

Principles of Reunification

Juche ideology also provides the guiding principles for unification policy. North Korea has been consistent in advancing a set of principles and a specific formula for national unification. National self-determination, peaceful means, and a grand unity of all Korean nationals have always been the underlying principles. The first and third principles are derived directly from *Juche* ideology.

Juche's principle of self-determination calls for the expulsion of foreign troops from the country and the denial of foreign involvement in the unification process. Viewed in this context, the stationing of U.S. troops in South Korea cannot be tolerated. Although Pyongyang has involved third countries such as the United States and China in exploring avenues to promote bilateral relations, it has not in principle invited them to talks pertaining to unification itself. Noteworthy here is the notion of "grand unity," which always includes Koreans living abroad. In every state of the union address since the inception of the system, overseas Koreans have been recognized as a vital part of the population.

Since the mid-1960s, North Korea has persistently adhered to the concept of confederacy as an approach to unification. The present unification proposal, the Confederate State of Koryo (another word for Korea), however, was created following the Sixth Party Congress in 1980. It was proposed as an intermediate stage whereby two governments and different ideological systems could cooperate until a more conducive climate was created for a unified state. There are conflicting interpretations of the intent behind this proposal. It is based on the premise that the two systems are basically incompatible in terms of their ideologies and system characteristics, and therefore a viable course toward unification must start with mutual acceptance and coexistence as separate systems under the rubric of a confederate state. The two sides would have equal representation in the national assembly, which would be the sole repository of authority.

According to one interpretation generally offered by South Korean authorities, this proposal may be designed to eventually overwhelm the South by indoctrinating the mass public in the South with the idea of unification and generating grassroots support for the more nationalist and solidified leadership of North Korea. The Seoul government has rejected this formula on the grounds that equal representation is unfair to the South, which has twice as large a population as the North. In addition, because this proposal recognizes separate systems and ideologies, North Korea can maintain its closed system without being disrupted by external influence, whereas the mass society in the South may become more vulnerable to northern "infiltration" because of its inherent openness. This eventuality is unacceptable to the Seoul government.

However, proponents of the proposal tend to stress that this confederate formula is the most realistic and workable solution to the inter-Korean impasse. The two systems have developed mutually incompatible institutions, norms and values, and behavioral traits to the extent that any direct effort at their immediate integration could only be counterproductive. According to this view, the two systems have promoted theories of regime legitimacy within their respective systems on the grounds of mutual rejection. In order to cope with this situation, there must first be a period (or stage) of coexistence for enhancing mutual understanding. In this period, common challenges must be dealt with in the spirit of coordination and cooperation. Yet the idea of permanent separation is guarded against in this proposal; Pyongyang has rejected the South Korean proposal of gradual integration as a ploy to establish permanent division. It seems that North Korea would not have advanced the idea of the Confederate State of Koryo had officials lacked self-confidence that *Juche* had sufficient merit and persuasive power and that the North could overwhelm the ideologically disjointed society of the South with the help of this ideology.

Although the summit meeting held in June 2000 and the ensuing developments may give the impression that the "frozen land" may be melting down as a result of the sunshine policy of South Korea, the reality is far different. I discuss the issue of inter-Korean relations, including the summit meeting, in more depth in the next chapter.

Notes

1. For a general discussion of North Korean foreign relations, see Kongdan Oh and Ralph C. Hassig, *North Korea Through the Looking Glass* (Washington, D.C.: Brookings Institution Press, 2000).

2. Georgiy Kaurov, "A Traditional History of Soviet–North Korean Nuclear Relations," and Alexander Zhebin, "A Political History of Soviet–North Korean Nuclear Cooperation," in James Clay Moltz and Alexandre Y. Mansourov, eds., *The North Korean Nuclear Program* (New York: Routledge, 2000).

3. The untouchables are the declassified people who do not have even a social class in the stratification system. The recognized social classes, in order of prestige, include the learned, farmers, craftsmen, and merchants.

4. As many as thirty-two of the 120 or so revolutionary heroes and heroines documented in the Revolutionary Museum of Northeast China in Harbin are identified as ethnic Koreans.

5. South Korean imports of weapons from the United States in 2000 ranked third in the world (*New York Times,* August 21, 2000).

6. U.S. secretary of state Colin Powell declared that the United States is prepared to talk with North Korea anywhere, anytime with no preconditions.

7. Ambassador Kim Hyong U made such a remark on the occasion of his participation in a bilateral conference with U.S. representatives in December 1999 at the University of Georgia, Athens, Georgia.

8. Opinion polls by *Yomiuri Shimbun* and *Asahi Shimbun* showed a drastic opinion shift.

9. The name *Kwangmyong Song* (translated as "Bright Shining Star") is Kim Jong Il's penname.

10. Kim Il Sung, *Selected Works,* vol. 5 (Pyongyang: Publishing House of the Workers' Party of Korea, 1975), pp. 236–249.

11. Hyon Ryong Sun, Li Jong Mun, Hoh Ryong Gu, Josonjok Peaknyon Sa Hwa, *Hundred Years of Koreans in China* (Shen Yang: Lianing Publishing House, 1984).

10

Inter-Korean Relations: A Legitimacy War

Without understanding the nature and structure of inter-Korean competition, one cannot properly comprehend the relationship between the divided halves of the Korean peninsula. This relationship is predicated upon the premise that both systems cannot be simultaneously legitimate; one of the systems must be illegitimate and therefore must disintegrate at some point in the future. The historical climate peculiar to the evolution of inter-Korean relations is unique. Each system has developed a political culture that contrasts with and often contradicts that of the other. Because political institutions, domestic policy behavior, and foreign policy postures are all founded on the norms and values that constitute the foundation of regime legitimacy, an understanding of the political culture regarding system legitimacy is particularly crucial in explaining and forecasting system characteristics and behaviors of both systems. By limiting analysis to the study of leadership characteristics or international contextual factors, even the most informed observers have consistently been puzzled by the unconventional nature of inter-Korean dynamics.

The purpose of this chapter is to discern the nature of the legitimacy competition and its ramifications for inter-Korean relations. Although the legitimacy war itself has never ceased, the pattern has shown appreciable transformation caused by contextual changes in domestic policy priorities and the international political climate. This evolution will also be examined.

Contrasting Bases of Regime Legitimacy

As alluded to earlier, analytical and empirical distinctions may be made between two bases of legitimacy. One is regime *performance* in meeting basic needs and promoting the prosperity of the people. In this case, people as the governed will authorize and support the regime in exchange for its performance in delivering what the people need and want. This basis of legitimacy is consistent with the classic democratic theory of social contract, as advanced by John Locke and adopted extensively by both participatory democracy and socialism. This theory simply suggests that the ruling elite can find the justification to possess and exercise power by helping people satisfy their needs and attain prosperity in their material and physical life environments. The second basis on which a regime pursues legitimacy is *ideology*. The ideological basis is more of a question of psychology and mass belief systems. In any political culture, there is a certain set of accepted norms and principles that cannot be easily compromised. In a liberal democracy, for instance, basic political rights such as speech, assembly, and due process are assumed to be so fundamental that they cannot be undermined if the polity is to be sustained as a legitimate system. Communist systems, however, uphold principles of distributive justice and centrist allocation of values. In reality, all systems are mixed systems in the sense that both performance and ideology are utilized in varying degrees of relative importance to maximize regime legitimacy.[1] However, some systems tend to weigh ideology more heavily than the utilitarian performance of the system. In general, neither North Korea nor South Korea has ever undermined the centrality of their relative ideologies. Indeed, the two systems have employed ideologies that are mutually incompatible to the extent that one system's ideology is predicated upon the rejection of the other's ideological system. Yet the two systems have encountered contextual changes in both domestic policy priorities and the international environment, forcing them to alter their basis of legitimacy to some extent. Although North Korea has almost always placed the emphasis on ideology, South Korea has shown great flexibility in pursuing pragmatic economic interests.

The Ascension of the Competing Systems

In the formative stages of both Korean regimes, a series of historical experiences decisively contributed to the shaping of their political systems. The fact that the nation's partition was engineered by external forces—the emerging superpowers—affected the nature of the Korean regimes. Following the Japanese surrender in 1945, U.S. and Soviet forces were to remain in Korea until an independent Korean government could be established. They were there to accept the Japanese surrender and facilitate the establishment of a Korean government. However, the post–World War II period was quickly dominated by the hegemonic conflict between the two, paving the way for their prolonged occupation of Korea. The United States was determined to curtail the communist forces that were riding the tide of global expansion. Thus, the country remained divided along the 38th parallel, with the United States occupying the south and the Soviet Union occupying the north. The line became permanent as the ideologically opposed hegemonic powers on the peninsula perpetuated the conflict. At the formal conclusion of their occupation in 1948, the occupying powers helped establish two separate governments with handpicked leaders.

Within two years of the establishment of governments in both halves of Korea, a civil war ensued.[2] It became an international conflict that placed the two Koreas on the frontline of the Cold War. During the war, the Korean people were devastated not only by the loss of many lives but by the separation of millions of people from their families. In the process of the bloody conflict and the ensuing decades of system developments sponsored and masterminded by the superpowers in the Cold War era, the two regimes have established not only mutually incompatible but fully hostile system characteristics.

The peninsula is still in a state of war. Even the end of the Cold War world order could not help terminate the division. No longer do the international forces commission the division. In this sense alone, the Korean partition is fundamentally different from the case of German division. Intense mutual distrust and latent hostility grew in the peninsula in the external context of Cold War world politics. Each system defines its jurisdiction and territorial boundary as inclusive of the entire peninsula. Even the seemingly conciliatory policy postures lately seen in the sunshine policy of South Korea could not change the fundamental stance that there could be only one legitimate state in the end. Although apparently similar to the divided China in this respect, unlike China, neither Korea accepts the notion of "two states in one nation" as an acceptable solution.

Legacies of the Korean War

What sets the Korean experience apart from the German experience is the fact that the divided Koreas engaged in brutal intra-ethnic conflict for three years. The conflict itself and the ensuing politics in both systems helped them further solidify their respective power bases and regime legitimacy.

The Korean War was described as a "moral war" in South Korea in that it was fought for the values and accompanying institutions of democracy. Needless to say, it was the United States as the "master" superpower who guided the politics of the surrogate power. Massive economic and military aid from the United States helped the Rhee regime (1948–1960) establish a "democratic" system that upheld, at least in the constitution, the ideals and institutions of participatory democracy in a country that had just been liberated from four decades of oppressive Japanese rule, a period of tutelage by the United States, and three years of a bloody conflict. Korea had been under centuries of dynastic rule. Thus, it is an understatement to say that South Korea was not prepared for the alien ideology and institution of democracy. Nonetheless, U.S. tutelage and the presence of the threat from the communist bloc left the Rhee and ensuing regimes with no alternative but to adhere to the norms and institutions of Western democracy. This course has been bumpy, with a series of constitutional revisions and military juntas. Yet, the consistent presence of a security interest on the part of the United States and its allies and the persistent threat from the North has allowed South Korean governments little room to maneuver away from the transplanted ideology. In the meantime, U.S. influence through educational and socialization processes has been so pervasive that democracy has found a relatively stable footing in the elite culture and mass belief systems.[3]

North Korea, however, has been induced to follow a completely different course. The Korean War was regarded as a continuation of the nationalist struggle against foreign domination, this time against the United States and its "surrogate" powers. North Korea felt a great sense of pride and fulfillment in representing itself at the signing of the armistice agreement, where its counterpart was the United Nations. Since then, Pyongyang has shown reluctance to treat South Korea as a sovereign system. At the same time, North Korea has campaigned almost single-mindedly for national sovereignty under the banner of *Juche* ideology. Although there have been various phases in the evolution of that ideology, no one can dispute the fact that it a form of ultranationalism.[4]

Diverging Ideologies: Democracy Versus Nationalism

From the inception of their respective systems, the two regimes adopted separate paths for their courses of political evolution. In the South, the

U.S.-educated Rhee Syngman assumed power with the blessing of the United States, setting the stage for democratic institutionalization. Power consolidation under Rhee was harshly anticommunist. The constitution was little more than a carbon copy of the U.S. Constitution with some elements of the British Constitution. There was nothing indigenous about institutional development in South Korea. What may be "indigenous" is the uneasy footing of democracy, which has shown symptoms ranging from violence to corruption. In the end, state-engineered capitalism faced profitable yet precarious encounters with the international market, paving the way to a model of "dependent" development.[5]

Power in North Korea was consolidated under the leadership of a young Soviet-trained military officer, Kim Il Sung, who had education and political experience in the underground nationalist movement.[6] He was able to consolidate his power base by eliminating factions who were in sympathy with the Soviets and with the South Korean leftist movement. In the meantime, the Chinese Communist Revolution was in full swing, most vigorously in northeastern China, where some 1.8 million ethnic Koreans had immigrated and established their residence. As discussed earlier, the success of Mao Zedong's revolution was in large measure due to its initial success in the northeastern region, where Korean residents made significant contributions. China literally rescued North Korea from certain defeat in the Korean War by intervening with a massive number of ground troops. It is estimated that a majority of the Chinese soldiers were "volunteers" from the Korean community in the region. This series of events helped the two communist countries develop a fraternal relationship that endured for decades.[7] The fact that Maoist ideological orientation was more in line with nationalism than Soviet-style communism made Mao's China exceptionally appealing to Kim Il Sung's North Korea. In fact, North Korean communism has always been predicated upon the premises and ideals of nationalism.

"State Capitalism" Versus *Juche*

Since the 1960s, the two systems' diverging development has progressed at an accelerated pace, resulting in even more intense legitimacy competition. South Korea found the basis of its legitimacy in capitalist development, whereas the North established a firm grounding in nationalist consolidation.

The course of South Korean democracy has been precarious. The Second Republic (1960–1961) under the leadership of Chang Myon, which replaced Rhee Syngman's First Republic (1948–1960), was overthrown by a military junta in 1961. An interim government took control and wrote a new constitution that replaced the presidential system with a parliamentary system. Yet another constitutional overhaul occurred with Park Chung Hee's Third Republic, established in 1963. Park's regime lasted until 1979, when the president was assassinated by the director of the Korean Central Intelligence Agency in a bizarre incident. After another interim government with Choi Kyu Ha as the president, General Chun Doo Hwan forced his way into power through another military insurrection. As expected, a new constitution was installed, this time limiting each president to one five-year term. The Chun regime (1979–1987) was succeeded by none other than another soldier-turned-politician, Roh Tae Woo (1987–1992). When a "civilian" government was installed under the leadership of Kim Young Sam with the help and blessing of the Roh government, the two generals (Chun and Roh) were subjected to a public trial on charges of corruption and eventually imprisoned. The Kim Young Sam government (1992–1998) soon became a public nuisance for gross corruption, especially fiscal irregularities involving his son and handpicked conglomerates (*chaebols*).[8]

Finally, this quasi-civilian regime was replaced by a genuine civilian government when the globally renowned human rights activist and opposition leader Kim Dae-jung won a highly contested election in 1998. However, the civilian government inherited a massive economic problem.[9] It was immediately forced to cope with an enormous amount of foreign debt of more than U.S.$150 billion; a virtually depleted foreign currency reserve; inefficient management on the part of conglomerates; and the imperative of restructuring the financial and economic system, making new loans, and accommodating intervention by international lenders such as the International Monetary Fund (IMF). Although the initial phase of Kim Dae-jung's government was plagued by enormous economic difficulties and labor disputes, the regime has shown its commitment to the principles of democracy.

Thus in South Korea, democracy was never firmly established, but the system could never abandon the ideology of democratic governance. Despite irregularities and turmoil in the process of instituting democracy, no one other than the most radical student and worker protesters has advocated socialism or communism. On the contrary, political integration and power consolidation have been promoted through the ideal of anticommunism. This phenomenon may be accounted for by the presence of North Korea as the antithesis of South Korea. In addition, in South Korea, the center of power has always exercised almost unlimited influence. When this is coupled with "political monism," whereby politics overwhelms all other sectors, the central power becomes almost omnipotent.

The government has always played a vital role in economic growth, yielding a pattern of development referred to as "state capitalism." Nowhere was this phenomenon more evident than in Park Chung Hee's Third Republic. Park, as the junta leader who assumed power through a military coup d'état, lacked legitimacy as a democratic leader. His regime was in need of supplementing his shaky basis of legitimacy by advancing system performance as the prime raison d'être of leadership. Park Chung Hee instituted multiyear economic plans with strong government intervention in all sectors of the economy. This practice was a drastic deviation from the laissez-faire principle of capitalism. Nevertheless, the South Korean ideology of democracy could never have distanced itself from capitalism, no matter how unconventional its practice might have been. Again, such actions result from the imperative of having a national identity opposed to the North Korean system. And even though Park was anything but democratic, he still claimed democratic credentials.

In short, the practice of strong government over civil society is in part due to the imperative of maintaining legitimacy against the presence of a threat from the North. To cope with this threat, the military has taken precedence to the extent that the entire society has embraced norms and values consistent with militarism. South Korea's military culture has deterred the maturation of its democracy, as militarism and democracy are often mutually incongruent in their value systems and operational dynamics. Militarism upholds such values as uniformity, a hierarchical authority structure, centralism, and enemy-driven belief systems, whereas democracy promotes diversity, articulation and aggregation of opinions from the bottom, a pluralist civil society, and bargaining and negotiation as consensus-building mechanisms.

North Korea, however, developed a unique breed of nationalism under the banner of *Juche*. This ideology systematically adheres to the premise that whatever South Korea stands for is wrong and illegitimate. It defies any form of reliance or dependence upon external powers. The self-reliance doctrine has led the system to alienate all foreign sources and, in doing so, to block off the people from the outside world. The evolution of *Juche* has shown a variety of phases and philosophical refinements, but one salient feature has always been nationalism.[10]

The extreme nature of North Korean nationalism has taxed the system in a number of spheres, including foreign relations, economic development, technological advancement, and functional literacy on the part of the people as the global community turns the corner into a new millennium. Yet Pyongyang is not in a position to embrace reforms and openness to induce economic growth. The regime fears that such a drastic move might endanger system stability and even cause system collapse. More important, the North Korean leadership cannot risk the basis of regime legitimacy by adopting reform policy measures that in effect negate its ideological legitimacy vis-à-vis South Korea.

With a demonstrated military capability that might include weapons of mass destruction, the Pyongyang regime is not expected to give in to foreign pressures and be swayed to embrace reforms. It has sufficiently demonstrated that it can endure economic hardships and diplomatic isolation. Furthermore, North Korea has a formidable enough military force to maintain significant bargaining leverage in the international community. However, the greatest strength of the North Korean system lies in its ideological solidarity, and the ideology of *Juche* has evolved in the process of legitimatization of the system as the antithesis of the South Korean system. The norms, values, and beliefs of a significant proportion of the people will not be altered overnight.

Ramifications for Unification: The Summit and Beyond

Any meaningful analysis of the prospect of reunification must focus on the motivational factors surrounding the dynamics of legitimacy competition between North and South Korea. As long as each side maintains its insistence on system legitimacy as proclaimed, a path of compromise for negotiated settlement toward reunification is not likely. All politically engineered gestures by either party are simply designed to demonstrate its relative superiority as a legitimate system.

Undoubtedly, the summit meeting between South Korean president Kim Dae-jung and North Korean leader Kim Jong Il that took place in Pyongyang on June 13–15, 2000, was a historic event. What is troubling is that most observers did not give enough attention to the psychological motivations on the part of the two leaderships, especially that of the North. For that reason, there have been several erroneous accounts of the event. First, a major mistake was to see the summit meeting as the ultimate success of South Korea's sunshine policy. If this policy is designed to open up North Korea and eventually foster the system's move toward accommodating economic and social reform and political change, then the summit meeting itself will probably do nothing to attain that objective. Related to this mistaken account is the widespread expectation that North Korea is surrendering its reclusive system to the world capital market in order to alleviate economic difficulties. Nothing is more remote from reality than this ideologically driven assessment. North Koreans have never shown any intention of altering policy orientations. Given these arguments, what was the motivation behind Kim Dae-jung's resolve to aggressively seek a summit meeting with Kim Jong Il and the latter's acceptance of the proposal? The answer is simple. They both calculated that the meeting would strengthen their respective systems' claims to legitimacy.

For South Korea's Kim Dae-jung, the meeting indicated the resounding success of his sunshine policy, thereby legitimizing the ideology of capitalist democracy. He expected that North Korea would be forced to open its door to South Korean investment and people, which would inevitably lead to system reform and social change. In this eventuality, Kim Dae-jung's policy would have given the Seoul regime a victory in the legitimacy competition. Furthermore, President Kim, as the first South Korean head of state to bring his reclusive North Korean counterpart to a summit meeting, could demonstrate his political capability in handling the North, thereby strengthening his political base. It was with these calculations that the announcement of the agreement to convene a summit was made on the eve of a general election in South Korea. Kim Dae-jung's personal desire to contend for the Nobel Peace Prize might have had some influence on his decisionmaking process as well. Certainly, the summit meeting would increase his support there. The only risk for Kim Dae-jung at the outset was the possibility of North Korea's noncompliance. In fact, he made the same overture to the North through such notable channels as Chung Joo-young of Hyundai Corporation and Park Po Hee of the Unification Church, wherein President Kim conveyed his desire to convene a summit meeting with Chairman Kim Jong Il, but the latter did not provide any positive reply until April 2000.

Observers were stunned when Pyongyang announced its willingness to accept President Kim's proposal. There were numerous speculations about Pyongyang's motivations for such an unexpected response. But most of them suggested that North Korea was finally coming out of the closet and that it was only a matter of time before Pyongyang began to reform in order to rehabilitate the failing economy through participation in the world market. Following the summit, a ranking official from Seoul made a pointed remark to an audience in Washington, D.C., that was widely shared by experts on North Korea: Kim Jong Il's coming out of the traditional enclave and embracing the South Korean leader at the airport was direct evidence that North Korea has surrendered to the South because of its failure as a socialist system. Nothing could be more wrong than this analysis. Pyongyang never gave in to anyone, let alone conceded defeat in the competition with the South for system legitimacy.

There are a few tangible events justifying the above observation. First, in recent months, the Pyongyang authorities reiterated the significance of a historical event that took place in May 1948, when Kim Il Sung assembled a group of nationalist leaders from throughout the peninsula, including a delegation from the South. On a little island in the Daedong River, a commemorative tower was erected on which the names of the participants were engraved. Kim Koo, who was a prominent nationalist leader, headed the southern delegation to the meeting. The northern delegation was led not by Kim Il Sung himself but by Kim Chaek. Kim Il Sung was elevated to the position of overarching leader who superseded all other leaders and actually presided over the meeting, thus demonstrating that he was the leader of all nationalist leaders. Also, the 1948 meeting took place in Pyongyang itself, suggesting that that city was the legitimate locus of unifying forces. It must have been in the mind of North Koreans that a summit meeting replicating the 1948 meeting would be a symbolic victory in the legitimacy competition, at least in the eyes of North Korean people. The meeting would boost North Korea's stance as a more legitimate government vis-à-vis the South. This calculation would have been a decisive element in making the decision to host the meeting.

Furthermore, Pyongyang might have thought that it could gain material and economic advantages from the South and its allies while gaining ground in the ongoing legitimacy competition. There is strong evidence to support this possibility. First, at the time of initial contact in Beijing to prepare for the 2000 summit meeting, the North Korean delegation, headed by Song Hyo Kyong, vice chairman of the Korea Asia Pacific Peace Committee, insisted that the meeting convene in Pyongyang and that it take the format of North Korean leader Kim Jong Il responding to the South Korean president's *request*. Second, the North Koreans insisted that the meeting in Pyongyang would be the only meeting and that there would be no obligation on Kim Jong Il to visit Seoul, reinforcing the symbolic implication that Pyongyang was the only locus of a unified Korea. Third, the North Koreans initially refused to name Kim Jong Il as Kim Daejung's counterpart; instead, they intended to name Kim Yong Nam, the nominal head of state. In this case, Kim Yong Nam would have played the role that Kim Chaek had in the aforementioned meeting of 1948.

The North Koreans appear to have played out this scenario. They secured a concession from the South that the summit meeting would be convened at the request of the South Korean president, at least in their version of the agreement. Pyongyang reported that the summit-meeting took place between Kim Dae-jung, president of South Korea, and Kim Yong Nam, president of the Presidium of the Supreme People's Assembly of the Democratic People's Republic of Korea.[11] Even though it was obvious that Kim Jong Il was the actual leader and that the summit meeting was between him and South Korea's Kim Dae-jung, the North Korean people were led to believe that their Dear Leader received the visitor and that the practical business meeting involved Kim Yong Nam. In fact, Kim Jong Il himself acted as host, with the clear intention of showing his warm hospitality and demonstrating his leadership attributes as the leader of the entire Korean people. North Koreans were led to believe that the terms of the agreement (see Box 10.1) signed by the two leaders in Pyongyang on June 15, 2000, were basically consistent with what Pyongyang has advocated for decades.

Article 1, which states that "the north and the south agreed to solve the questions of the country's reunification independently by the concerted efforts of the Korean nation responsible for it," was seen as affirmation of the *Juche* ideology of self-reliance. This item also suggests that the stationing of U.S. troops in Korea cannot be justified. Article 2 accepts the notion of a confederacy as an initial approach to unification, in that the "low level" of North Korea's Koryo Confederacy is similar to the initial stage of South Korea's (Kim Dae-jung's) Three-Stage Approach.[12] For the first time in inter-Korean relations, the concept of North Korea's confederacy was accepted as a legitimate approach by the South Korean government. In the North, this was deemed a significant victory in the long-standing struggle with the South for regime legitimacy. Article 3 involves two humanitarian concerns. South Korea wanted to secure Pyongyang's agreement to the exchange of separated family members, who are believed to be in the millions. In addition, the South agreed to return war prisoners whom it has detained. There may be as many as eighty prisoners, each of whom has been documented by North Korea. Pyongyang has been demanding their return for decades. The return of additional prisoners will help North Korea's cause of boosting patriotism and enhancing relative legitimacy. Article 4 spells out the principle of developing the national economy throughout the peninsula by facilitating economic integration. This article is interpreted as a sign of South Korea's willingness to divert considerable economic and technological resources to the North, without necessarily obligating Pyongyang to open the system or to reform

---

Box 10.1   Text of the Agreement

1. The north and the south agreed to solve the question of the country's reunification independently by the concerted efforts of the Korean nation responsible for it.
2. The north and the south, recognizing that the low-level federation proposed by the north and the commonwealth system proposed by the south for the reunification of the country have similarity, agreed to work together for reunification in this direction in the future.
3. The north and the south agreed to settle humanitarian issues as early as possible, including the exchange of visiting groups of separated families and relatives and the issue of unconverted long-term prisoners, to mark August 15 this year [the date of national independence from Japanese colonial rule].
4. The north and the south agreed to promote the balanced development of the national economy through economic cooperation and build mutual confidence by activating cooperation and exchange in all fields, social, cultural, sports, public health, environment, and so on.
5. The north and the south agreed to hold an authority-to-authority negotiation as soon as possible to put the above-mentioned agreed points into speedy operation.

Source: Pyongyang Times, June 17, 2000.

---

economic and political measures. It means an enormous economic gain on the part of the North, at least in the short run. Finally, the invitation of Kim Jong Il by Kim Dae-jung and a possible visit by the North Korean leader to Seoul are dealt with as peripheral issues. A supplementary document simply states that Kim Jong Il will visit South Korea at an appropriate time. When that "appropriate time" will be or what conditions might make the time appropriate is yet to be known.

In the final analysis, it is erroneous to assume that Pyongyang's acceptance of the summit meeting is a prelude to a fundamental change in North Korea's system characteristics. On the contrary, Pyongyang's rational calculation prevailed in that the summit meeting enhanced North Korea's position in the legitimacy competition with the South and, at the same time, provided much-needed economic assistance. Furthermore, the conciliatory gesture surrounding the summit meeting will also help

Pyongyang secure cooperation from the United States and other Western countries. One should notice that Washington did not waste time easing trade sanctions against North Korea. The lifting of U.S. sanctions became effective almost immediately after the inter-Korean summit. Other countries, including Japan and Canada, have shown their desire to improve relations with Pyongyang. By the end of 2001, most European countries had normalized diplomatic relations with North Korea. This development would not have been possible without a summit meeting and the sunshine policy of the South Korean government. The South Korean side, of course, had its own scenario that favored its capitalist democracy as the dominant force that will stimulate the North to compromise its longstanding ideology of *Juche*. In short, the two leaders had "different dreams in the same bed."

We have witnessed the passing of the Cold War, the fall of socialist systems in Europe following the demise of the Soviet Union itself, and drastic economic and legal reforms in China. All of these events, however, were unable to move the Korean peninsula out of the Cold War status quo.

In this chapter, I have maintained that in order to properly understand the history and dynamics of inter-Korean relations, observers must focus on the nature of legitimacy competition between the two systems. The competition has never slowed down, let alone having been settled in favor of market economy–oriented South Korea. Since the inception of the two separate regimes following Japanese surrender at the end of World War II, the difference between the competing systems has grown to the point at which they became mutually incompatible. The process of this diversion was fueled by the Cold War politics in which the two Korean governments confronted each other as enemies. More significantly, they have advanced and refined ideologies and system characteristics that are mutually exclusive. Each has sought the basis of regime legitimacy on the grounds of rejecting what the other stands for. The politics and policies in both Korean systems, as well as inter-Korean relations, suggest clearly that the legitimacy competition explains the underlying motivations and ensuing policy behaviors for both regimes.

The recent inter-Korean summit meeting was a historic event, and the world was shocked by the unexpectedly conciliatory gestures extended, especially by North Korea's Kim Jong Il. The media hype surrounding the meeting has led not only Koreans but foreign observers to raise their hopes for a speedy improvement in inter-Korean relations and for rapid structural and political reforms in North Korea. Yet all indications in this nascent postsummit era are that these hopes were raised too high and prematurely. One thing is certain: North Korea has not given in to pressures from within or without. The legitimacy competition is still intact.

In this sense, the Korean conundrum is uniquely complex. One has to dig into the political culture and system characteristics to be able to shed light on the seemingly endless string of mysteries posed by the behavior of the Korean systems toward each other.

Notes

1. On the basis of legitimacy along this line, see John Schaar, *Legitimacy in the Modern States* (New Brunswick, N.J.: Transaction Books, 1981). For extensive references on this topic, see Han Shik Park and Kyung Ae Park, *China and North Korea: Politics and Integration and Modernization* (Hong Kong: Asia Research Service, 1990), chap. 2.

2. On the origins and for a detailed account of the Korean War, see Bruce Cumings, *The Origins of the Korean War*, vols. 1 and 2 (Princeton, N.J.: Princeton University Press, 1981 and 1990); and William Stueck, *The Korean War* (Princeton, N.J.: Princeton University Press, 1995). The two authors offer conflicting interpretations about the origins of the war.

3. The process of the evolution of democracy in South Korea is carefully examined by John Kie-chiang Oh in *Korea: Democracy on Trial* (Ithaca, N.Y.: Cornell University Press, 1968) and *Korean Politics* (Ithaca, N.Y.: Cornell University Press, 1999).

4. The ideology of *Juche* was conceived as a simple form of antiforeignism, but as it was used as an instrument of regime legitimacy, its content has evolved to counter the South Korean ideology of capitalist democracy.

5. The concept of "dependent development" is used as the antithesis to the *dependencia* school of thought, which decries the intervention of external powers who will exploit and impoverish indigenous economies.

6. For an extensive discussion of the underground nationalist movement, see Suh Dae-Sook, *The Korean Communist Movement, 1918–1948* (Princeton, N.J.: Princeton University Press, 1967); and Chong-sik Lee and Robert Scalapino, *Communism in Korea*, 2 vols. (Los Angeles: University of California Press, 1972).

7. The Chinese government granted the Korean community in the northeastern region the status of an "autonomous region" during the Korean War on September 5, 1952. This policy action was generally regarded as a reward for the contribution that the Koreans in China made to the Chinese involvement in the Korean conflict. See Ma Min, ed., *Jungkuk sosuminjok sangsik* (The Chinese minority nationalities) (Beijing: Nationalities Publication House, 1983).

8. For a concise and credible discussion of the leadership crisis and economic difficulties in this period, see Oh, *Korean Politics*, chap. 9.

9. The outstanding external liabilities at the end of 1997 were U.S.$154 billion, of which U.S.$68 billion was short-term debt.

10. On the evolution of *Juche*, see Han S. Park, "The Nature and Evolution of *Juche*," in Han S. Park, ed., *North Korea: Ideology, Politics, Economy* (Englewood Cliffs, N.J.: Prentice Hall, 1996).

11. Article 11 of the constitution adopted in 1998 designates the president of the presidium of the Supreme People's Assembly as the head of state.

12. For a detailed introduction to Kim Dae-jung's three-stage concept, see Kim Dae-jung, *Kim Dae-jung's Three Stage Approach to Korean Reunification* (Los Angeles: Center for Multiethnic and Transnational Studies, University of Southern California, 1996).

11

The Unconventional Wisdom in Negotiating Behavior: The Weapons Controversy and Beyond

In the early 1990s, the entire world was puzzled for a prolonged period of time over the "mysterious" behavior of North Korea surrounding the suspected construction of nuclear power plants at Yongbyon. U.S. negotiators characterized North Korea as unpredictable, stubborn, irrational, and even mad. Many condemned North Korea for playing "brinkmanship" diplomacy.[1] Yet in the end, North Korea seemed to have outmaneuvered and out-"negotiated" everyone else in a way that served its pragmatic and ideological national interest.

Although the International Atomic Energy Agency (IAEA) and Pyongyang were finally able to come up with an agreement in October 1994, the road to full implementation is expected to be bumpy and difficult to a point at which it may still be derailed. Negotiations went from one deadlock to another, until the IAEA realized that the conundrum was becoming increasingly more difficult to comprehend. Most of this complexity and mystery stems from the world's inability to understand North Korea's behavioral motivations. Repeatedly, the IAEA and the United States have been frustrated by the seemingly unpredictable and "untrustworthy" patterns of behavior shown by North Korea.

However, one must realize that foreign policy behavior is seldom irrational or random. It always manifests the attitudes, norms, and values of the ruling elite in the process of pursuing what is perceived to be best for national interest. Therefore, in order to analyze the foreign policy behavior of North Korea, one must first examine the belief system (or political culture) of the ruling elite and concurrently the perceived national inter-est. With respect to the issue of the nuclear weapons program, one must examine how North Koreans perceive themselves and the political envi-ronment surrounding the peninsula and how they perceive the implica-tions of the nuclear weapons program for their own national interest.

There seems to be an unbridgeable gap between the typical perception of North Korea held by outsiders (especially Westerners) and North Korea's self-perception.[2] The painful reality demonstrated by the recent nuclear conundrum suggests that self-perception determines the course of North Korea's policy. The seemingly puzzling behavior of Pyongyang will not be as mysterious when viewed in the context of the *Juche* ideology as discussed in this book. Therefore, it is essential to put oneself in the shoes of the North Koreans, who have conditioned themselves with *Juche* ideas and devised policy goals and strategies in accordance with the norms and beliefs of that peculiar ideological orientation. North Koreans seem to view themselves as the protectors of socialism in the world and also as surrounded by massive forces threatening their survival.

North Korea's Reasons for Going Nuclear

If North Korea's nuclear weapons program is to be discouraged, efforts must be directed toward neutralizing the incentives for such a program. As long as North Korea sees a greater payoff in maintaining the development of weapons than in discontinuing it, the country will not comply with the expectations of the nonproliferation regime. In this sense, North Korea is just as rational as any other nation-state. What makes North Korea differ-ent from other systems is the complexity of behavioral motivations behind the nuclear program. Dealing with North Korea requires a complete and synoptic approach. Simply to set aside North Korea as an irrational and erratic outcast in the world community is not only dangerous but wrong; all foreign policy measures should be considered rational means of attain-ing national goals and interests. Now, what might underlie North Korea's nuclear decisions?

Political Motivations

The nuclear issue is directly related to the survival and stability of the system itself. Self-reliance in national defense has long been promoted as the essential requirement of political sovereignty. North Korea has opted to develop unconventional weapons as a measure to secure national survival.

Regime survival and stability. Visitors who have had direct contact with ranking officials in North Korea tend to agree that they perceive the possession of nuclear weapons as guaranteeing the existence of the country. Although publicly denying the existence of the nuclear weapons program, North Korea has made it clear both in words and deeds that it is militarily prepared to deter any aggression and defend itself without having to rely on external assistance.

No country in the world has consistently spent as high a percentage of its gross national product for defense as has North Korea in the post–World War II era. The defense burden has always been felt by North Korean citizens to what many would consider an unbearable degree. But all the inconvenience and hardships caused by militarization have generated little complaint from the public because they are led to believe that the alternative is no less than the demise of the sovereign state itself. Economic life in North Korea has been invariably difficult because of the shortage of consumer goods and daily necessities, but in no way has the difficulty forced the government to compromise its defense priority. The people are constantly reminded of the fact that once the military burden is alleviated, it will take virtually no time for the nation to prosper.

North Koreans realize that South Korea has a stable military alliance with the United States and that it has achieved admirable economic prosperity through industrial and commercial development. Even when President George Bush (senior) announced that all U.S. nuclear weapons had been removed from foreign territories and President Roh Tae Woo confirmed the absence of the U.S. nuclear arsenal in South Korea in the fall of 1991, Pyongyang never doubted the presence of such weapons across the border. Because the development of an adequate conventional weapons program requires a sound economic and technological base, North Korea realized that it was in a disadvantaged position in its competition with the South. Furthermore, Pyongyang believes that the epidemic demise of Eastern European communist systems, including that of East Germany, could not affect North Korea because of its military and ideological preparedness. In short, North Korea has never been apologetic for its military development because it believes that development to be necessary for the survival of the system itself.

The orchestration of Kim Jong Il's charismatic leadership has a great deal to do with the military modernization program, including the development of nuclear programs. Any successor to a charismatic leader faces the formidable challenge of "filling the shoes" of the previous leader. When the outgoing leader is a "charismatic giant," as is the case with Kim Il Sung, this challenge is almost insurmountable.[3] The ruling elite in Pyongyang witnessed the inevitable de-charismatization in the cases of Joseph Stalin and Mao Zedong, and they sought an answer to the structural dilemma of instability and power conflict following the passing of charismatic leaders. They decided to explore a type of leadership succession that would not undermine the Great Leader's authority even after his death and so paved the way for Kim Jong Il's ascension to leadership. In a Confucianist culture, being loyal to the father is only natural, and to that extent, loyalty to Kim Il Sung is not likely to disappear as long as the son is in charge.

The promotion of militarism in recent years, especially following the demise of European socialist systems, coincides with the building of Kim Jong Il's leadership. As the supreme commander of the People's Army with the newly attained rank of marshal, the orchestration of Kim Jong Il's charisma is based on projecting him as a military genius. In this context, he is credited for the highly publicized "success" of bringing Americans to a bilateral negotiation, leaving aside the Seoul government. In this way, the nuclear issue has served the political purposes of power solidification and regime stability.

Prestige and leverage. As all nations do, North Korea seeks to be esteemed in the international community, but the community it has in mind is the nonaligned countries of the Third World. Those countries that have had bitter experiences of colonialism and maintain a nationalist culture are providing North Korea with moral support, as the latter single-handedly resists the immense pressure from the Western powers. Visitors from those countries openly praise the Pyongyang leadership for its refusal to submit to the pressure, and North Korea's media exploits the situation to further promote the legitimization of the system.[4]

Pyongyang sees its possession of nuclear capability as benefiting its leverage and bargaining power in the international community.[5] All indications from current negotiations (and lack thereof) seem to support that perception, and North Korea has taken advantage of the "nuclear card" to achieve its policy goals. The goals in this case are twofold: gaining the time Pyongyang needs to further develop weapons programs and securing concessions from the United States. North Korea has fared remarkably well in terms of these goals. It remains to be seen whether the "nuclear card" has been exhausted.

Security and Deterrence

In coping with what it saw as Pyongyang's incomprehensible behavior regarding the nuclear question, the IAEA failed to recognize the stark reality that Pyongyang cannot and will not negotiate away what it views as the "strategic equalizer."[6] Furthermore, North Korea's relative diplomatic isolation from its traditional allies (China and other socialist systems) has pushed Pyongyang in the direction of self-defense. South Korea's success in opening diplomatic and economic ties with China, Russia, and virtually all socialist countries in Central Europe justifiably made Pyongyang feel isolated in the international community. In fact, the demise of the Soviet Union coupled with the ideological reorientation of China has made North Korea feel that there is no external ally on which it can rely in the event of a security threat. In this political climate, Pyongyang moved rapidly to its own rescue with the three principles of militarism: militarization of the entire population (*chon inminui muchang hwa*), the commissioning of all soldiers (*chon gun ui ganbu hwa*), and the encirclement of the entire land (*chon gunto ui yose hwa*). These three principles are the guiding doctrines with which every person is inculcated.

Undoubtedly, North Korea believes that once it is known as a nuclear power, aggression by all adversaries, including the United States, Japan, and South Korea, will be deterred. In addition, South Korea may take Pyongyang more seriously when it comes to negotiations. Not unlike any other government, "negotiation from strength" is what Pyongyang desires.

Economic Incentives

Since 1990, Pyongyang has openly acknowledged difficulties in its economic situation, especially in the provision of basic necessities, including food. Initially, Pyongyang attributed the difficulty to the consecutive years of poor harvests. But still unable to recover from a shrinking economy, the leadership has shifted its policy emphasis to the production of light industrial goods and international trade. In October 1992, Pyongyang introduced a set of sweeping joint venture laws designed to attract foreign capital and technology. In his 1994 New Year's Message, Kim Il Sung reiterated the importance of expanding the production of consumer goods and improving economic relations with other countries, especially with capitalist developed countries.

The defense burden. People of all walks of life in North Korea seem to agree that the inordinately heavy defense burden is the single obstacle to their economic growth. One military officer who was assigned to a commanding post at the demilitarized zone (DMZ) indicated that "it is a matter of prioritization that forces us to absorb economic hardships." He observed that "no country will be able to maintain economic prosperity if it is burdened with defense expenditures amounting to some 25 percent of the gross national product."[7] Indeed, massive defense expenditures over such a prolonged period have denied the North Korean economy the possibility of igniting a takeoff. Pyongyang believes that it is imperative to cut military spending if it is to promote economic growth. Because of this belief, the government has devoted its efforts to securing unconventional weapons, including the nuclear bomb. In fact, once a few bombs are developed, the maintenance of defense preparedness might be far cheaper than continuously indulging in an arms race with the South.

Foreign currency. It is ironic that the heavy concentration of resources in defense might be the primary reason for defense and scientific development, including, but not limited to, nuclear physics. For although these expenditures have been a burden on the economy, the weapons developed with this money currently provide North Korea with one of its primary sources of foreign currency, earning at least U.S.$100 million annually. North Korea seems to be of the opinion that it is time for the defense sector to cash in. It is known that Iran, Iraq, Libya, and Syria have all made trade deals with North Korea for Scud missiles.[8] Reportedly, North Korea concluded a deal with Iran to barter Scud missiles and related technology for oil that may have been worth several hundred million dollars.[9]

Once North Korea's nuclear capability is conceded by the international community, the country will be in a position to export technology and equipment to the Organization of Petroleum-Exporting Countries (OPEC) if the nonproliferation regime becomes ineffective.[10] One must consider the reality that North Korea has no choice but to explore alternative avenues for economic advancement, and these avenues are severely limited.

Technological development. Technology has a spin-off effect. Nuclear energy and the nuclear weapons program are mutually interchangeable. Technology, once obtained, is inevitably improved. North Korea asserts that the attainment of "indigenous technology" could have far-reaching beneficial consequences because then it could not be subjected to foreign sanctions and manipulations.

Although North Korea's indigenous industrial technology is not expected to be among the foremost in the region, let alone in the world, the nation has made concerted efforts to promote research and technology at all levels. It is commonplace at primary schools that students are required to participate in at least one science project, and this practice is called "an investment in the future." In this respect, one might observe that North Korea views weapons technology not in isolation from overall technological development but as a part of it. In short, North Korea has turned to the development of nuclear technology not for irrational reasons but because of a number of well-thought-out "rational" considerations.

Psychological Motivations

One must not forget that North Korea is a country of paternalist supervision by the "benevolent" Great Leader. As such, any major decision, not to mention such a crucial decision as that regarding weapons programs, is made at the highest levels of leadership. As a leader who was never without an irreconcilable enemy, initially Japan and subsequently South Korea and the United States, Kim Il Sung was engaged in an arms struggle throughout his life. When he was a teenage student at Yungmum Middle School in Jilin, China, Kim seldom ceased organizing terrorist activities against Japanese authorities. Activities such as bombing police headquarters, attacking military installations, and assassinating Japanese officers characterized his adolescent life. He bought guns whenever he managed to save some money. He developed the belief that military capability was the only method of gaining independence from a colonial power.[11]

To Kim Il Sung, the Japanese military seemed invincible and the emperor's resolution of militant nationalism was unshakable. But then a dramatic event captured Kim Il Sung's attention—the surrender of Japan after the demonstration of the awesome power of atomic bombs. Having witnessed the magic of the bomb, he was intrigued by the idea of developing it himself. In fact, he attributed the defeat of the great Japanese empire to the superiority of Western science and military technology. One might suggest that his desire to develop nuclear weapons was prompted by these events.

Despite the claim that Kim Il Sung, the creator of the *Juche* ideology, was a great philosopher, he was always more of a man of the sword than a man of the pen. One might even suggest that during his long tenure as a leader, Kim Il Sung developed an obsession with weapons preparedness. In this context, the decision to go nuclear on the part of this leader is neither irrational nor inexplicable.

In the final analysis, one must realize that North Korea has a huge stake in the nuclear program, no less than the survival of the system itself. The motivations and incentives to go nuclear are far-reaching, and they all seem to be consistent with what North Korea believes to be its national interest.

Notes

1. On brinkmanship diplomacy, see Scott Snyder, *Negotiating on the Edge: North Korean Negotiating Behavior* (Washington, D.C.: United States Institute of Peace Press, 1999). On U.S. strategies to cope with North Korea's peculiar negotiating behavior, see Leon Sigal, *Disarming Strangers: Nuclear Diplomacy with North Korea* (Princeton, N.J.: Princeton University Press, 1988).

2. To this date, the most accurate description of North Korea's self-perception has been made by Manwoo Lee, whose observation was made after a personal visit to Pyongyang. Refer to his work, "How North Korea Sees Itself," in Eugene Kim and B. C. Koh, eds., *A Journey to North Korea* (Berkeley, Calif.: Institute of East Asian Studies, University of California, 1982).

3. The concept of charismatic giant was introduced by Robert Tucker in his theory of charisma formation. The final stage of charismatic giant is preceded by charismatic aspirant and charismatic luminary. See Robert Tucker, *Stalin as Revolutionary: 1879–1929* (New York: W. W. Norton, 1973).

4. This practice was evident from television programs in Pyongyang, on which foreign visitors were interviewed to express their admiration for North Korea's heroism.

5. Richard Fisher, among others, suggests that North Korea views nuclear weapons as a means of increasing its prestige among radical states. Richard D. Fisher, Jr., "Responding to the Looming North Korean Nuclear Threat," *Backgrounder* (Heritage Foundation), Working Paper no. 19 (January 1992), p. 5.

6. Andrew Mack, "The Nuclear Crisis on the Korean Peninsula," *Asian Survey* 33, no. 4 (April 1993), pp. 341–344.

7. A colonel in charge of the "concrete wall" area made this remark to me when I visited there in 1998.

8. For a concise presentation of North Korea's missile trade, see Peter Hayes, "International Missile Trade and the Two Koreas," Monterey Institute of International Studies, Working Paper no. 1.

9. "North Korea Country Profile." *Journal of Commerce*, November 16, 1993. Economist Intelligence Unit, China, p. 87.

10. In agreement with this assessment, Richard Perle maintains that North Korea will not hesitate to sell nuclear weapons and related technology and com-

ponents to other countries. See Perle, "Policy Implications of North Korea's Ongoing Nuclear Program," U.S. House of Representatives, Subcommittee on East Asian and Pacific Affairs of the Committee on Foreign Affairs (Washington, D.C.: U.S. GPO, 1992), p. 5.

11. This observation is based on Kim Il Sung's autobiography, *Segiwa doburo*, published in a series of eight volumes beginning in 1992.

12

North Korea Sees Itself: Perceptions of Policy Goals, Strategies, and Tactics

The Korean peninsula is the most heavily armed area in the world in terms of both manpower and weaponry. One need only to travel to the DMZ to view the massive forces confronting each other. What is not visible to the casual observer is the pervasive mistrust that exists between the two systems, mistrust that makes the security system all the more precarious. North Korea is often vilified as irrational, unpredictable, and lacking in civility. Such criticisms are made of North Korea with little knowledge about the thought processes, policy motivations, and behavioral traits of this alienated system. Simple labels such as reclusive system, Stalinist state, irrational actor, and rogue regime have not been very helpful in explaining its policies. In the previous chapters, I attempted to shed light on the nature of the North Korean "mindset" in the hope that a better understanding of the norms, values, and beliefs pervasive in the political culture might help us in comprehending the behavior of the system. In this chapter, I go further to more concretely explore the way in which North Korea perceives itself and others when it makes vital choices regarding policies, strategies, and tactics in the context of the post–Cold War world order. The orientation employed in this chapter, as throughout the book, may be called a "phenomenological perspective," in that North Korea's perceptions constitute the reality and they must be articulated from the standpoint of the perceiver.[1]

The Last Hope for Socialism

When the Soviet Union disintegrated, North Koreans contended that Gorbachev's flirtation with capitalism caused the demise. When the socialist systems of Romania, Czechoslovakia, Hungary, Yugoslavia, and Poland collapsed, Pyongyang attributed the collapse of its allies to the fact that all of them were dependent on the Soviets and thus lacked self-reliance. When East Germany was absorbed into West Germany, North Korea criticized that country's lack of a self-reliant economy and a consolidated salient ideology. In the national media, especially on television, Pyongyang has concertedly advanced the view that all the systems that betrayed socialism are experiencing enormous economic distress, social dislocations, and human sufferings far worse than they were during the socialist era. The public is told that such a grim reality will become the unavoidable fate for North Korea as well if its socialist system fails to withstand the massive tide of capitalist conspiracy.

The leadership tells the North Korean people that their country is the last reservoir of socialism in the world and that they have the predestined mission and obligation to defend and revitalize the ideology against the adversarial force of world capitalism. They are even told that they are the last and only hope for humanity.

In the 1990s, Pyongyang felt a deep sense of betrayal from its trusted allies. First, China under the leadership of Deng Xiaoping did not waste much time in normalizing relations with the United States. A fatal blow struck North Korea when Beijing announced the normalization of diplomatic relations with South Korea in 1992. The Soviets also recognized the Seoul government as a legitimate sovereign state, followed by nearly every socialist system in Europe. Furthermore, Pyongyang had to deal with another fatal defeat in diplomacy when the United Nations voted to admit both North and South Korea as separate independent states. It had always been Pyongyang's position that Korea should be one nation and that any effort by anyone to split the nation would be regarded as harmful to it. Pyongyang felt a deep sense of humiliation and betrayal from allies who could have blocked the vote. At the same time, it was a diplomatic victory for South Korea, which had advocated and campaigned for its admission to the international organization.

The changing political map of the region and the world not only made Pyongyang uncomfortable but also threatened its security and system survival. The criticism within the country of former socialist systems has been mounting. Pyongyang did not hesitate to criticize even Beijing for its allegedly revisionist approach to development. Pragmatism devoid of ideological sensitivity was unacceptable to Pyongyang.

As pointed out above, the end of the Cold War era signified a major disturbance for North Korea, inhibiting economic growth and forcing diplomatic isolation. To Pyongyang, all its allies, including China, betrayed its trust. Pyongyang lost its support system in the international community so abruptly that it had no time to make gradual adjustments. To ride out the tide of socialist change was not an option for North Korea. Such a course of action could have meant the demise of the system itself as it would have been forced to compete with the Seoul regime on terms vastly advantageous to the South. By the time Beijing chose to establish diplomatic relations with Seoul in 1992, Pyongyang felt a deep sense of isolation and even more resolve to protect its national identity. The regime accelerated the course of ideological purification, along the lines of portraying itself as the antithesis to capitalist consumerism and socialist revisionism. It is instructive to note how Pyongyang perceives the collapse of the Eastern European socialist countries. Pyongyang attributes the demise of the socialist systems to three major factors: first, the lack of spiritual preparedness to resist material temptations associated with capitalist decadent culture; second, the inability, especially on the part of the Eastern European socialist systems, to defend themselves militarily; and third, the inability to cope with confusion following the succession of political power from a charismatic leader. Pyongyang sees potential challenges coming from these three areas and has made resolute efforts to prepare itself.

Pyongyang sees itself surrounded by hostile and evil forces that are undermining its legitimacy. It further believes that these forces are constantly preparing to overthrow the system by force or other means. During the Cold War era, Pyongyang's primary concern was to prepare itself against possible military provocation by the United States and South Korea. But in the post–Cold War world order, Pyongyang also feels its existence to be threatened by subversive means of inducing changes and reforms that are designed to destroy the very fabric of the political system, thus causing system collapse. In addition to the traditionally adversarial systems of the United States and its "puppet" South Korea, Japan has joined the ranks of Pyongyang's primary enemies.

Pyongyang has never forgotten the stark reality that the Korean War has never ended. It is in a state of temporary truce. The continuing presence of U.S. forces in South Korea, including some 36,000 ground troops, is keenly felt in North Korea as a formidable and direct threat to the security of the region. The annual military exercises by the joint forces of the United States and South Korea, termed Team Spirit, cause the utmost alarm throughout the country. I witnessed more than once how the entire city of Pyongyang felt itself to be in a state of war whenever a Team Spirit exercise was in progress, paralyzing the entire city. Functions and activities at workplaces, private homes, and public buildings all ceased as though the country was on the verge of being attacked. For the duration of the exercise (generally two weeks), no normalcy was restored.

The explosive economic expansion of South Korea, which coincided with difficulties in the North, has been no source of comfort for Pyongyang. After German reunification, in which the socialist east was absorbed by the capitalist west, the Seoul government acted as though the collapse of the Pyongyang regime was imminent. The Seoul government even contended that the fate of North Korea was in its hands. Furthermore, Seoul has changed its longstanding position by publicly maintaining that the collapse of the Pyongyang government would not be in the interest of South Korea. Seoul is open about its reluctance in assuming what it terms as the "burden" of reunification. Since the beginning of Kim Young Sam's government in 1992, it has been Seoul's official position to induce reform and changes in the North Korean system, as opposed to a sudden collapse. The much-orchestrated "soft landing" policy of the Kim Young Sam administration resulted from this consideration. This policy was designed to force North Korea to terminate the journey of socialism by inducing an economic soft-landing through gradual reforms rather than crashing into a sudden collapse. It was little more than an insult to and humiliation of the North Korean system. As expected, this policy did not generate any sympathy from Pyongyang. It was indeed a policy of gradual absorption rather than a peacefully negotiated integration. It is not surprising that the sunshine policy of the Kim Dae-jung government is also seen in this light.

Victory in Sight: The Destiny of the Legitimacy War

The mythical notion of saving humanity from consumerism and the decadent culture of capitalism is seldom taken seriously by North Koreans. This visionary concept is only for rhetoric and propaganda, except for a small number of blind believers. But North Koreans are deadly serious about the ongoing legitimacy war with the South. As discussed in Chapter 10, the survival of the system is directly linked to the regime's legitimacy competition with the South. The nature of this competition is "unconventional" in the sense that economic prosperity is of little relevance. It is the support for the system (the citizens' state of mind) that determines whether it is legitimate or illegitimate. In this sense, what matters is the subjective basis on which regime legitimacy is established rather than such objective factors as economic output or material life conditions. Although prolonged deprivation of basic needs such as food may lead to criticism of the government and diminishing support for the leadership, material life conditions do not determine system legitimacy directly or immediately. Viewed in this context, we can see that North Koreans may well be persuaded that the spiritual and ideological solidarity of the North might generate a broad basis of support, not only in the North but in the South as well.

To the South Korean journalists who visited following the historic summit in June 2000, Kim Jong Il reportedly said that "we can make a great unified country when South Korea's economic and technological assets become empowered with North Korea's spiritual and ideological achievement."[2] This comment was clearly meant to indicate that North Korea is the ideologically fit Korean nation because of its strong nationalism and spiritual integrity. Kim Jong Il's apparent concession that South Korea is economically and technologically more advanced in no way undermines Pyongyang's position in its age-old legitimacy war with the South. On the contrary, the comment was an open affirmation to the South Korean audience of North Korea's longstanding insistence that nationalist ideology provides legitimacy to the Korean nation and that the Pyongyang regime is, therefore, a more legitimate system. North Korea is encouraged by the apparent acceptance of Kim Jong Il himself among South Koreans as an able and sophisticated leader and the rising popularity of northern entertainers, artists, and sportsmen who have visited the South following the summit.

To Pyongyang, the rapidly changing public opinion among the South Korean people in the second half of the year 2000 was encouraging indeed. As discussed in Chapter 10, the terms of the summit agreement seem to be consistent with the long-held North Korean policies of national self-determination and confederacy, which gives Pyongyang sound grounds for claiming a victory in the legitimacy competition. This "victory" was publicly and tangibly demonstrated by the return of sixty-eight prisoners of war who had been held in South Korea since the Korean War.[3] None of them denounced their loyalty to the North Korean regime for some fifty years. Some of the returnees will be included in the aforementioned documentary series, *Nation and Destiny.* This series will be used to dramatically and concretely demonstrate the ideological resolve on the part of the war heroes and their successful homecoming as a result of the benevolent nationalist leadership of Kim Jong Il.

Policy Action, Not Reaction

North Koreans seem confident that their way is best for them. In other words, they think that they know better when it comes to the question of their own destiny. They refuse to listen to others because they believe that the world is not trustworthy. North Korea's negotiation tactics earned the label of a brinkmanship approach because they defy the conventional wisdom. Also, as discussed earlier, Kim Jong Il's acceptance of the summit meeting with South Korea's Kim Dae-jung stunned the world, as it too defied what would have been conventionally expected from North Korea.

When Kim Il Sung died in 1994, the world expected his son Kim Jong Il to succeed him as president. It would have been highly unconventional to leave the post of head of state unoccupied for a prolonged time. Indeed, much speculation followed Kim's death. Many observed that the delay in succession was due to the young Kim's inability to establish firm control immediately following his father's death. Others even suggested that Kim Jong Il's health was unfit for the position. Still others speculated that some sort of power conflict was under way to eventually give birth to a collective leadership. None of these ideas were accurate. Kim Jong Il was in complete control of the system, his health was quite normal, and no sign of power conflict was detected. In the end, Kim Jong Il emerged as the undisputed leader of the country. In fact, his leadership was never in doubt. It was just that North Koreans did not show any reaction to outside speculation. When South Korean papers erroneously reported the "breaking news" that Kim Il Sung had died, North Koreans kept silent for two weeks until Kim himself appeared at the Pyongyang Airport to welcome the visiting Mongolian president. They never reacted to those reports.

In short, one reason for the common notion that North Korea is unpredictable is the fact that the people there do not readily show the kind of behavior that is normally expected of them, simply because they choose not to react or respond to others' behaviors or perceptions. They like to act, not react. This preference can be interpreted as an extension of the *Juche* belief that their way of thinking and mode of behavior should not be determined by others. Yet it does not mean that their behavior is irrational.

Salient Goals, Uncompromising Strategies, and Unconventional Tactics

The national goals of the North Korean system have been remarkably salient and consistent. The decisionmakers seem to have a clear sense of goals, strategies, and tactics. People from all walks of life share their perceptions. Once the center (meaning the Party) makes a decision, it will be efficiently transferred to the rank and file through the most effective channels of Party cells, community residential units, workplaces, and all the aforementioned agents of socialization.

The goals of North Korea are not fundamentally different from those of any other system, in that it pursues first and foremost system survival and a stable leadership. Like any other system, North Korea seeks prosperity as much as possible but not at the expense of system survival. Furthermore, North Korea's desire to establish a system identity is by no means unique to that country. In other words, North Korea has a set of goals shared by any system: survival, prosperity, and identity.

With respect to the goal of system survival, what is unique about North Korea is the nature of the system itself. The goal is not just keeping the leadership in power or maintaining the political entity without being swallowed up by another system. It means the perpetuation of the system characteristics that tend to be unique and peculiar. Once these characteristics are compromised, the system faces the danger of being absorbed into the South. The system simply cannot stay alive by being similar to the South; it would only be poorer, inferior, and less popular among the people. Pyongyang has been vigorously waging the legitimacy war against South Korea since the inception of its system. One must realize that North Koreans believe for good reason that system change means system collapse. Therefore, their resistance to change is in fact their resistance to collapse. Viewed from this perspective, it is not hard to understand why the North Korean leadership has refused to compromise its stance on the question of reforms and opening to the outside. It is a huge dilemma for North Korea that it cannot participate in the global market to make best use of its high-quality labor force, rich mineral resources, and strategically placed geographical location, which may well bring the necessary comparative advantage in market competition. This fixation on survival constrains the choice of acceptable strategies and tactics for the goal of system identity. The identity of the system cannot be easily altered from an ideological (*Juche*) system to a pragmatic system without losing the legitimacy war with the South, thereby risking system survival.

The imperative of system survival in the peculiar context of North Korea at this historical juncture requires a specific set of conditions. Among the central conditions are the defense of the country from military provocation, the preservation of system legitimacy vis-à-vis South Korea, and the protection of the population from disruptive, capitalist, decadent culture. These conditions have led to the development of a series of policy strategies and tactical maneuverings.

First and foremost, information control is an indispensable strategy. To criticize North Korea for maintaining a closed system whereby the population is protected from external forces without considering the aforementioned adversarial conditions is irresponsible. No government will allow its system to drift into a course of feared demise. Pyongyang has every reason to shield the population from the same forces that swallowed up the former socialist systems in Eastern Europe. It is true that Pyongyang does not allow undesirable information and materials to be smuggled in. It is true that tourists coming into the country as part of the Hyundai project at Mt. Kumkang are carefully monitored and guarded so that the population will not come into contact with the tourists and their consumerist lifestyle. It is true that the border is not open. It is true that there is no diversity in the content of mass media outputs, which are strictly controlled by the government. These seemingly "undemocratic" practices may be a source of displeasure to the outside observers, but one can hardly characterize the strategic policy postures as being irrational or abnormal. Considering Pyongyang's perception of the demise of the Soviet Union and the socialist systems in Europe, it is only natural for the leadership to protect the population and system from the same adversarial forces that induced their collapse in the first place.

For Pyongyang, it is also imperative to view the reforms and "democratization" in those countries as mistakes that only worsened the situation. Therefore, it is not unusual for Pyongyang to claim that the "former Soviet Union and Eastern European countries are grieving and repenting today . . . countries where capitalism is restored presented a serious lesson to the people . . . if one defends socialism, it is victorious and if one discards socialism it is death."[4]

Second, North Korea's strategic move at this time has to do with alleviating grim economic realities. The country has been suffering from extremely severe economic hardships. Although no accurate account of the number of deaths resulting from starvation is available, it is generally assumed that "since 1995, two million people of a population of 24 million have died of hunger and disease."[5] Malnutrition and inadequate health care are so pervasive that the government places the highest emphasis on alleviating these problems, and all policy efforts are geared in this direction. Western observers tend to attribute the food shortage problem to the failure of the socialist system, a generalization that has routinely been made with respect to the European socialist experience. But the North Korean case is far more complicated. There are multiple reasons for the food shortage and accompanying economic difficulties. The first and most obvious reason was indeed the disruptive weather. Heavy rainfall and floods swept away as much as 40 percent of the arable land in 1996. Since then, the weather conditions have never been favorable. Also true is the fact that much of the hillside farming areas are no longer arable because of erosion that may have been exacerbated by the practice of removing trees and natural vegetation in an effort to expand much-needed arable plots. Another major cause of general economic difficulty is the cessation or reduction of trade relations with North Korea's traditional partners, including China. The vacuum created by the drastic and abrupt change in the political spectrum of the socialist bloc has never been filled with alternative economic ties with the international market.

In seeking humanitarian aid, Pyongyang has restrained itself from making overtures that would be excessively embarrassing to the dignity of the people. Furthermore, the leadership has been constrained by the imperative of protecting the population from contact with capitalist consumerism. In fact, Pyongyang often points to Western relief efforts as nothing more than an excuse for the capitalists to infiltrate North Korea and seize upon the misfortune of a people to achieve political and economic objectives. The government's determination to solve the food shortage problem has steered efforts in boosting agricultural productivity. Pyongyang does not enjoy the status of being a "bread basket." It has tried to develop agricultural and livestock industries by allowing its scientists to go abroad to learn about transferable technology, more productive seeds, and improved animal husbandry.[6] The current mass campaign to increase the use and productivity of potatoes should be seen as an attempt to add options to the people's diet beyond rice. Pyongyang's desire for increased agricultural productivity has forced it to agree to "invite" U.S. inspectors to the Kumchangri underground site, which was suspected to be a hidden site for the nuclear weapons program. At first, North Koreans refused to open the site to foreign inspectors on the grounds of protecting national sovereignty. But in the end, they agreed and allowed inspection. The agreement called for a bilateral "agricultural pilot project" that included the farming of potatoes.

One of the policy strategies aimed at increasing agricultural productivity without relying on external intervention is found in "localization" efforts. In fact, Jagang Province, under the governorship of former prime minister Yeon Hyong Muk, has been singled out as a model case of regional economic self-help. Small power plants by the thousands have been constructed to promote self-reliance in electricity at the local level. The popularity enjoyed by the windmill project provided by a California-based organization, Nautilus Institute, can be seen in this same light. In short, Pyongyang has been responding to the challenge of food shortage concertedly and concretely.

Third, the new leadership under Kim Jong Il has adopted a policy strategy that placed a premium on ultranationalism. The only rational course of action on the part of the new leadership was nationalism. Pyongyang had to be alarmed by the massive tide of market forces and reformist ideology that had swept the socialist world. Especially alarming in this regard was the absorption of East Germany by West Germany. After German unification in 1989, most observers predicted that the North Korean system would inevitably follow in the footsteps of East Germany, giving it a limited lifespan ranging from a few months to no more than three years. These observers predicted that the North Korean system might survive under the charismatic leadership of Kim Il Sung but that it could never survive the death of the revered leader. Pyongyang could not simply disregard these observations and do nothing to cope with the new political dynamism in the region and the world. The nationalism of Kim Il Sung had helped solidify power and consolidate the diverse and competing factions in the formative stage of the republic. After his death, that same nationalism was used by the current leadership to protect regime stability and integrate the political system.

A fourth policy strategy involves the military. Following the death of Kim in 1994, the junior Kim's efforts were devoted to the promotion of the military in the belief that defense preparedness precedes any other national goal, including even the people's livelihood. The principle of militarism is not new in North Korea. It has always been sustained since the Korean War. What is relatively new is the supremacy of the military leadership in the political system itself. At no time in the past was the military given the ultimate authority in policymaking that it has today. The new constitution, adopted in September 1998, clearly endorses the centrality of the military, as evidenced by the ascendance of the chairman of the Military Commission as the supreme commander and the ultimate reservoir of state authority. The doctrine of military supremacy, however, does not advocate control by physical force alone. In fact, the ideology of *Juche* has been undergoing a transformation from being an abstract worldview to a concrete nationalist doctrine that employs the principle of militarism as the policy yardstick.

Coincidental with this development was the defection of Hwang Jang Yop, who was believed to be the leading architect of *Juche* ideology. His defection reinforced criticism among intellectuals in North Korea of *Juche* for having been little more than a useless armchair philosophy, as typified by the works of Hwang. Thus, one of the challenges Pyongyang faced was to redirect *Juche* as a practical ideology. This challenge led the leadership to reinstate the centrality of pragmatic socialism, as opposed to the abstract notion of humanism.[7]

Another area of strategic and tactical change can be seen in Pyongyang's approach toward Seoul and Washington. Both South Korea and the United States have lately shown more conciliatory gestures toward Pyongyang, using recently coined terms such as "sunshine policy" and "engagement policy." Yet, Pyongyang is not in a position to welcome them. To Pyongyang, the sunshine policy is even more subversive and conspiratorial than the previous policy of a soft landing. Pyongyang objects to the assumption inherent in this policy that North Korea will voluntarily take off the socialist jacket when the "sunshine" makes it unbearably hot. Both policies advanced by South Korean administrations have relied on the same political strategy of opening up the North Korean economy and providing its citizens with the opportunity to interact with their counterparts from the South and to witness the "superior lifestyle" across the border. Pyongyang views this strategy as subversive and vicious in its intention.

The policy of separation of business from politics, initiated unilaterally by the Kim Dae-jung government, is not viewed favorably either. The much-heralded tourism at Mt. Kumkang, set up by Hyundai tycoon Chung Joo-young, is viewed by Pyongyang simply as a businessman's calculation in making a long-term investment. At best, Chung's efforts are seen as showing his personal desire to make a contribution and homage to his birthplace, something any old person would like to achieve. Pyongyang has expressed its appreciation for this aspect of the project. It is the subversive aspect of the sunshine policy that prompted Pyongyang to apply constraints on the tourists' movements, especially any encounters with North Korean residents. Pyongyang's contention is that any subversive efforts from the South must be countered with the utmost caution. By the end of 2000, more than 300,000 South Koreans had participated in the tour. If Seoul's intention was to open up the population and society of North Korea, it failed to achieve that goal. Pyongyang has succeeded in protecting and shielding its people from the tourists.

As for the U.S. engagement policy, Pyongyang has never shown any degree of enthusiasm for it. Pyongyang views engagement as a unilateral concept whereby only North Korea is to be engaged with the United States and the West. Pyongyang observes that the engagement policy does not call for U.S. engagement with North Korea, as evidenced by the fact that the lifting of the U.S. economic embargo against it has never been implemented. This U.S. policy is also predicated upon the expectation that North Korea will have to reform if it is to engage with the outside world, especially the global market system. Also, North Korea has not failed to point out that the notion of "engagement" is essentially imperialist. Pyongyang contends that the policy implies that North Korea is the "subject" that is to adjust its behavior in order to conform itself to foreign norms and practices, rather than the United States searching actively for means and ways in which it can engage itself with North Korea.

In being more pragmatic, Pyongyang has made a series of tactical gambles, including acceptance of the plan designed by the Korean Peninsula Energy Development Organization and the convening of the inter-Korean summit meeting. Acceptance of the KEDO deal was a landmark gamble for Pyongyang. It is absurd to suggest that Pyongyang received two light water reactors and the supply of crude oil from the consortium countries "at no cost" to the North Koreans, as former U.S. secretary of state James Baker claimed in his 1999 essay in the *New York Times*.[8] It is absurd because Pyongyang had to pay a rather hefty cost in the form of giving up the bargaining leverage and the new source of electricity expected from the nuclear power plants that had been under construction. The 1994 Geneva Framework effectively suspended the construction of two graphite-powered nuclear power plants in Yongbyon that would have produced weapons-grade plutonium. According to a senior government official with whom I had a meeting in 1997, had the construction proceeded without interruption, the plants would have been completed by now, and the additional electricity would have helped the economy and eased people's lives. Whether such an assessment is scientifically accurate is not of great concern here. What is important is that Pyongyang perceives strongly that the KEDO agreement was a deceptive tactic that was never designed to help the North Korean economy by providing safer and more efficient modern reactors. The unwillingness (or inability) of the United States to deliver the crude oil as scheduled, according to Pyongyang, is a sufficient reason for North Korea to abandon the agreement. Furthermore, considering the fact that such unexpected occurrences as the infamous submarine incident, the launching of a missile/satellite over Japan, and the suspicion that Kumchangri was being used as a nuclear development site have affected the timetable of the KEDO project, Pyongyang feels that the fate of the project itself is uncertain at best. Accordingly, Pyongyang feels that it may have prematurely suspended the Yongbyon plants and that the gamble of trusting the adversarial parties might have been a mistake.

The Four-Party Talks, designed to establish a peace treaty to replace the armistice agreement signed in 1953, are another pending issue of which Pyongyang is especially wary. Because Pyongyang chose not to honor the old agreement, it is imperative that a new peace arrangement be established. The parties that stationed ground troops in the Korean War—the United States and China in addition to the two Koreas—have been meeting to attain that objective. It is Pyongyang's intention to negotiate for concessions on such pending issues as the withdrawal of U.S. troops and the de-nuclearization of the peninsula. Although the outcome of these negotiations is hard to predict, one might suspect that the process will be long and tedious. There still are major policy differences between the negotiators, and the negotiation will be plagued by lack of mutual trust.

The missile talks with the United States are yet another forum about which Pyongyang is extremely cautious. It will not lightly relinquish its assets in missile technology and production. After all, it is the intercontinental ballistic missile launching capability that makes any weapon of mass destruction a meaningful threat. In addition to their military value, missiles can be and have been a commodity in high demand in lucrative global markets. Once this asset is relinquished, Pyongyang's leverage in political relations with the adversarial countries will dissipate. The North Korean leadership is keenly aware of this fact and its subsequent ramifications.

Since Pyongyang did not initiate any of the proposals discussed above, North Korea has been reactive and suspicious, as opposed to proactive and affirmative, in responding to the pending issues. Pyongyang is inclined to say, "We know you enter these talks to make us change, and there is no reason for us to change just because you want us to."

Protecting Bargaining Leverage

The North Korean leadership is well aware that its bargaining leverage is limited and should be treasured. Two such forms of leverage stand out.

First and foremost, Pyongyang is mindful that its greatest bargaining leverage is its military capability, especially the ability to produce long-range missiles, nuclear bombs, and other chemical and biological weapons. North Korea would not be what it is today without the suspected nuclear weapons program in the early 1990s. North Korea would not have attracted Japanese attention as much as it has without the launching of a long-range missile over its territory in 1998. Should North Korea exhaust this leverage, it will become merely a less developed country, and the Pyongyang leadership is more keenly aware of this than anyone. Related to this weapons leverage is the mystery or uncertainty surrounding the weapons program and intentions of the leadership. To this day, no one knows for sure whether North Korea has produced nuclear bombs. The suspicion and mystery help Pyongyang in maintaining leverage, and it will not be inclined to relinquish it. This fact suggests that continuously maintaining a system closed to outsiders and thereby protecting the leverage itself in the mind of the leadership is a rational course of action.

Interestingly, the very closed nature of North Korean society can act as important leverage. It is not easy for a foreigner to enter North Korea. For a South Korean to enter is even more difficult. Each entry visa is issued after rigorous assessment of the merit of the visit. Every visit is by invitation only. There is no tourism industry. No tourist agency, foreign or domestic, is commissioned to bring in tourists. Furthermore, there is no physical infrastructure to handle large numbers of visitors or unexpected requests. As a result, the demand for foreigners, South Koreans, and overseas Koreans to visit Pyongyang is extremely high. Even businesses aspiring to enter North Korea are competing with one other, giving Pyongyang a bargaining edge. South Korean conglomerates have been making competitive business offers from which Pyongyang can choose. When Daewoo, following chairman Kim Woo-joong's numerous visits to Pyongyang, made an agreement to construct a textile plant in Nampo City, Hyundai responded with dramatic gestures, including the infamous shipment of cows on trucks across the demilitarized zone and the ensuing deal involving the much-publicized tourism at Mt. Kumkang. The Unification Church also explored business opportunities, securing the right to build an activity center in the heart of the capital city along the Potongkang River. The church's founder, the Reverend Sun Myung Moon, had visited Kim Il Sung in Pyongyang. The host wanted and expected the visitor to make business investments and monetary contributions to his fatherland and hometown, which he had left during the Korean War as a teenager. Moon, however, dreamed of promoting his religious doctrines in North Korea through business and educational channels he might establish there. Yet, to this date, no appreciable overtures from the church have been made. Even the Hyundai tourism project, which attracted so many people from the South, could not make North Korea open its society, nor could it force the common people to be exposed to the South Korean tourists. In short, the system is not going to be open freely to the outside world and South Korea anytime soon.

North Korea has earned a reputation as a tough bargainer. The toughness is largely due to the simple fact that Pyongyang tends to see its course of action not as an alternative but as an imperative. The notorious label of "brinkmanship diplomacy" that North Korea has been given is a relatively new concept in diplomacy studies. It simply suggests that once a country is pushed into a corner, leaving little room for maneuver, the country does not tend to retreat because space has run out. It is not difficult for an empathetic observer to see this limitation on North Korea's behavior and to understand, but not necessarily agree with, the behavioral pattern exhibited by Pyongyang.

Risk Management Strategy

If the Kim Il Sung era can be characterized as an era of risk avoidance, the Kim Jong Il era can be called a risk management era. The end of the Cold War and the massive current of globalization have forced Kim Jong Il to change policy strategies and tactics. Pyongyang can no longer ignore the rapidly changing global economic system. Nor can it continue to shield the country from the rest of the world. From the KEDO agreement in 1994 (the same year as Kim Il Sung's death) to the inter-Korean summit meeting in 2000, North Korea explored avenues to induce foreign investment and establish diplomatic ties with other countries, especially the United States. It succeeded in securing diplomatic recognition from Italy (the first Group of Seven country to officially recognize North Korea), Australia, Canada, and the Philippines. Additionally, the United States partially lifted trade sanctions it had imposed on North Korea since the Korean War. Pyongyang responded affirmatively to numerous proposals for talks and negotiations with the United States and Japan for the eventual goal of normalizing diplomatic relations. Eventually, the ultimate shock materialized in the invitation of Kim Dae-jung to Pyongyang and the convening of a summit meeting. These changes in Pyongyang's behavior should be seen as tactical changes, as opposed to fundamental changes in system goals.

The goals of system perpetuation, maintenance of system identity, and promotion of economic development have not been compromised or altered.

As discussed earlier, as long as North Korea feels its national security is threatened, Pyongyang will not ease its military preparedness. Furthermore, as long as the leadership feels the political system is threatened, the ruling elite will do everything possible to prevent its demise. These premises are not unusual, nor are they only relevant to North Korea. Since the fall of the Soviet Union and much of that support system, North Korea's security requirements have become multifaceted and include both external and internal sources of destabilization.

The fear of external threats has never eased since the Korean War. The continued stationing of U.S. ground troops along with sophisticated weapons has been the single most vivid reminder that the war has not ended. Even in the midst of emotional détente in the Korean peninsula following the 2000 summit meeting, Pyongyang was reminded of (and alerted by) the presence of the South Korea–Japan–U.S. security alliance. As long as these conditions are unchanged, Pyongyang will not ease its military and psychological preparedness for national defense. It is in this context that the current Four-Party Talks, the missile negotiations between Washington and Pyongyang, and the overall inter-Korean rapprochement will face formidable challenges.

The external threat felt by Pyongyang has recently come to include Japan. Since North Korea launched a missile/satellite in August 1998, Japan has shown anger against Pyongyang, not to speak of its reluctance to cooperate with KEDO arrangements. In North Korea itself, the Japanese reaction has produced great alarm, for people fear that it signals the resurgence of militarism and the beginning of rearmament. Furthermore, the intensification of weapons preparedness along the Taiwan Strait is also feared as an another kind of security threat.

The renewed alliance among the United States, Japan, and South Korea and possibly even Taiwan has become a grave concern for Pyongyang. It views the proposed missile defense umbrella in the region as a unified offensive effort by adversarial forces. All these developments suggest that any one country cannot guarantee East Asian security but that it takes a regional comprehensive structure involving all the parties concerned.

To make the security issue even more complicated, Pyongyang no longer seems to view national security merely as an external issue. The lessons from German reunification and the fall of the Soviet Union and other socialist countries have prompted Pyongyang to cope with the forces that threaten the political system from within. This danger became more serious as a result of the more extensive interaction with the South following the summit meeting. As discussed earlier, particular attention has been given to protecting the population from sources of "spiritual pollution" by maintaining a policy of strict information management and selective exposure. This policy will undoubtedly affect foreign economic and cultural policies.

Although the North Korean system has shown a remarkable degree of resiliency, people's basic needs cannot go unmet indefinitely. Ideology alone cannot be a sufficient basis for regime legitimacy. The government in Pyongyang has and will continue to make concerted efforts to alleviate economic difficulties at the most basic level. Each year, North Korea promotes a certain policy goal in an annual slogan. In 1998, the pronounced goal was apparent in the slogan, "Though the road is bumpy, let us march with a smile," indicating that the economic hardships must be taken in stride. Since 1999, the slogan changed to, "Let us make this a momentous year to build a strong and great nation," implying a heightened emphasis on military preparedness and the development of science and agriculture. The government and the system it employs will inevitably be evaluated by their performance in the areas of the announced objectives.

Notes

1. Edmund Husserl, *The Idea of Phenomenology*, trans. by W. P. Alston and G. Nakhnikian (The Hague: Martinus Nijhoff Press, 1966), and Husserl, *The Crisis of European Sciences and Transcendental Phenomenology*, trans. by David Carr (Evanston, Ill.: Northwestern University Press, 1990).

2. *Chosun Ilbo*, August 25, 2000.

3. Conservative circles in South Korea criticized Kim Dae-jung for returning the prisoners, some of whom were North Korean spies during and after the Korean War. They claimed that returning prisoners was even less justified when no South Koreans who might be held in the North were to be retuned in exchange. See *Chosun Ilbo*, August 25, 2000.

4. *Rodong Shinmun*, February 13, 1999.

5. *Washington Post*, March 13, 1999; Tony Hall, a member of the U.S. House of Representatives from Ohio, affirmed this estimate after his visit to North Korea in November 2000.

6. At the invitation of the University of Georgia, an agricultural delegation from North Korea consisting of six top officials and scientists visited research laboratories and facilities in Georgia, the Purina (animal feed) Company in St. Louis,

and farms in Minnesota in August 1997. The Academy of Agricultural Sciences of North Korea extended an invitation to the University of Georgia for a reciprocal visit in October 2000.

7. After Hwang's defection, the Academy of *Juche* Science was dissolved, and the ideology developed in the direction of a pragmatic worldview.

8. James A. Baker, "North Korea Wins Again," *New York Times*, March 19, 1999, in the Op-Ed section.

13

System Stability and Vulnerability

Any evaluation of the *Juche* ideology's functions and dysfunctions must examine the tangible contributions *Juche* has or has not made to the system and what possible adverse effects and consequences are expected from the pervasive and intensive application of this belief system. As with all political ideologies, *Juche* has been used by the ruling elite as a powerful tool for generating public support. As in all political systems, the people in North Korea have been subjected to political education and indoctrination. As documented throughout the preceding chapters, what is truly unique about the North Korean experience is the thoroughness and completeness of these processes.

Sustenance of the System

The foremost contribution that *Juche* has made to the system is to keep it from collapsing. Numerous North Korea watchers predicted the collapse of the system, especially after the death of Kim Il Sung. The collapse thesis is based on two events: the severe economic difficulty, as evidenced by the much-publicized food shortage; and the possibility of a power conflict in the leadership itself, as signified by the defection of Hwang Jang Yop, a secretary of the Workers' Party of Korea and a leading theoretician.[1]

The collapse thesis is not new. When Kim Il Sung was alive, the predominant view on North Korea by foreign experts was that the system would not survive Kim's death. When he finally died at the age of eighty-two in July 1994, most experts predicted that the system would follow the fate of East Germany and other socialist systems within months, if not weeks. But the leadership centered around Kim Jong Il has survived for over seven years amid unceasing speculations and reports doubting his leadership position. When the top posts of general secretary of the Party and the presidency of the state were left unfilled following Kim's death, most observers inferred that Kim Jong Il was unable to consolidate his power position. Nevertheless, the younger Kim waited until the third anniversary of his father's death before assuming those positions. After their dismal failure at predicting the demise of Eastern European socialist systems and the Soviet Union itself, scholars have been overly anxious to forecast the fate of one of the very last surviving socialist systems in the world. Their views are generally insensitive to (and ignorant of) the system, the people, and their peculiar circumstances. The collapse thesis advocates are plainly guided by their ideological or even emotional bias against a system that refuses to recognize the egocentric pride of Western systems.

I shall proceed with my analysis by examining the two bases of the collapse thesis, poverty and power conflicts, and by discerning those forces that sustain the system, forces that have been largely neglected by outside observers. First, will economic difficulty lead to system collapse? An inordinate amount of attention has been focused on the simple question of whether North Korea has a genuine food shortage and economic crisis. The long-held notion that North Korea, along with other rogue nations, is not trustworthy has exerted a lingering effect on how seriously outsiders perceive the repeated appeal for food aid by the World Food Program and other international organizations, as well as by North Koreans themselves. The food shortage in North Korea is real. The situation may be described accurately by four words: serious, pervasive, dangerous, and chronic. It is serious in the sense that scores of people have died, and more are dying. After visiting Pyongyang and Shinuiju in May 1997, I came to the conclusion that "the entire population is in the process of slow death."[2] The devastating flooding in 1995 and 1996 resulted in the loss of vast tracts of land in northern Pyongan and northern Hwanghae Provinces, and the food shortage is so severe that not only has the amount of food distributed been drastically reduced, but the timing of it has been erratic. The problem is pervasive in the sense that virtually everyone is hungry. Hunger is not limited to pockets of people; it extends to teachers, government officials, office workers, and farmers and factory workers. It is dangerous because the military leadership may become nervous about the possibility of having to release food and oil reserved thus far for the military. If such an eventuality should become a reality, the military may choose to use force against targets across the border. I am convinced that under no circumstances will military leaders in North Korea raise their hands and surrender. They will surely use guns instead. Finally, the food shortage is a chronic problem in the sense that it will be a lingering headache for North Korea for many years to come.

To what does Pyongyang attribute the food shortage? Three reasons are commonly cited: the successive floods in the 1990s; the decrease in food supply from China and the former Soviet Union; and the "suffocation" of the national economy by international imperial forces. All these are external sources, and therefore, the government should not be blamed for the economic hardship.

The issue is not how serious the economic problems are, but rather whether the economic difficulties will threaten the survival of the regime. In North Korea, economic hardships for the people will not undermine the regime itself. One has to realize that few countries in the history of mankind have collapsed simply because of the deprivation of people's basic needs. The linkage is warranted only under two conditions: when economic problems bring about a legitimacy crisis for the regime and when the leadership is incapable of silencing the voice of dissent. As discussed earlier, in North Korea, regime legitimacy has little to do with economic conditions. In theory, there are two bases upon which a ruling elite seeks and attains legitimacy: their performance in satisfying people's needs and aspirations and the creation of a political culture to win the support of the governed. Although all governments must use both bases, the extent to which one is more central than the other varies. In representative and participatory democracies, regime performance is crucial for generating the support of the people. When the leadership is unable to help the people meet basic needs and enjoy continuous prosperity, it tends to be viewed as illegitimate. But when regime legitimacy is based on inculcating a belief system, as in a religious community, the leadership's survival is not directly linked to its ability to satisfy people's basic physical needs. As discussed earlier, North Korea is the most striking example of a system that uses values and beliefs as the foundation of power and authority.

The current economic difficulties are not expected to bring about the demise of the regime for at least two reasons. First, the remarkable level of equality in economic life among the general population precludes the rising of "relative deprivation," which usually precedes social unrest. This does not mean that there is no privileged class in North Korea; in fact, there is. But the small number of privileged people are regarded differently from the masses. This form of elitism may be reinforced by North Korea's age-old despotic culture, in which the ruling elite is expected to have a different domain of responsibility as well as privilege. Second, the people in North Korea are sufficiently convinced of the notion that their economic difficulties are due to the hostile international community and natural disasters, for which the regime is not to blame. In fact, the leadership has been quite effective in manipulating the external hostile environment, whether it is real or perceived, for domestic political expediencies.

The economic difficulty thesis of regime collapse is untenable even as a general theory. Few regimes, if any, have collapsed because of poverty. Regimes collapse only when they lack the basis for the justification of power and legitimacy. The linkage between economic poverty and political illegitimacy is not clearly present in North Korea.

If poverty is not a sound basis for the collapse thesis, then, will there be a serious power conflict within the leadership? Competition and conflict are inevitable in any political leadership. North Korea is not an exception. There have been conflicts among various factions since the inception of the regime in 1948. During the first ten years, which included the Korean War, Kim Il Sung had to deter challenges from contending communist factions from Yenan, the Soviets, and the southern part of the Korean peninsula. It took the turbulent years of the war and the *Chollima* campaign in the late 1950s for Kim's partisan faction to solidify its power base. However, to assume that North Korea is experiencing a similar kind of factional struggle today is grossly misplaced. At the time of Kim Il Sung's death, there was no evidence that his leadership was challenged by any competitor, and there appears to be no evidence today that Kim Jong Il's position is challenged by anyone in the leadership. It took several decades for the regime to establish a political culture in which the Kims have been idolized, although it is common knowledge that the son's charisma is not as sound as that of his father, who has been almost immortalized since his death. In fact, the masses are led to believe that the two leaders are inseparable, that one is the other. In fact, one might observe that Kim Il Sung, dead for more than seven years, is still ruling North Korea under the proclamation of "governance by the will of the deceased."

The current leadership in North Korea did not observe the three-year mourning period after Kim's death in July 1994 solely to allow the people to express their sorrow and pay tribute to the late leader. In fact, the three-year period was essential in constructing a bond between the two Kims. Now, to challenge Kim Jong Il amounts to discrediting and challenging Kim Il Sung himself, which is unthinkable in the context of North Korean political culture. As a result, a power conflict is extremely unlikely at the highest level of leadership, but it may be waged at lower levels to seek favoritism and access to the inner circle surrounding Kim Jong Il. What form will such a secondary level conflict take? Will such conflict threaten the stability of the regime itself? A cursory observation suggests that the power conflict might take the form of rivalry within a given sector, as opposed to intersector confrontation. In other words, there could be rivalry and intense competition within the military, bureaucracy, intelligentsia, and social and labor organizations. This form of conflict is not expected to cause political unrest and regime instability at the systemic level.

Thus far, it has been observed that economic difficulties, even including famine, cannot be a singular cause for the collapse of a system. It has also been observed that a power conflict, given the expected nature of it, is not going to destabilize the system. If both these observations are true, what will cause a possible demise of the system itself? As a universal law, a system will fail when it experiences an unmanageable degree of legitimacy crisis. How sound is the basis of regime legitimacy for North Korea under the current leadership of Kim Jong Il? If legitimacy is to be based on the satisfaction of basic needs and economic prosperity, the North Korean regime is in profound trouble. If legitimacy is to be drawn from the status of human rights, defined as civil rights and political freedom, the Kim Jong Il regime is doomed. In fact, a typical system throughout the world bases its regime legitimacy on human needs, economic prosperity, and political-civil liberties. If we assume that North Korea is such a system, we can safely conclude that the collapse of the regime in Pyongyang is inevitable and imminent. However, North Korea is not a typical system in this regard.

Regime legitimacy for North Korea is anchored, to a large extent, on the ideology of *Juche*, as opposed to economic prosperity or political freedom. A number of factors have contributed to the formation of such an ideology. First, Kim Il Sung's leadership was founded on the belief that he was the liberator of the nation from Japanese colonial oppression. *Juche* was originally conceived as an antiforeign doctrine, thereby promoting the belief that Korea cannot rely on any external power. This belief suggests that all foreign powers are essentially imperialist and exploitative, in consonance with the once-popular *dependencia* theory. Second, the lingering rift between the communist superpowers, China and the Soviet Union, made Pyongyang's position precarious, thereby forcing it to maintain a policy of equidistance from them or self-reliance toward them. Third, the presence of South Korea as a system against which Pyongyang has had to defend itself and with which it has competed for legitimacy at the grassroots level has strengthened the ideology. Indeed, much of the postindependence era with respect to inter-Korean relations has been marked by a legitimacy war, in which each system on the peninsula has claimed to have greater legitimacy. This confrontational setting led the Pyongyang regime to explore policy orientations in such a way as to repudiate that for which Seoul stood: a system of capitalism, ideological pragmatism, dependence on alliances for defense, reliance on the world market for economic development, and a social system open to the international community. When the South became the envy of many developing systems as a result of its economic success, Pyongyang had to move in a direction opposite to Seoul's, resulting in the development of an ideology that defies capitalism, pragmatism, foreign dependence, and an open system of communication.

Juche has been effective in facilitating nationalism, antiforeignism, and a distrust in market forces as detrimental to the cultural system. The ideology has further embraced human determinism, which proclaims that man is the center of the universe and should not be subservient to material objects. The North Korean system has made concerted efforts to instill in the masses a belief that rejects material prosperity as a symbol of success. Human dignity, according to this belief, has little to do with economic or material life; in fact, material abundance is often viewed as a trap in which human dignity gets lost. In this way, poverty and dignity have become companions in the peculiar context of North Korea. An intriguing issue here is the fact that Confucianism has always pointed to "clean poverty" as a source of human dignity, particularly in times of corruption and material domination. This attitude suggests that the task of socialization for poverty reverence might not have been insurmountably difficult, especially in the presence of an "antithesis" across the southern border.

Even at the height of the food shortage in spring 1997, the regime refused to give in to pressures to open up the society to foreign food suppliers, thus avoiding the danger of exposing the people to "unhealthy" external stimuli. Pyongyang's dilemma has been in balancing system integrity and pride based on the principles of self-reliance and nationalism with the need to obtain food aid from those very systems, especially the South, toward whom it has waged a legitimacy war for the entire duration of the system's existence. Being pragmatic, in this case, would amount to repudiating the ideological foundation of legitimacy, thus undermining it. North Koreans are keenly aware of the fact that they will become second-class citizens if they play the pragmatic (material) game and compete with the South on Seoul's terms. They are fearfully aware of the German experience, in which East Germany was absorbed into the West just as soon as it was swirled by the tide of capitalism and Western values.

In the above discussion, I have attempted to establish the thesis that North Korea is a system whose behavior and policy postures cannot be explained by the conventional wisdom that human needs and rights must be satisfied for the regime to claim legitimacy. Further, I have maintained that the ideology of *Juche* has worked as a basis for regime legitimacy in the unique context of the inter-Korean confrontation. The question is, will this strategy work continuously and indefinitely? That depends largely on whether many people in North Korea are true believers and who they are. It also depends on whether their belief systems are strong enough to withstand the global trends that might challenge their beliefs.

Can the North Korean regime maintain legitimacy while the people are continuously deprived of basic needs and rights? Any distortion of such basic human needs can be maintained only in a unique social and political setting and in a specific historical context. Therefore, if the setting changes, the basis of legitimacy will become vulnerable. Furthermore, if the deprivation of basic needs continues over a considerable period of time, the ideological basis upon which power is justified will suffer serious setbacks.

The unique social and political setting alluded to above refers to a group of system characteristics. The first characteristic is the maintenance of a system closed to external influence. It is crucial for the "political man" to be stable and to be exposed selectively to information and social contacts, especially with foreign and South Korean sources. A "political man" is formed through a process in which he perceives, is exposed to, and retains new and alien information *selectively*. To accomplish this end, the ruling elite must have total control of information. For this reason, Pyongyang authorities cannot subject the people to "unhealthy" information originating from the capitalist West and South Korea. In this category of controlled information, the leadership is also extremely cautious about material that might be spiritually or culturally polluted. For example, upon entering Pyongyang through Soon-an Airport, one is likely to be searched for and often interrogated about publications, pictures and photos, and video material by border patrol officials.

The second aspect of the unique setting is the continuity and salience of the content of political socialization because of the longevity of the Kim Il Sung/Kim Jong Il leadership. The singular goal of all the political education and socialization has been the creation of charisma in the two leaders, not one at a time but rather as an inseparably integrated whole. This integration was necessitated by the fact that the young Kim could effectively use the people's unwavering devotion to his father's authority, even after his death.

Third, the perpetuation of a rigid political culture is aided by the presence of an imminent threat from U.S.-backed South Korea, with its superior economic base and more sophisticated weapons. The immense fear of aggression from the South, actual or perceived, is conducive to solidifying power and consolidating mass beliefs. The process of this consolidation is reinforced greatly by the aforementioned legitimacy war with the South. In this context, one can easily understand why North Korea has opposed every norm and each value for which the Seoul regime has stood.

Fourth, the aforementioned "spiritual determinism" looms large here. What sets *Juche* ideas apart from conventional socialist norms has to do with the spiritual determinism of the former and the material determinism of the latter. By spiritual determinism, two related notions are implied. First, it includes the traditional Confucian belief that "if there is an iron will, even a mountain can be moved." This norm has helped North Koreans endure physical and economic hardships. Second, the formation of a semireligious culture with *Juche* as the principle doctrine has been aided by the pervasiveness of spiritualism in the mass belief system. Indeed, political socialization in North Korea has consistently been designed to imbue the system of mass beliefs with the quality of fanatical religion. These elements of the unique setting may not endure the test of time. How long will it take for the North Korean system and its people to overcome them? No one can tell for sure, but given the nature of the system and the incumbent leadership, it is fair to suggest that their dismantling through a process of gradual reform may take considerable time, even decades.

Thus far, I have discussed the thesis that the collapse of the North Korean system is not likely in the foreseeable future. This observation is based on a number of factors discerned from the characteristics specific to the North Korean system, ranging from the domestic factors of leadership structure, political culture and the mass belief system, and social structure and organizational life to the external factors of international and inter-Korean politics. The stability of the system, however, does not suggest that people's needs and wants are satisfied. It is an anomaly that a political regime can survive when people's basic needs are unmet. It is an anomaly that in such a case people will not revolt against the government. It is also an anomaly that an ideological doctrine can supersede the government's performance in meeting people's basic needs in gaining legitimacy. It is certainly an anomaly when a system is ruled by the guidelines and "teachings" of a leader who has passed away. Will these anomalies be maintained? If so, for how long? The answers rest with the system's ability to deal with the dysfunctions of the ideology discussed below.

Sources of Vulnerability

Although it is undeniable that *Juche* has helped the North Korean system distance itself from the trend of the collapse of socialist systems, the extraordinary phenomenon surrounding the ideology might lead to expected and unforeseen consequences in a number of areas.

Political Integration and Social Consequences

Juche as an official ideology has been an effective institutional means for the government to solidify its power base and integrate the political community. The authority structure has become centrist and hierarchical. The government has successfully guarded the system from developing what David Apter called the "pyramidal authority structure."[3] Politics has become highly personalized, as opposed to institutionalized. Some of these developments, while helping the regime achieve political integration, have had profound long-term effects on the political system.

In promoting a paternalist society with the Great Leader and his successor as its fathers, the institution of the traditional family has ironically been affected in a most unexpected way. The fact that political authorities and Party functionaries can penetrate into the family may have virtually destroyed the traditional institution of the family itself. Within the otherwise Confucian family, where the head of the household is the father who assumes almost absolute power, the intervention of the state authority may have led to the demise of the father's authority. Young children who refer to the Great Leader as "the father" will soon realize that his authority supersedes that of their own biological fathers. They may experience what psychologists call "cross-pressures" and confusion. In the end, their loyalty to the nation and the Great Leader will become overwhelming.

Another area in which the social consequences of political integration by *Juche* may be seen is the formation of a new class structure, in line with what Milton Djilas has termed the "new class."[4] As discussed earlier, there is a Party representative in every work unit, who mediates between the workplace and the Party headquarters and enjoys a wide range of power, including on personnel matters. In fact, the Party members, whose membership has reached as high as 15 percent of the population, occupy an elitist position. Below this elite group, there are functional experts, including bureaucrats, technicians, and educators, who are still respected in the cultural system. The workers, including industrial and agricultural laborers, are symbolically heralded as the masters of society, but in reality, they are hardly in control of the political apparatus. However, many Party members and functionaries come from the working and farming classes, suggesting that the society is much more egalitarian than the apparent occupational structure may indicate.

In North Korea, life aspirations are rather homogeneous. Success for anyone in North Korean society means becoming a Party member and moving up the ladder of promotion in the unique power hierarchy. This uniformity of values causes efficient competition in all walks of life. In fact, contrary to the widely held belief that North Korea, being a "totalitarian socialist system," frowns on incentives for competition, the system is exceedingly competitive. The competition, however, is never by individuals but by groups. Group competition is indeed fierce. Agricultural production teams compete for larger harvests; factory workers for more production; and schoolchildren for excellence. All groups and organizations compete in a variety of sports and arts. In most instances, there are national tournaments of all conceivable kinds throughout the year. Winners in competitions will be rewarded to the extent that one might be led to believe that North Koreans go to work to win competitions. Schoolchildren at all levels, for example, put forth extraordinary efforts and train themselves in sports and the performing arts to compete for recognition.

In a strange way, the competition itself promotes even greater homogeneity and a one-dimensional political culture. To expect any kind of diversity or pluralism in the society is out of the question. Thus, the prospect for the emergence of a civil society appears to be ever so remote.

Ideological Consolidation and Cultural Consequences

The motto "all for one and one for all," which signifies perfect ideological consolidation, has produced a number of important consequences in the cultural life of North Koreans. Complete cultural integration means the denial of a private life for individual citizens. The fact that every individual's conduct is subject to public scrutiny deprives the society of privacy. Conformity to the center and the collective societal organism is the rule, and any deviation from it would constitute abnormality and be subjected to sanction. In this context, individual creativity can be seriously hampered, which could be a profoundly adverse consequence of *Juche* that was not originally intended. In fact, the ideology is constructed on the premise of human creativity as an inherent quality of man, but in the process of its development, *Juche* has discouraged and might even have destroyed creative impulses.

Culturally, *Juche* has also promoted a monolithic value system whereby diverse interpretations of any social phenomenon or political event are strictly prohibited. In theory, individuals are encouraged to voice their ideas and preferences in meetings at various levels of the society, but these meetings tend to be oriented toward "self-criticism," in which confessions and evaluations of job performances are made and directives from the Party center are communicated to the grassroots level. In the end, the people have become overly reliant upon the system and the Party, contrary to being independent and self-reliant as called for by *Juche* ideology. Yet even in this collective society where individualism is regarded as a vice, the unit of creativity may also be at the group level. The ideology of *Juche* itself must be understood as a product of the collective society, although it is said to have been created by the Great Leader. It is crucial to understand that individuals are considered meaningless apart from the political-social body, and therefore, the latter, not the former, processes the quality of creativity. This deification of the social collective body may be subject to scholarly debate, but there seems to be no one in North Korea seriously challenging it.

One should not underestimate the sentiment of racial and ethnic superiority that could result from the ideology of *Juche*. The ideology is characterized as the "eternal truth," without which the world situation of dehumanization and exploitation and eventually self-inflicted extinction cannot be stopped. As such, the Koreans are depicted as a people with the responsibility to save all the oppressed peoples in the world. If historical experiences are any indication, this sense of a "chosen people" can lead to reckless and often hostile behavior toward others. This belief of racial superiority is systematically encouraged as citizens go through the process of political socialization.

Self-Sufficiency and Economic Consequences

As discussed earlier, the self-reliance doctrine does not allow for import substitution industrialization and balanced growth. As a result, it has hampered North Korean economic expansion. One should view this in the global perspective, in which most of the successful Third World economies exploited the growing international market with their advantageous assets of cheap labor and raw material. In fact, it was mostly in the 1960s and 1970s that the developing economies took off as a result of their aggressive economic interaction with many postindustrial economies. The developed industrial powers themselves invited the participation of developing economies in their joint ventures and expansionist policies. High labor costs, increasingly restrictive environmental guidelines, and intensifying market competition among the industrial nations themselves have driven corporations out of their own territorial boundaries. The presence of "pollution havens" throughout the Third World, where environmental restrictions are relaxed and a quality labor force is inexpensive, attracted corporations from the advanced economies. In the process of economic globalization, many underdeveloped economies, especially in Africa and Latin America, became helplessly dependent upon the supply of basic needs from the developed world. The "dependency school" considers this linkage to be detrimental to the health of underdeveloped countries. At the same time, however, many other countries, especially in Asia, have successfully induced economic growth, mostly by becoming integrated into the international economic system. The newly industrializing countries of East Asia, including South Korea, have demonstrated that the lesser economies can attract capital investment and technology from advanced countries. The NICs often employ what is referred to as "state capitalism," in which the government assumes the initiative in implementing "export-led" economic policies.

North Korea has long opted for a policy of denouncing the "exploitive" orientations of the developed Western economies and has echoed the "dependency school" perspective. As a result, the economy has been isolated from the global economic network, forcing it to lag further behind the NICs, especially South Korea. This is not to suggest that the policy of economic self-reliance is without any merit, especially in its efforts for distributive justice. What is being observed, however, is the undeniable trend that the global economy has moved toward specialization and that economic growth cannot be realistically expected without participating in the international market. Thus, for what North Korea has gained in terms of economic self-reliance and balanced growth, it has had to sacrifice the promotion of light industry and gross economic expansion.

Self-Defense and Security Consequences

If national security is defined narrowly to mean military self-defense, North Korea has made impressive achievements. It might even have developed the necessary technology to produce nuclear bombs as well as conventional weapons. One finds it difficult to believe that North Korea has such an advanced level of military capabilities, considering its undeveloped economic base. It is only with the realization of the centrality of self-defense that one can understand the remarkable achievement in military preparedness.

However, national security is more than self-defense; it also involves social stability, economic prosperity, ideological consensus, and even the credibility of the system in international society.[5] Of these extramilitary conditions, North Korea seems to have achieved a respectful level of ideological consensus and social stability, but it appears to be lagging behind in terms of economic conditions and international credibility. These shortcomings might affect social stability and ideological consensus in the long run. Nevertheless, the extent to which these factors will affect political stability cannot be predicted with any degree of accuracy. What is certain is that if the regime is unable to meet people's basic needs on a continuing basis, especially after the era of Kim's charismatic leadership, social unrest cannot be avoided.

In short, the ideology of *Juche* has affected North Korean society in a most profound way. This ideology may have saved the system from certain collapse when the Soviet Union and all its satellite countries suffered the fatality of system demise. Yet, it is the very ideology that may be preventing economic and social change and precluding the system from prospering.

Notes

1. A typical work along this line is Nicholas Eberstadt, "Hastening Korean Reunification," *Foreign Affairs* 76, no. 2 (March–April 1997).

2. Han S. Park, remarks cited in "Hungry North Korea Swallows Some Pride," *New York Times*, May 29, 1997.

3. David Apter, "The Role of Traditionalism in the Political Modernization of Ghana and Uganda," in Jason L. Finkle and Richard W. Gable, eds., *Political Development and Social Change* (New York: John Wiley and Sons, 1966).

4. Milton Djilas, *The New Class* (New York: Praeger, 1957).

5. See Han S. Park, "Self-Reliance and National Security," in Edward Azar and Chung In Moon, eds., *National Security in the Third World* (London: Edward Elgar Publishing, 1988).

14

Conclusion: The Challenges Ahead

Human history has seen a wide variation of political systems. But at no time in history has the world witnessed a system of governance that is as truly unique as North Korea. This system is so uniquely crafted that it is a natural experimental setting, where a number of significant theories and propositions may be tested, among them: (1) To what extent can a political belief system alter the seemingly inherent structure of basic human needs and wants? (2) Can one expect the replication of a fundamentalist religious experience in a large society? (3) Will a reclusive system avoid by policy choices and political maneuvering the certain fate of most socialist systems, as witnessed in Eastern Europe and the Soviet Union itself? (4) Can a government maintain its legitimacy when the people are exposed to an open environment that may lead them to develop a sense of relative deprivation? In this book, I made an effort to address these questions.

I advanced the central theme that North Korea may have achieved a political culture that is so pervasive that no study of the system and politics can be complete without placing *Juche* at the center of analysis. To unravel the mystery of the ideology, I made deliberate efforts to examine the cognitive and affective structure of North Korean beliefs from a phenomenological perspective; that is, I attempted to "empathize" with the believers themselves. Using this perspective, I found that North Koreans have not been irrational or unpredictable in their policy choices and behavioral manifestations. On the contrary, they have been extremely consistent in their objective of maximizing national interest. They may have been unconventional, but no one can say that they were unwise in pro-

175

moting their own national interests. In fact, the problems and challenges North Korea faces are by no means unusual or unique, in that they have to do with meeting people's basic needs, maintaining regime stability, promoting national identity, and expanding economic and cultural prosperity. Given the shortage of natural resources and limited arable land, coupled with the disappearance of support systems in the world, Pyongyang could not have done better than it has without really risking the very survival of the regime itself.

North Korea survived the fatal blow of the collapse of the socialist systems throughout Europe, the disintegration of the Soviet Union, a reformed China, and alienation by the Western world from international financial institutions. Furthermore, it survived economic hardships, natural disasters, and most of all, the death of the Great Leader. However, the ability to survive all these adversities does not mean that North Korea's problems and challenges are not formidable. They are.

In assessing the challenges for North Korea, one should consider two factors. First, it is unlikely that the North Koreans are immune to the universality of human nature. Second, there must be a limit to ordinary people's tolerance of hardship. The study of human nature suggests that there are certain needs and rights so universal and natural for every individual that no political power or philosophical teaching can undermine or suppress them effectively for a prolonged period of time. North Koreans cannot be exempt from this characteristic. Of all needs and rights, life itself is most salient and is one to which every person is *entitled*. The sustenance of life requires basic needs such as food, safety, and security. When these basic needs are threatened, people are generally willing to allow the government to curtail other rights or privileges, such as freedom and civil liberties, if such a measure is believed to be necessary for the leadership to alleviate the threat. In general, people are willing to "trade off" their political and civil rights for survival.[1] But if the government shows little or no capability to cope with the life-threatening situation on a sustained basis, the people cannot and will not suffer the hardships indefinitely. The current food shortage has been around since the poor harvest that resulted from the massive flood in 1995, followed by drought, hail, and other bad weather patterns in the succeeding years. As discussed earlier, the natural disaster was a key cause of the famine, but the shortage of food is not expected to disappear. Natural disasters cannot provide the regime with effective excuses indefinitely for its inability to cope with the problem. In the end, people will question the merit of the doctrine of economic self-reliance.

Identity is commonly suggested as another kind of human need or right. The destruction or restriction of individual identity leads to unstable and often unpredictable personality and behavioral traits. The absence of a clear identity for a group might lead to its dissolution. The absence of identity on the part of a nation-state will deprive it of its sovereign character. In an ideal society, its members are supposed to have a satisfying degree of identity at all levels. In the context of North Korea, one might find a great degree of imbalance among individual identity, group identity, and national identity. A cursory observation suggests that individual identity is neglected as being unimportant. Personal values and beliefs unique to the individual are considered counterproductive for the society and are discouraged. In North Korea, diverse beliefs and perspectives by different individuals are strictly prohibited. At the collective level, however, there seems to be a strong sense of group identity along the lines of official norms articulated by the Workers' Party of Korea and the center of the leadership. Every group or organization in the society is charged with a concrete and clear sense of mission and the values necessary to carry it out. Because of the high degree of in-group cohesiveness, group members retain a sense of belonging and identity. And at the national level, North Koreans are almost obsessed with nationalism. The process of education and political socialization is loaded with nationalist themes and ethnic pride. This phenomenon has been greatly reinforced by the need to idolize Kim Il Sung, who is portrayed as the emancipator of the nation from colonial Japan and the guardian of the people from the hegemonic superpowers throughout the Cold War era. The norm of nationalism is so central to *Juche* ideology that one might define the ideology as developmental nationalism rather than Marxist socialism. In the final analysis, one would be mistaken to suggest that North Koreans are struggling with an identity crisis. Although unable to appreciate the importance of individual identity, the average person in North Korea appears to have maintained a satisfactory degree of group identity.

The third component of human rights is the right to make choices. The literature on freedom and civil liberty documents ample justification for choicemaking as an inalienable universal right for all human beings. It is in this area of human rights and needs that the North Korean system has been unable to make much progress. However, one should not make a blind and uneducated assumption that North Koreans have been oppressed by the iron hand of the "Great Leaders," as might be expected in a typical police state of totalitarianism. The overwhelmingly submissive and compliant attitude displayed by the people at all levels of society has resulted from a consistent and carefully engineered process of lifelong political socialization. Thus, North Koreans have developed extremely effective self-censorship as well as a system of incentives and rewards for compliance and submission. Major decisions (choices) are made by the leadership, but the people tend to believe that they are for their own good. The ordinary people submit themselves voluntarily to elite authority because they are not provided with alternatives or oriented toward doubting the virtue of the leadership. Here lies another anomaly, namely, that people do not feel discontented or choose not to express grievances in spite of the fact that their right to choose is obviously undermined. Will this anomaly continue indefinitely? Under what conditions will this situation be altered? Only time will tell.

Prognosis

The collapse thesis—the dominant view among North Korea watchers and policymakers in South Korea as well as in the Western world—is obviously predicated upon erroneous assumptions and superficial information. A more insightful observation suggests that the political regime of North Korea is not likely to collapse as long as the following two conditions are met.

First, the unique domestic and external environments must be preserved to a satisfactory extent. They include the perpetuation of political education, the belief that Kim Jong Il is the embodiment of Kim Il Sung's spirit and mind, the presence of external hostility, and the control of information at all levels of the society. Although the leadership is capable of managing these requisite conditions, it will face a dilemma when preserving them might systematically undermine economic development and universal rights. Thus, the leadership must find a "golden mean" whereby pragmatic measures for economic growth can be explored without disturbing the equilibrium of the system. One desirable path might be creating a way in which the domestic socialist economy becomes consistent with and conducive to interaction with the international market economy. Other systems in Europe have failed at this task, but if North Korea is to remain a true anomaly, it must face this challenge as a last test.

Second, the deprivation of basic needs and rights, especially food and life, cannot be prolonged over a span of many years. The effectiveness of ideological education and spiritual preparedness for adversity will be diminished rather drastically if people's basic needs are not satisfied. In order to promote food production, North Korea has accelerated its efforts to attract foreign capital and technology, not only to the Rajin-Sonbong economic free zone but also to the rest of the country. It also expanded its efforts to develop the livestock industry as exemplified by sending delegations of scientists to the United States and other areas. As mentioned earlier, solving the North Korean food shortage is a long-term proposition. For the immediate and intermediate future, a large quantity of grain must be imported. Because grants of aid in this area are unlikely to materialize, the government must generate hard currency. For this reason, North Korea is expected to aggressively seek loans and grants through international monetary communities such as the IMF, World Bank, and Asia Development Bank. In order to make this effort viable, Pyongyang is expected to seek the improvement of relations with the United States and European systems as a top diplomacy goal.

It is a great irony that Hwang Jang Yop's warning that the Kim Jong Il leadership is fully prepared for and willing to wage a long-awaited war will give Pyongyang greater bargaining leverage. Given the plain fact that North Korea's offensive military capability is formidable and includes weapons of mass destruction and that any military provocation will be countered by an even more deadly and sophisticated retaliation, an actual confrontation is frightening, but the possibility is always there. This scenario becomes more credible when one factors in the possibility of a conflict caused by the psychological game of a preemptive strike on the part of either side.

Postscript

In this book, I attempted to observe issues and problems in and around the Korean peninsula from a perspective that might be taken by Pyongyang. In hard politics, perception is reality. The way Pyongyang perceives itself and the world has to be taken as its reality and incorporated into policy considerations by all parties interacting with North Korea. There is nothing more dangerous and counterproductive than epistemic imperialism, whereby concepts are defined and behavioral orientations are characterized by a third party. Viewed from this perspective, I have concluded that the security issue in the Asia-Pacific region that involves North Korea is not one-dimensional. It is complex and multifaceted.

Given the fact that North Korea has an immense military capability and every reason to preserve and enhance it, finding a simple policy to curb Pyongyang's current policy goals and strategies is not only ill-advised but destined to fail. One should also be reminded of the fact that South Korea is heavily armed and further reinforced by the U.S. presence. As a result, the Korean peninsula has the heaviest concentration in the world of military personnel and sophisticated weapons. Any misstep on either side will lead to certain catastrophe.

It is clear that Pyongyang is not going to give in to external pressures if those pressures undermine the system itself. In fact, small sovereign states in the post–Cold War era have not been easily swayed by a large state's military coercion. The era of physical domination creating a peaceful world order is over. One has to develop a system of mutual coordination and complementarity that is based on the acceptance of diversity in values and governing styles. It is clear in the Korean conundrum that military or economic might on the part of one party cannot guarantee peace. It takes the courage and wisdom of all parties concerned to create a situation in which relations are guided by the win-win premise, not a zero-sum game. This we must create because peace is not an option; it is an imperative.

Note

1. This phenomenon is evident in any political system, including the United States. In the "war against terrorism" after the September 11, 2001, attacks, U.S. citizens showed willingness to allow the government to conduct surveillance of their lives that could infringe upon their civil rights, as long as such activity was necessitated by protecting lives and homeland security.

Bibliography

Alexander, Francesca, and Michele Rollins. 1984. "Alcoholics Anonymous: The Unseen Cult." *California Sociologist* (Winter), pp. 33–48.

Almond, Gabriel, and James Coleman, eds. 1960. *The Politics of Developing Areas*. Princeton, N.J.: Princeton University Press.

Almond, Gabriel, and Sidney Verba. 1963. *The Civic Culture: Political Attitudes and Democracy in Five Nations*. Princeton, N.J.: Princeton University Press.

Apter, David. 1966. "The Role of Traditionalism in the Political Modernization of Ghana and Uganda." In Jason L. Finkle and Richard W. Gable, eds., *Political Development and Social Change*. New York: John Wiley and Sons.

Balch, Robert W. 1980. "Looking Behind the Scenes in a Religious Cult: Implications for the Study of Conversion." *Sociological Analysis* 41, no. 2 (Summer), pp. 137–143.

Choson jonsa. 1979–1982. Written by the Research Institute of Social Sciences. 33 vols. Pyongyang: Encyclopedia Publishers.

Cumings, Bruce. 1981. *The Origins of the Korean War*, vol. 1. Princeton, N.J.: Princeton University Press.

———. 1990. *The Origins of the Korean War*, vol. 2. Princeton, N.J.: Princeton University Press.

Deuchler, Martina. 1992. *The Confucian Transformation of Korea: A Study of Society and Ideology*. Cambridge, Mass.: Harvard University Press.

Djilas, Milovan. 1957. *The New Class*. New York: Praeger.

Dorpat, Theodore L. 1996. *Gaslighting, the Double Whammy, Interrogation, and Other Methods of Covert Control in Psychotherapy and Psychoanalysis*. Northvale, N.J.: Aronson.

Eberstadt, Nicholas. 1997. "Hastening Korean Reunification." *Foreign Affairs* 76, no. 2 (March–April).

Eckstein, Harry. 1988. "A Culturalist Theory of Political Change." *American Political Science Review* 82, no. 3.

181

Festinger, Leon. 1957. *A Theory of Cognitive Dissonance*. Evanston, Ill.: Row Peterson.

Finkle, Jason L., and Richard W. Gable, eds. 1966. *Political Development and Social Change*. New York: John Wiley and Sons.

Fisher, Richard D., Jr. 1992. "Responding to the Looming North Korean Threat." *Backgrounder*. Working Paper. Washington, D.C.: Heritage Foundation.

Frank, Andre Gunder. 1969. *Latin America: Underdevelopment or Revolution?* New York: Monthly Review Press.

Hayes, Peter. "International Missile Trade and the Two Koreas." Working Paper no. 1. Monterey Institute of International Studies.

Hunter, Helen-Louise. 1999. *Kim Il Sung's North Korea*. Westport, Conn.: Praeger.

Husserl, Edmund. 1966. *The Idea of Phenomenology*. Trans. W. P. Alston and G. Nakhnikian. The Hague: Martinus Nijhoff Press.

———. 1990. *The Crisis of European Sciences and Transcendental Phenomenology*. Trans. David Carr. Evanston, Ill.: Northwestern University Press.

Kang, Hosuck Thomas. 1979. "Changes in the North Korean Personality from Confucianist to Communist." In Jae Kyu Park and Jung Gun Kim, eds., *The Politics of North Korea*. Seoul: Institute for Far Eastern Studies.

Kaurov, Georgiy. 2000. "A Traditional History of Soviet–North Korean Nuclear Relations." In James Clay Moltz and Alexandre Y. Mansourov, eds., *The North Korean Nuclear Program*. New York: Routledge.

Keiser, Thomas W., and Jacqueline L. Keiser. 1987. *The Anatomy of Illusion: Religious Cults and Destructive Persuasion*. Springfield, Ill.: Thomas.

Kim, Dae-Jung. 1996. *Kim Dae-Jung's Three Stage Approach to Korean Reunification*. Los Angeles, CA: Center for Multiethnic and Transnational Studies, University of Southern California.

Kim Il Sung. 1975. *Selected Works*, vol. 5. Pyongyang: Publishing House of the Workers' Party of Korea.

———. 1980. *Works*. English ed. Pyongyang: Foreign Language Publishing House.

———. 1986. *The Mission of Contemporary Literature*. Pyongyang: Foreign Language Publishing House.

———. 1992. *Encyclopedia*. New Delhi: Vishwanath.

———. 1992. *Segiwa doburo* (With the century). Pyongyang: Korea Labor Publishers.

———. *Answers to Questions Raised by Foreign Journalists*. English ed. Pyongyang: Foreign Language Publishing House.

Kurian, George. 1979. *The Book of World Rankings*. New York: Facts on File.

Lee, Chong-Sik, and Robert Scalapino. 1972. *Communism in Korea*, 2 vols. Los Angeles: University of California Press.

Lee, Manwoo. 1982. "How North Korea Sees Itself." In Eugene Kim and B. C. Koh, eds., *A Journey to North Korea*. Berkeley, Calif.: Institute of East Asian Studies, University of California.

Levine, Edward M. 1980. "Deprogramming Without Tears." *Sociology* (March–April), pp. 34–38.

Lifton, Robert Jay. 1961. *Thought Reform and the Psychology of Totalism: A Study of "Brainwashing" in China.* New York: W. W. Norton.

Ma Min, ed. 1983. *Jungkuk sosuminjok sangsik* (The Chinese minority nationalities). Peking, China: Nationalities Publication House.

Mack, Andrew. 1993. "The Nuclear Crisis on the Korean Peninsula." *Asian Survey* 33, no. 4 (April).

Mo, Han Chang. 1984. *Jarip kyungje riron* (Theory of economic self-reliance). Pyongyang: Publishers of Social Science.

Mukherjee, T. B. 1983. *The Social, Economic, and Political Ideas of the Great President Kim Il Sung.* Pyongyang, North Korea: Foreign Language Publishing House.

"North Korea Country Profile." 1993. *Journal of Commerce*, November 16. Economist Intelligence Unit, China.

Oberdorfer, Don. 1997. *The Two Koreas: A Contemporary History.* Reading, Mass.: Addison-Wesley.

Oh, John Kie-chiang. 1968. *Korea: Democracy on Trial.* Ithaca, N.Y.: Cornell University Press.

———. 1999. *Korean Politics.* Ithaca, N.Y.: Cornell University Press.

Oh, Kongdan, and Ralph C. Hassig. 2000. *North Korea Through the Looking Glass.* Washington, D.C.: Brookings Institution Press.

Ottenberg, Donald J. 1981. "Therapeutic Community and the Danger of the Cult Phenomenon." *Marriage and Family Review* (Fall–Winter), pp. 151–173.

Palmer, Spencer. 1984. *Confucian Rituals in Korea.* Berkeley, Calif.: Asian Humanities Press.

Park, Han Shik. 1983. "Chu'che: North Korean Ideology." In Eugene Kim, ed., *Journey to North Korea.* Berkeley, Calif.: Institute of East Asian Studies, University of California.

———. 1984. *Human Needs and Political Development: A Dissent to Utopian Solutions.* Cambridge, Mass.: Schenkman Press.

———. 1987. "*Juche* as a Foreign Policy Constraint in North Korea." *Asian Perspective* 11, no. 1.

———. 1988. "Self-Reliance and National Security." In Edward Azar and Chung In Monn, eds., *National Security in the Third World.* London: Edward Elgar Publishing.

———. 1996. *North Korea: Ideology, Politics, Economy.* Englewood Cliffs, N.J.: Prentice Hall.

Park, Han Shik, and Kyung Ae Park. 1987. "The Bases of Legitimacy in North and South Korea." *Korea Observer* 11, no. 2, pp. 33–44.

———. 1990. *China and North Korea: Politics and Integration and Modernization.* Hong Kong: Asia Research Service.

Park, Therese. 1977. *A Gift of the Emperor.* Duluth, Minn.: Spinster's Ink.

Perle, Richard. 1992. "Policy Implications of North Korea's Ongoing Nuclear Program." U.S. House of Representatives, Subcommittee on East Asian and Pacific Affairs of the Committee on Foreign Affairs, Washington, D.C.

Pye, Lucian. 1985. *Asian Power and Politics: The Cultural Dimensions of Authority.* Cambridge, Mass.: Harvard University Press.

Ri, In Mo. 1997. *My Life and Faith: Memoirs.* Pyongyang: Foreign Language Publishing.

Sargant, William W. 1957. *Brainwashing.* New York: Doubleday.

Schaar, John. 1981. *Legitimacy in the Modern States.* New Brunswick, N.J.: Transaction Books.

Sigal, Leon. 1988. *Disarming Strangers: Nuclear Diplomacy with North Korea.* Princeton, N.J.: Princeton University Press.

Snyder, Scott. 1999. *Negotiating on the Edge: North Korean Negotiating Behavior.* Washington, D.C.: United States Institute of Peace Press.

Stueck, William. *The Korean War.* Princeton, N.J.: Princeton University Press, 1995.

Suh, Dae-Sook. 1967. *The Korean Communist Movement, 1918–1948.* Princeton, N.J.: Princeton University Press.

———. 1988. *Kim Il Sung: The North Korean Leader.* New York: Columbia University Press.

Sun, Changjiang. 1991. "Chinese Society, Chinese Confucianism, and the Modernization of China." In Silke Krieger and Rolf Trauzettel, eds., *Confucianism and the Modernization of China.* Mainz, Germany: V. Hase and Koehler Verlag.

Sun, Hyon Ryong, Li Jong Mun, Hoh Ryong gu, and Josonjok Peaknyon Sa Hwa. 1984. *One Hundred Years of Koreans in China.* Shen Yang: Lianing Publishing House.

Tucker, Robert. 1973. *Stalin as Revolutionary: 1889–1929.* New York: W. W. Norton.

Westerhoff, John H. *McGuffey and His Readers.* Nashville, Tenn.: Parthenon Press, 1978.

White, Steven. 1979. *Political Culture and Soviet Politics.* New York: St. Martin's Press.

Winn, Denise. 1983. *The Manipulated Mind: Brainwashing, Conditioning, and Indoctrination.* London: Octagon Press.

Zhebin, Alexander. 2000. "A Political History of Soviet–North Korean Nuclear Cooperation." In James Clay Moltz and Alexandre Y. Mansourov, eds., *The North Korean Nuclear Program.* New York: Routledge.

Ziegler, Harmon. 1988. *Pluralism, Corporatism and Confucianism: Political Association and Conflict Regulation in the United States, Europe, and Taiwan.* Philadelphia: Temple University Press.

Index

Academy of *Juche* Science, 36, 160(n7)
Acrobatics, 82
Afterlife, 37
Agricultural production, 83, 87, 92–93, 151–152, 159(n6); in China, 100–101
Ahn Joong Keun, 79
Almond, Gabriel, 9
Ancestor worship, 12, 67
An Chang Ho, 24, 29(n8)
Anticolonialism, 21
Anticommunism, 122
Antiforeignism, 18, 23, 130(n4), 166
Antihegemonism, 21–22
Apter, David, 169
Arable land, 83, 93, 151
Architecture, 77
Arirang, 76
Armistice agreement, 104, 120, 155
Arms sales. *See* Weapons sales
Asia Development Bank, 103, 179
Asian tigers, 23, 95
Atheism, 48

Baker, James, 165
Bangchang, 75–76
Basic needs provision, 163–164, 167, 176, 178. *See also* Food aid; Food production; Food shortages

Belief systems, 4, 9, 63
Brain. *See under* Political-social body doctrine
Brainwashing, 1, 41–42
Brinksmanship diplomacy, 157
Bureaucracy, 89–90
Bush, George H. W., 135
Bush, George W., 105

Calendar, 39, 83
Cancer treatment, 81–82, 84(n4)
Capitalist development, 3–4, 71, 121, 130(n4), 144, 145, 150, 151; in South Korea, 121, 123, 172; state, 172
Chaebols, 122
Chang Myon, 121
Changuisong, 28, 35
Charisma formation, 25, 68, 71–72, 136, 140(n3)
Charismatic leadership, 7, 10, 42, 46, 167; of Kim Il Sung, 14, 21, 22, 25–26, 46, 71–72, 86, 136; of Kim Jong Il, 25, 136. *See also* Legitimacy
Children's Palace, 52, 76
China, 44, 90; ethnic Koreans in, 100–101, 110–111, 121; Korean autonomous region in, 101, 130(n7); and Korean War, 101, 110, 121,

185

130(n7); North Korea policy toward, 100–102, 151; post–Cold War, 144; and South Korea relations, 62, 111, 144; and Soviet Union relations, 8, 14, 19, 21, 44

Choe Hong Hee, 80–81

Choi Kyu Ha, 122

Chollima campaign, 8, 164

Choson jonsa (history volumes), 32

Chosonmunhak (literary journal), 78

Choson University (Japan), 62, 111

Christian theology and practice, 36, 38, 40(n11), 47–48

Chun Doo Hwan, 122

Chung Joo-young, 125, 153

Citizen interaction. *See* External contact

Civil rights, 176, 177, 180(n1)

Civil society, 170

Class, 163, 169–170

Clinton, William Jefferson, 103, 105, 106

Cold War, 44, 100, 119. *See also* Post–Cold War

Coleman, James, 9

Collapse thesis, 161–169, 178

Collective farms, 83, 87, 93

Collectivism, 35–36, 45, 48, 88, 89, 170–171; Confucian, 65

Colonialism, 14. *See also* Japan, and occupation of Korea

Comfort women, 108

Committee on Overseas Compatriots, 112

Commodity goods. *See* Consumer goods

Communications. *See* Media

Communism, 79, 101, 121

Communist party. *See* Workers' Party of Korea

Competition, 53, 93, 170

Confederate State of Koryo (reunification proposal), 113, 127

Confucianism, 10–13, 25, 64–67, 81, 166, 168, 169

Consciousness, 28. *See also Uisiksong*

Constitution of 1998, 88, 131(n11), 152

Consumer goods, 93–94, 96, 138

Consumerism, 48, 145, 151, 166

Creativity, 28, 35; individual, 170–171. *See also Changuisong*

Cross-pressures, 45, 63, 169

Cultural exchanges, 128(box)

Cultural heritage, 32, 70. *See also* Confucianism

Cultural integration, 170–171

Cultural Revolution (China), 8, 10, 22, 90

Cultural study, 9–10

Daewoo, 156

Dams, 93

Dance, 82

Defense preparedness. *See* Military preparedness

Democracy, 120–123, 150

Deng Xiaoping, 144

Dependencia school of development, 24, 28, 121, 130(n5), 165, 172

Dependent development, 100, 121, 130(n5)

Deuchler, Martina, 11

Development assistance, 96

Diplomatic relations, 45, 129; and brinksmanship, 157; post–Cold War, 144, 145, 157

Distributive justice, 94–95, 118, 172

Djilas, Milton, 169

East Germany, 144, 146, 152

Eckstein, Harry, 9

Economic assistance, 96, 100, 103, 179

Economic dependence, 100. *See also Dependencia* school of development; Dependent development

Economic free zone, 179

Economic globalization, 3–4, 103, 171–172

Economic growth, 2, 137–138, 178

Economic hardship. *See* Basic needs provision

Economic integration, 97, 103, 127, 128(box), 137–138, 151, 172, 178; and bargaining leverage, 156–157. *See also* Energy production

Economic sanctions, 103, 106, 129, 154, 157

Economic self-reliance, 23–24, 90, 92–96, 100, 135, 147, 150–151, 159; and economic globalization, 3–4, 103, 171–172; and local self-help, 152. *See also* Basic needs provision

Education, 22, 106; extracurricular, 52–53; higher, 53–54; mass, 58–59; through media and arts, 54–57, 76, 97–98; party, 57–58; preschool, 51–52, 76; primary, 52–53, 76; technical and vocational, 53–54; workplace, 27, 54, 56, 78. *See also* Political-social body doctrine; Political socialization; Self-criticism

Elite, 7–8, 22, 164–165

Embargo, 154

Energy production, 96, 152. *See also* Korean Peninsula Energy Development Organization

Entertainment, 56–57

Epistemic imperialism, 9, 179

Erosion, 83, 93, 151

Eternal life, 36–39, 42, 46–48, 63, 65, 71, 92

Ethnic homogeneity, 18, 29(n2), 89

Expatriate Koreans. *See* Overseas Koreans

Experts and reds, 90

Export-led economies, 23, 28, 95, 172. *See also Dependencia* school of development

Export production. *See* Weapons sales

External contact, 45, 61, 62, 150, 153–154, 156, 157. *See also* Information control

Factory colleges, 27, 54

Family, 11–13; leadership as, 65–67, 169; separated, 127, 128(box)

Famine, 43, 93, 176

Federation of Koreans (Japan), 62

Film, 78, 97

Floods, 83, 93, 151, 162

Food aid, 96, 101–102, 166, 179

Food production, 179. *See also* Agricultural production

Food shortages, 2, 43, 96, 101–102, 151, 162–163, 176, 179; and starvation, 2, 96, 150

Foreign contact. *See* External contact

Foreign currency earnings, 24, 92, 138

Foreign investment, 137, 157, 179

Foreign policy, 23, 99–100. *See also* China; Japan; Inter-Korean relations; Nonaligned nations; Overseas Koreans; United States

Four-Party Talks, 106–107, 155, 158

Geneva Framework (1994), 154

Global market system. *See* Economic globalization

God, 37, 38, 48–49

Government by legacy, 39

Graphite-powered nuclear power plants, 154

Great Leap Forward (China), 8

Group of 77, 28

Hairstyles, 82–83

Haksop, 27

Han Wan Sang, 79

Health care, 2, 81–82, 151

Heroes, 78–79, 97

Honor: in family, 11; in political-social body, 65

Housing, 95

Human determinism, 166

Human dignity, 28, 166

Humanitarian assistance, 105, 151

Human mind. *See* Individual in society; Man in universe; Political-social body doctrine

Human nature, 26–27, 34, 38, 176; perfected, 37, 38, 48–49

Human nursery phenomenon, 63
Human rights, 176–178
Hwang Jang Yop, 2, 19, 29(n3), 97, 153,
    161, 179
Hyundai, 156

IAEA. *See* International Atomic Energy
    Agency
Identity: group, 89, 177; national,
    43–44, 69–71. *See also* Individual in
    society
Immortality. *See* Eternal life
Imperialism, 71, 109, 154
Imports, 96
Income distribution, 94
India, 23
Individual in society, 32, 33, 35–38,
    40(n12), 48, 64, 65, 88, 89, 170–171,
    177; Confucian, 13, 65. *See also* Man
    in universe; Political-social body
    doctrine
Industrial technology, 139
Industry, 87–88, 100; light, 93–94, 137;
    military, 91–92, 94. *See also* Export-
    led economies; Trade
Information control, 54, 62, 150, 159,
    167. *See also* External contact
Inter-Korean relations: and legitimacy,
    23, 44, 102, 117–118, 121–126, 129,
    130(n4), 146–150, 168; and military
    attack, 45, 68, 158; and nuclear
    power project, 104–105; and popular
    attitudes, 147; and post–Cold War
    security, 145–146; and presidential
    visits, 126, 128; and prisoner release,
    127, 128(box), 147–148, 159(n3); and
    separated families, 127, 128(box);
    and sunshine policy, 105, 114, 124,
    129, 146, 153–154; and U.S., 45,
    103–105. *See also* Armistice
    agreement; External contact; Inter-
    Korean summit; Korea, division of;
    Korean War; Reunification; South
    Korea
Inter-Korean summit (1948), 126

Inter-Korean summit (2000), 69, 93, 96,
    114, 124–130, 157; agreement of,
    127–128
International Atomic Energy Agency
    (IAEA), 91, 133, 137
International Institute of *Juche* Ideas, 71
International loans, 179
International Monetary Fund, 103, 122,
    179
Irrigation, 93
Isolation, 43–45

Jajusong, 28, 33, 34, 64
Japan, 104, 106, 156, 157; Koreans in,
    41, 62, 111–112; and missile launch,
    108, 114(n8), 155, 158; North Korea
    policy toward, 107–109; and
    occupation of Korea, 12, 14, 18, 20,
    32, 42–43, 91, 97, 98(n6), 107–108
Joint ventures, 137
Jolgawha, 76
Juche, 4, 13, 148; defined, 17; evolution
    of, 20–29, 29(n1), 153, 160(n7);
    historical conditions for, 13–15,
    18–19, 42–43; humans as locus in,
    13, 26–28, 32–35, 64, 71, 166;
    international scope of, 71, 109–110,
    136, 140(n4); public support of, 39;
    religious ideology of, 4, 36–49, 63,
    71, 72, 168; and social values, 171;
    and system stability, 161–173. *See
    also* Collectivism; Economic self-
    reliance; Education; Identity;
    Individual in society; Leadership;
    Legitimacy; Mind conditioning;
    Nationalism; Neo-*Juche;* Political-
    social body doctrine; Spiritual
    determinism
Jucheization, 57
Juche Tower, 110
Jusok, 88
Juvenile delinquency, 53

Kang, Hosuck, 12

KEDO. *See* Korean Peninsula Energy Development Organization
Kim Chaek, 126
Kim Chaek Technological University, 54
Kim Dae-jung, 105, 122, 124, 125, 127, 146
Kim Hyong U, 81
Kim Il Sung, 109, 156; charisma of, 14, 21, 22, 25–26, 46, 71–72, 86, 136; and China, 44, 100; death of, 39, 46, 48, 67, 85–86; designations for, 52, 53, 56, 66–67; and development of *juche,* 17, 19–25, 32, 33, 35; and economy, 137–138; and Japan, 14, 107, 111; and military capability, 18, 139–140; at national inception, 121, 126; and Soviet Union, 100; writings of, 46–47, 77, 79–80, 91, 96–97, 109
Kim Il Sung University, 53
Kim Jong Il, 26, 40(n4), 67, 102, 114(n9); designations for, 52, 53, 56, 59(n1), 66–67; and inter-Korean relations, 147; and inter-Korean summit, 124–127; leadership of, 2, 25, 66, 98(n1), 136, 148, 157; and military, 8, 152; succession by, 2, 26, 36, 67, 86, 162, 164
Kim Koo, 24, 79, 126
Kim Woo-joong, 156
Kim Yong Nam, 102, 126, 127
Kim Young Sam, 79, 122, 146
Korea, division of, 19, 44, 103, 118–119, 121. *See also* Armistice agreement; Inter-Korean relations; Korean War
Korean Central News Agency, 54, 62
Korean Peninsula Energy Development Organization (KEDO), 104–105, 154–155, 158
Korean War (1950–1953), 14, 21, 103, 119–120, 145–146; China in, 101, 110, 121, 130(n7). *See also* Armistice agreement
Kumchangri site, 151, 155
Kye Sun Hui, 80

Labor, international division of, 24, 28
Leadership, 25, 63, 85–87; Confucian, 65; by legacy, 39, 87–88, 164; and political integration, 22, 169–170; and power conflicts, 164–165; selection of, 62; succession in, 25–26, 36, 67, 89, 136, 145, 162. *See also* Charismatic leadership; Eternal life; Kim Il Sung; Kim Jong Il; Legitimacy; Paternalism; Political-social body doctrine; Presidency; Regime stability; Regime survival
Legitimacy, 22, 25, 44, 85–87; and economic conditions, 163–164; and inter-Korean relations, 23, 102, 117–118, 121–130, 130(n4), 146–150, 168; and *Juche,* 165–168; post–Cold War, 145; and regime performance, 118; social contract theory of, 16, 29(n10), 62, 88, 118; and spiritual integrity, 147. *See also* Basic needs provision; Military preparedness; Nationalism; Regime stability; Regime survival
Li Chi Su, 37
Life expectancy, 81
Lifestyle, 95
Light-water reactors, 154
Literature, 77–80
Livestock, 87, 93, 179
Locke, John, 118
Long-range intercontinental ballistic missiles, 108
Loyalty, 35, 89

Madden, Harrison D., 107
Malnutrition, 150
Man in universe, 13, 26–28, 32–33, 64, 71, 166. *See also* Individual in society
Mankyongdae, 19, 25, 26
Mao Zedong, 22, 44, 101
Market economy. *See* Economic globalization
Martyrdom, 37
Marxism-Leninism, 22, 33–35, 64

Mass media, 54–55
Mass rallies, 58–59, 59(n4)
Material prosperity, 166
Media, 54–56
Mediating orientations, 9
Medicine, 81–82
Migrations, to China, 100–101
Militarism, 137; in South Korea, 123.
    See also Military preparedness
Military alliances, 97
Military defense treaties, 100
Military exports. *See* Weapons sales
Military leadership, 8, 152
Military preparedness, 18, 20–21,
    68–69, 90–92, 106, 123, 135–137,
    152–153, 172–173; as bargaining
    leverage, 124, 155–156; and
    economic conditions, 2, 24, 135, 137,
    138; post–Cold War, 145, 152, 158,
    179–180. *See also* Missile defense;
    Nuclear defense; Nuclear weapons
    production
Mind conditioning, 61–72
Minjok Unmyong (*Nation and Destiny*,
    literary series and film), 78, 97, 148
Missile defense, 8, 18, 69, 99, 108,
    114(nn 8, 9); of Asian-U.S. alliance,
    158
Missile launches, 108, 114(n8), 155,
    156, 158
Missile sales, 92, 106, 108, 138, 155
Missile talks, 155, 158
Moon, Sun Myung, 156
Mt. Kumkang, 150, 153, 156
Mukherjee, T. B., 66
Museum of Revolutionary Struggle, 70
Music, 56, 72, 75–77

National identity, 43–44, 69–71
National independence: from Japan, 18,
    21
Nationalism, 14, 18–20, 22–24, 28, 97,
    120, 121; *juche* as, 22–23, 31–32,
    123–124, 166, 177; post–Cold War,

152. *See also* Political self-
    determination; Political sovereignty
Nationalist activists, 108
National missile defense (NMD, United
    States), 69, 158
National Museum of History, 70
National superiority, 18, 23, 70, 98, 171
Nation and Destiny (*Minjok kwa
    Unmyong,* literary series and film),
    78, 97, 148
Nautilus Institute, 152
Neo-*Juche,* 97, 98(n5)
Neutrality, 8. *See also* Antihegemonism
Newly industrializing countries (NICs),
    23–24, 28, 172
Newspapers, 54–55
New York Times, 154
NICs. *See* Newly industrializing
    countries
NMD. *See* National missile defense
Nobel Peace Prize, 125
Noesu, 34
Nonaligned nations, 23, 28, 71, 99,
    109–110, 136
Nonviolent resistance, 24, 29(n8)
North Korean policy: conceptual
    approaches for study of, 7–10
North Korea–South Korea relations. *See*
    Inter-Korean relations
Nuclear defense, 8, 18, 24, 68, 99, 137
Nuclear disarmament, 155
Nuclear inspections, 91, 151
Nuclear power plant construction,
    104–105, 133, 154
Nuclear technology, 138–139, 141(n10),
    154
Nuclear weapons production, 24, 91,
    100, 134–140, 140(n5), 156

Olympic Games (1996), 80
Opium War (1839–1842), 18
Organization of Petroleum-Exporting
    Countries (OPEC), 138
Overseas Koreans, 101, 110–113,
    114(n4), 121, 130(n7)

Palmer, Spencer, 12
Paradise on Earth (slogan), 43
Park Chung Hee, 122, 123
Park Po Hee, 125
Party in political-social body, 34, 65–66, 88–90. *See also* Workers' Party of Korea
Paternalism, 10, 25–26, 66, 139, 169
Patriarchal society, 13, 66, 67
Patriotism, 52, 78–79, 97
People's Hall of Great Learning, 77
Performing arts, 56–57, 76, 82
Perry, William, 106
Personality cult, 1, 67, 72
Phenomenological viewpoint, 9, 143
Physical appearance, 82–83
Pibada (*Sea of Blood*, opera), 56, 76, 97
Poetry, 76, 78
Policymaking and implementation, 2–3, 90–91; and institutional structure, 8, 27; national self-perception in, 4, 8–10, 143–159, 179; and political self-determination, 90, 96–98
Political culture, 10. *See also* Confucianism; *Juche*
Political education. *See* Education; Political-social body doctrine; Political socialization
Political integration, 22, 169–170
Political isolation. *See* Isolation
Political parties. *See* Workers' Party of Korea
Political rights, 176, 180(n1)
Political self-determination, 28, 48, 90, 96–98
Political-social body doctrine, 34–37, 46, 48, 64, 65, 88–89; brain in, 34, 64, 88, 89; leadership in, 34, 39, 65, 66, 88; and political-social life, 36, 38, 46, 48, 63. *See also* Collectivism; Individual in society; Leadership; Man in universe; Political sovereignty
Political socialization, 51–59, 63, 67, 71, 75, 177–178

Political sovereignty, 22–24. *See also* Political self-determination
Post–Cold War, 106, 143–159; and collapse of socialism, 2, 4, 144–146, 150, 152
Potato farming, 151
Poverty, 162, 164, 166
Powell, Colin, 114(n6)
Power relations, 7, 8
Predestination, 32
Presidency, 88, 91, 126, 127, 131(n11)
Prisoner release, 78, 79, 127, 128(box), 147–148, 159(n3)
Privacy, 170
Public services, 58
Pye, Lucian, 11

Radios, 56
Rajin-Sonbong economic free zone, 179
Rallies, 58–59, 59(n4)
Red Flag Youth campaign, 8
Reds and experts, 90
Regime legitimacy. *See* Legitimacy
Regime stability, 123–124, 135–136
Regime survival, 149–150; and collapse thesis, 161–169, 178
Religious community: conditions for creation of, 41–49, 72
Religious fundamentalism, 4
Religious ideology, 36–49, 63, 71, 72, 168
Reunification, 99, 112–114; soft-landing policy for, 146, 153. *See also* Inter-Korean summit (2000)
Rhee Syngman, 23, 120, 121
Rice, 92, 101
Ri In Mo, 78, 79, 97–98
Rocket technology, 108
Rodong Sinmun (newspaper), 54–55
Roh Tae Woo, 122, 135

Sacrifice, 36, 37, 92
Sarochong, 39, 58
Sea of Blood (*Pibada*, opera), 56, 76, 97

Security: post–Cold War, 137, 158–159, 172–173
Segiwa doburo (With the century, literary series), 79–80, 96–97
Self-censorship, 178
Self-criticism, 27, 54, 57, 171
Self-determination. See Jajusong; Political self-determination
Self-sufficiency. See Juche
Shijo, 76
Siege mentality, 42, 45
Sixth Party Congress (1980), 25, 113
Social change. See Political-social body doctrine
Socialism: of Koreans in China, 101; Korean-style, 1, 14, 28–29, 35, 47, 69–70, 144; post–Cold War collapse of, 2, 4, 144–146, 150, 152; pragmatic, 153. See also Marxism-Leninism; Paternalism
Socialist Youth League, 39, 58
Social values, 170, 171
Society and individual. See Individual in society; Man in universe; Political-social body doctrine
Song Hyo Kyong, 126
South Korea: and China relations, 62, 111, 144; economic development in, 121–123, 146; education in, 52, 59(n2); institutional development in, 120–123, 131(n9); military in, 122, 123; and U.S. security relations, 14, 21, 68, 69, 98, 99, 102–104, 112–113, 127, 145–146, 155, 158. See also Inter-Korean relations
Soviet Union, 21, 100; and China relations, 8, 14, 19, 21, 44; and division of Korea, 44, 118–119
Spiritual determinism, 33–35, 48, 168
Sports, 80–81
Submissiveness, 177–178
Sun, Changjiang, 13
Superiority, 18, 23, 70, 98, 171
Supernatural being, 37, 48–49
System survival. See Regime survival

Table tennis, 81
Tae kwon do, 80
Team Spirit military exercises (South Korea), 68, 146
Technical assistance, 100
Technological development, 33
Television, 55–56, 62, 94
Theocracy. See Juche, religious ideology of
Third World nations. See Nonaligned nations
Three Revolutions Campaign, 33, 40(n4)
Three-Stage Approach (reunification proposal), 127
Totalitarianism, 35–36
Tourism, 45, 153, 156, 157
Trade, 100, 137, 151; sanctions, 103, 106, 129, 154, 157
Transcendentalism, 36–40
Travel, 61–62
Tucker, Robert, 25, 71

Uisiksong, 28, 34, 35, 37
Ultranationalism, 120, 152
Unification. See Reunification
Unification Church, 156–157
United Nations, 144
United States, 69, 97; and economic sanctions, 103, 129; and engagement policy, 105–106, 114(nn 6, 7), 153, 154, 157; and missile talks, 155, 158; North Korean policy toward, 102–107; and nuclear facilities, 91; and partitioning of Korea, 118–119; and South Korea security relations, 14, 21, 68, 69, 98, 99, 102–104, 112–113, 127, 145–146, 155, 158. See also Korean War; National missile defense
Untouchable social groups, 101, 114(n3)
Urisik sahoejuii, 28

Verba, Sidney, 9
Visitor contact. See External contact
Visual arts, 76

Wealth, 94, 95
Weapons of mass destruction (WMD), 105, 106, 124
Weapons production, 94, 105. *See also* Nuclear weapons production
Weapons sales, 24, 91–92, 94, 100, 138; by U.S. to South Korea, 104, 114(n5); missile, 92, 106, 108, 138, 155
West Sea irrigation, 93
White, Steven, 10
Windmill projects, 152
With the Century (*Segiwa doburo,* literary series), 79–80, 96–97
Workers' Party of Korea, 22, 39, 47, 56–58, 177; membership of, 57–58, 169–170

Working class, 19, 33, 56
World Bank, 179
World Food Program, 162

Yeon Hyong Muk, 152
Yi (Chosun) Dynasty, 11, 12, 14, 91
Yongbyon power plants, 154
Youth education, 58
Yo Woon Yong, 24
Yuhoon, 47, 88
Yuhoon jongchi, 39, 87
Yun Isang, 78–79
Yun Isang Institute, 78
Yun Isang Symphonic Orchestra, 78

Ziegler, Harmon, 66

About the Book

Despite isolation, an impoverished economy, mass starvation, and the challenge of leadership succession, North Korea's socialist state continues to survive. Han S. Park explores the reasons for this resilience, concentrating on the implications of mass beliefs and political ideology for the country's political life.

Park begins with an examination of *Juche*, or self-reliance, the ideology that so pervasively penetrates the entire spectrum of North Korean society and guides political behavior at all levels. Drawing on personal interviews and on-site observations, he finds a belief system that is comparable to a theology and a society that exhibits many characteristics of a religious community. In this context, he discusses regime legitimacy, the economy, foreign and defense policy, and the politics of reunification, as well as the regime's reaction to the market forces of globalization.

It is *Juche*, Park concludes, that is the locus of North Korea's political culture and is central to understanding its politics and policies. Though far from proposing a single explanation of the North Korean system, he demonstrates convincingly that an understanding of the country's doctrine of self-reliance is essential to an understanding of the country itself.

Han S. Park is professor of political science and director of the Center for the Study of Global Issues at the University of Georgia. His numerous publications include *China and North Korea: The Politics of Integration and Modernization*, *North Korea: Ideology, Politics, Economy*, and *Human Needs and Political Development*. He has visited North Korea regularly since 1981.

Job #: 112256

Author Name: Park

Title of Book: North Korea

ISBN #: 9781588264039